PAINT SHOP PRO 8

STEPHEN COPESTAKE

in easy steps

BARNES & NOBLE BOOKS
NEW YORK

In easy steps is an imprint of Computer Step
Southfield Road . Southam
Warwickshire CV47 0FB . United Kingdom
www.ineasysteps.com

This edition published for Barnes & Noble Books, New York
FOR SALE IN THE USA ONLY
www.bn.com

Notice of Liability
Every effort has been made to ensure that this book contains accurate and current information. However, Computer Step and the author shall not be liable for any loss or damage suffered by readers as a result of any information contained herein.

Trademarks
Paint Shop Pro® is a registered trademark of Jasc Software Incorporated. All other trademarks are acknowledged as belonging to their respective companies.

Printed and bound in the United Kingdom

ISBN 0-7607-5420-9

Contents

First steps

In this chapter, you'll learn to use the Paint Shop Pro screen (including guides, grids and palettes) and work with files. You'll also customize your working environment and create new toolbars. You'll rescale images (and resize the underlying canvas) then go on to learn about special screen modes. You'll also zoom in and out on images; use the Magnifier and Overview palette; and reverse/redo amendments. Finally, you'll learn how to work with background/foreground colors and swatches; run the Product Tour; and use Quick Guides.

Covers

Chapter One

The Paint Shop Pro screen

The Paint Shop Pro screen is exceptionally easy to use. When you run the program, this is the result (minus the loaded picture):

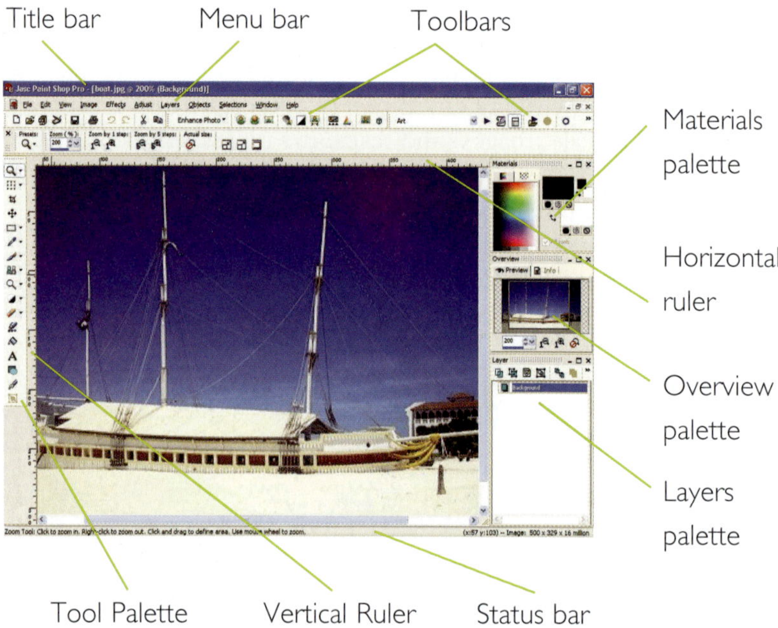

Your screen may look slightly different – in particular, you may have different or more palettes displaying. That's the fun of Paint Shop Pro 8: you can pretty much get your working environment looking the way ***you*** *want it. See pages 11–15.*

For more on the Overview palette, see page 26.

Keep your installation of Paint Shop Pro 8 up to date. Jasc provides free patches on: ***www.jasc.com/patches.asp?#psp8****.*

Toolbars

These are collections of icons. By clicking an appropriate icon, you can launch a specific feature. Many other screen features (e.g. the Status bar) are also classed as toolbars. In addition, palettes function as toolbars . . .

The Tool palette

A specialized toolbar that you use to launch a variety of tools (e.g. the Zoom tool – see page 23). (The Tool palette is sometimes referred to as the Tools toolbar.)

The Materials palette

An easy and convenient way to access Paint Shop Pro's color selection tools (see pages 30–31).

Using guides

You can create guides in Paint Shop Pro pictures. Guides are useful alignment devices because you can ensure that:

- selections
- vector objects
- brush strokes

are automatically aligned with guides when they come within a specific distance.

To specify the distance at which objects snap to guides, double-click a ruler. In the dialog, select the Guides tab. Type in a distance (in pixels) in the Snap influence field – the default is 15.

Creating guides

1 Ensure rulers are currently displayed (see page 11)

2 Ensure guides are currently displayed (see page 11)

3 Click in the vertical or horizontal ruler and drag to produce a guide

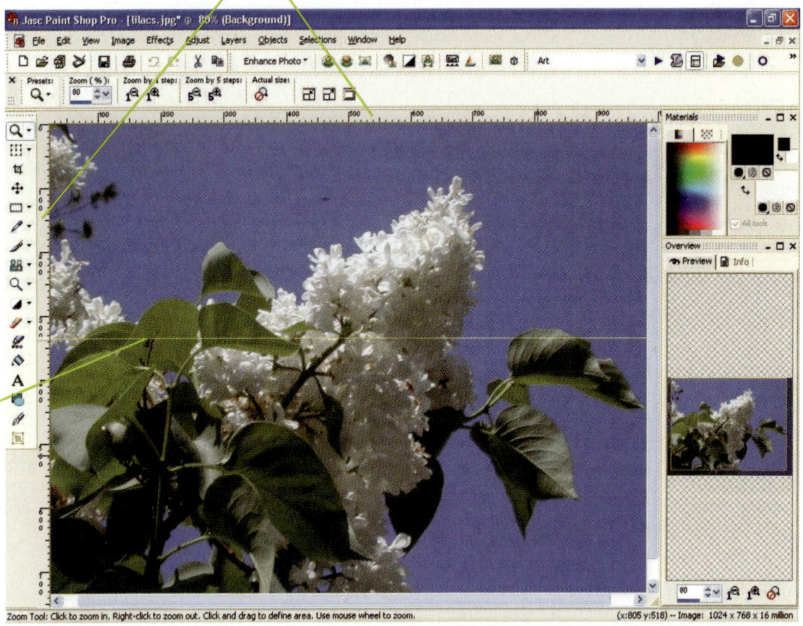

This is a horizontal guide:

You can also have Paint Shop Pro apply a grid to images. Grids are a lattice of horizontal/vertical lines that you can use to align objects more accurately.

To view (or hide) the grid, press Ctrl+Alt+G. To refine it (e.g. change the color), double-click a ruler and complete the dialog that appears.

You can perform a variety of editing actions on existing guides.

Moving guides

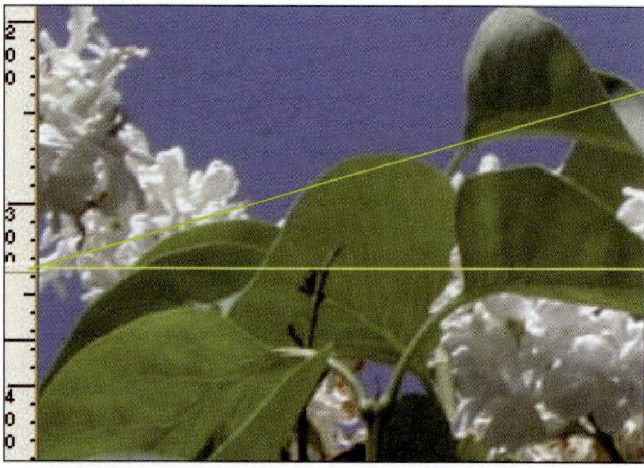

1 Drag the handle to a new location

Recoloring guides

By default, guides are blue – this isn't always suitable since it often clashes with images. To apply a new color:

If an image has both guides and a grid active, the grid is ignored.

1 Double-click a guide's handle

To delete a guide, drag it by its handle till it's off the image window.

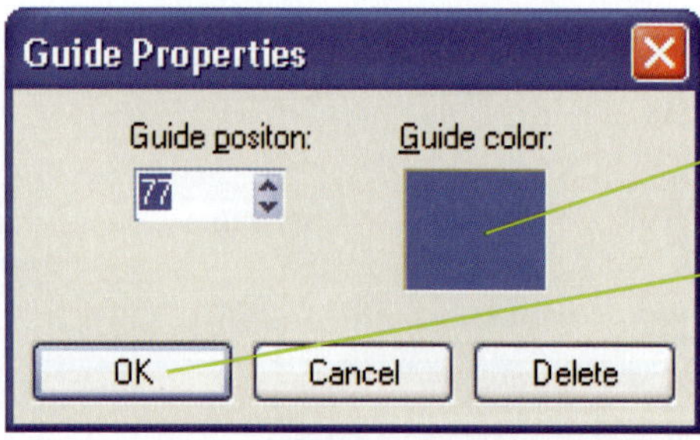

2 Click here

4 Click OK

To have selections/vector objects align with guides, the Snap To Guides feature must be turned on. If it isn't, pull down the View menu and click Snap To Guides.

3 Refer to the Color ring at the top of the Color dialog. Drag on the outer ring to select a hue, then drag in the inner square to adjust the saturation. When the Current color box shows the correct color, click OK

Customizing screen components

You can use two techniques to specify which screen components display:

Displaying the grid, guides or rulers

Pull down the View menu and do the following:

*It's a good idea to calibrate your monitor before using Paint Shop Pro to any extent (calibration improves image quality). Fire up your browser and go to **www.jasc.com/monitor1.asp** – follow the instructions.*

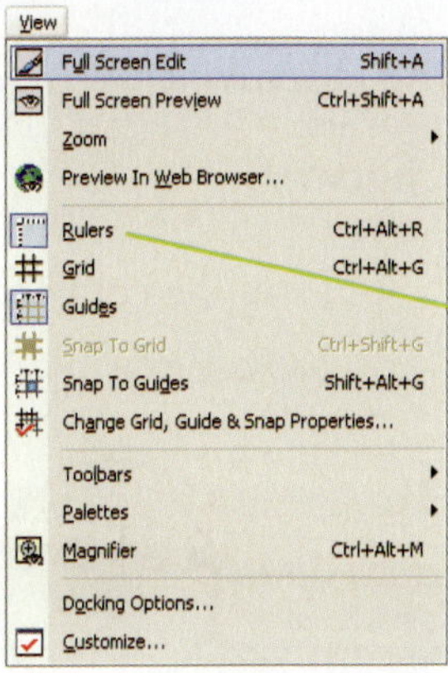

1 Click Grid, Guides or Rulers to enable or disable them

Viewing/hiding toolbars

To view or hide a toolbar, follow step 1 above but select Toolbars instead

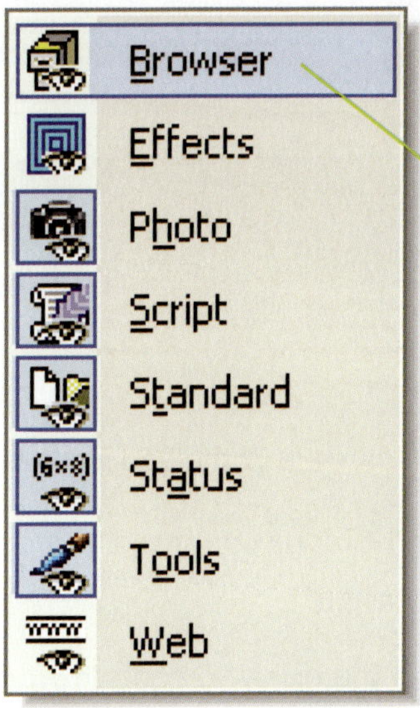

2 Click a toolbar entry (if it's lit on the left, it's active)

Customizing menus and toolbars

Paint Shop Pro is now almost infinitely customizable. You can:

- add program commands to toolbars, menus or palettes
- create your own toolbars
- allocate keyboard shortcuts to menu commands

Adding or moving commands

1 Choose View, Customize

3 Drag the command to a toolbar, menu or palette

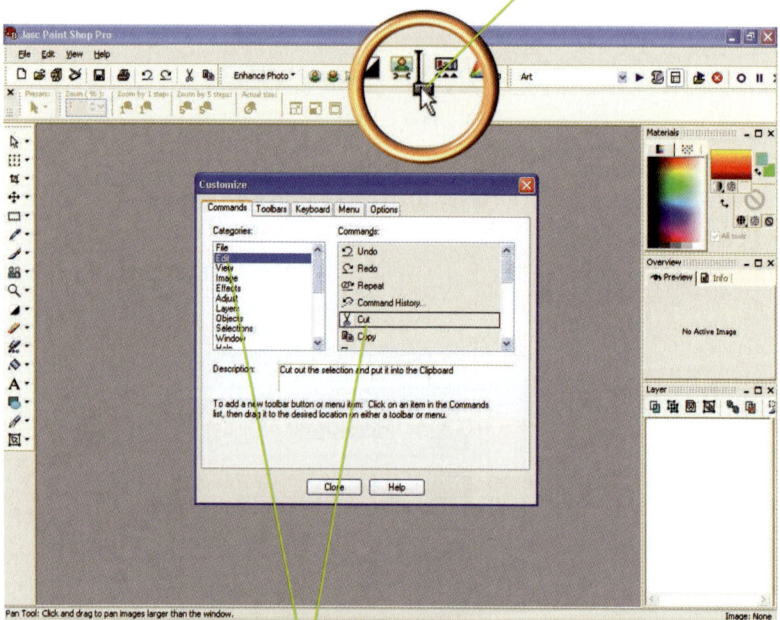

2 Select a category on the left then a command on the right

To remove a menu, toolbar or palette command, follow step 1. Then drag the command into the work area and release the mouse button.

4 To move an existing command, just drag its icon to a new menu, toolbar or palette

5 Hit Close in the dialog to confirm your changes

Creating toolbars

Want your own toolbar? No problem.

Want bigger icons in toolbars? Select the Options tab and then check Large Icons.

You can also use this dialog to specify which toolbars display. Just uncheck any you don't presently want onscreen.

If you're a Microsoft Office user and really like its personalized menus feature, you can get this in Paint Shop Pro 8, too. In the Options tab, check Menus show recently used commands first.

1 Choose View, Customize

2 Select the Toolbars tab

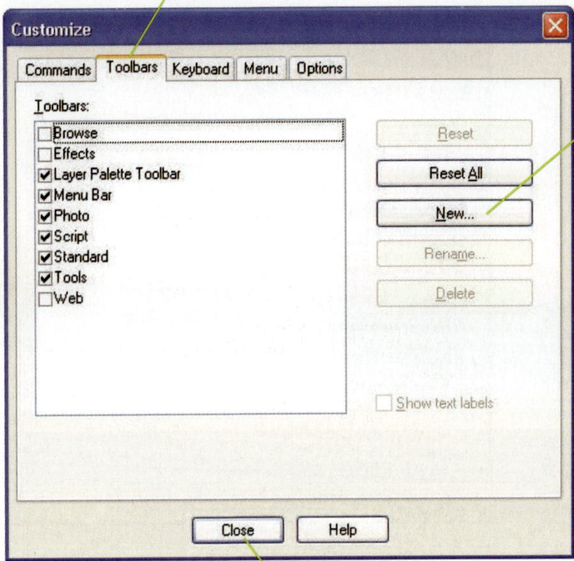

3 Click New

6 Confirm

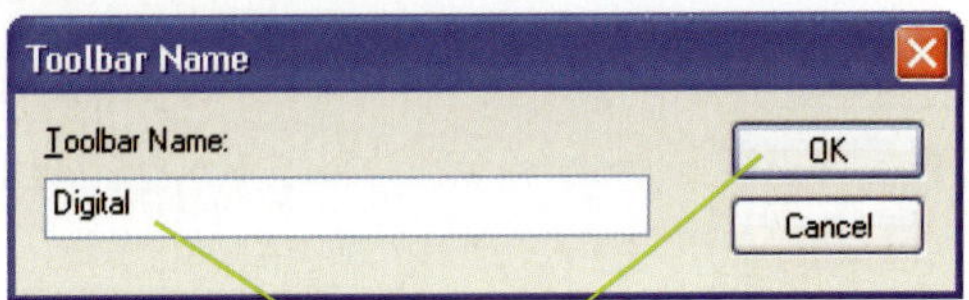

4 Name the toolbar and click OK

5 To populate the new toolbar, select the Commands tab then drag the relevant commands onto it

Assigning keyboard shortcuts to commands

Being able to launch a command via a keyboard shortcut like Ctrl+Shift+F8 can save a lot of time and effort.

You can also assign shortcuts to scripts – you can find them under the Bound Scripts category.

1. Choose View, Customize
2. Select the Keyboard tab

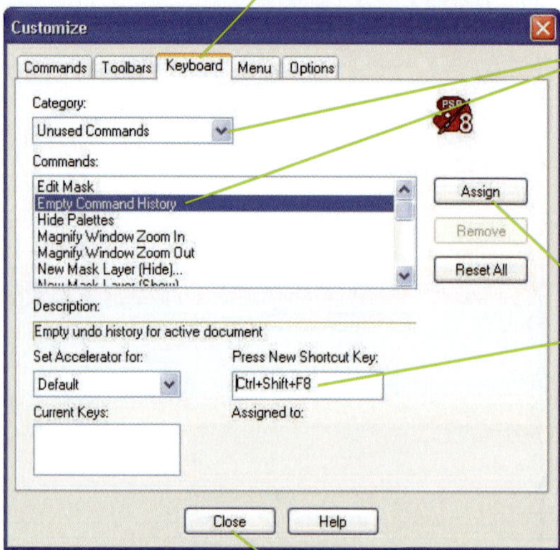

3. Select a category then a command
4. Press the relevant keys then hit Assign
5. Confirm

Click in Set Accelerator for and choose whether you want the shortcut to work in the program itself (Default) or the Browser.

Viewing all shortcuts

1. For an overview of all Paint Shop Pro shortcuts, choose Help, Keyboard Map

To print the shortcut list, click the Print icon:

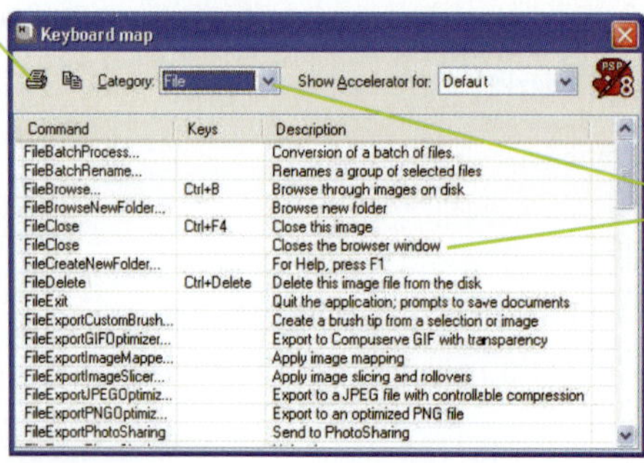

2. Shortcuts display by category/command

Using palettes

Paint Shop Pro 8 organizes many of its key commands in "palettes". Palettes work just like toolbars. By default, they're positioned ("docked") on the right of the screen but they can also be dragged out like toolbars.

When they're functioning like toolbars, palettes automatically "roll-up" when not in use, to free up space. If you don't want this, click the arrow on the right of the Title bar so it looks like this:

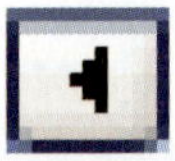

Hiding/showing palettes

1 Choose View, Palettes. In the submenu, click any palette entry to display or hide it

Making palettes float

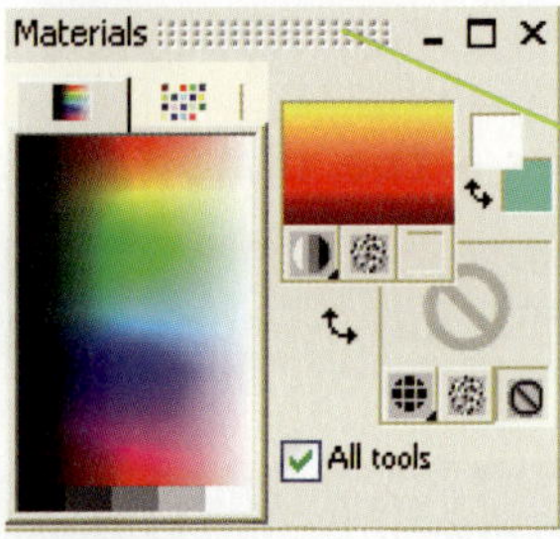

1 Double-click the palette's Title bar or drag it onto the work area

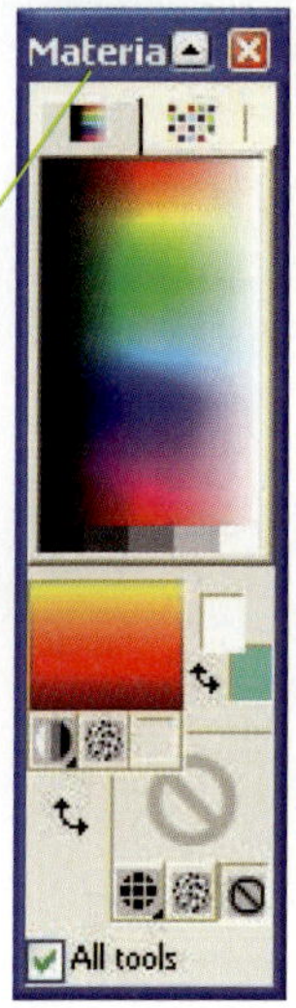

2 The "floating" palette – double-click the Title bar to redock it

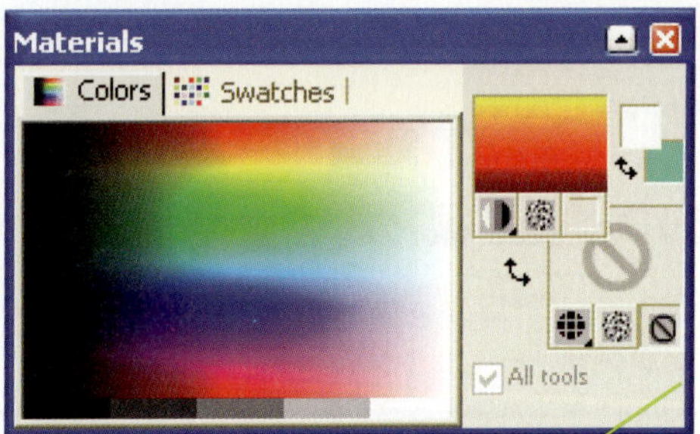

3 You can resize the palette, too, just like any window

Opening files

Paint Shop Pro will open (i.e. read and display) around 60 separate graphics file formats. These fall into two broad categories: raster and vector – see Chapter 7 for details of some of the principal image formats supported by Paint Shop Pro. When you tell Paint Shop Pro to open an image, it automatically recognizes which format it was written to, and acts accordingly. It does this by taking account of the file suffix. For example, for TIFF (Tagged Image File Format) images to be opened in Paint Shop Pro, they must end in: .TIF. (This is no hardship, since they always do.)

HOT TIP: In the Open dialog, highlight an image and click Details for information about it before you open it.

When an image has been opened, press Shift+I for the same information. Additionally, select the Creator Information tab and enter your own image information (e.g. the artist's name and brief details). Or, if the picture was imported from a digital camera, hit the EXIF (Exchangeable Image File Format) tab for camera details (e.g. the time and date the image was taken and exposure information).

Not all of the supported formats, however, can be written to disk. (See page 21 for how to save/export files.)

You open files via the Open dialog, or via a special Browser.

Opening images – the dialog route

1 Pull down the File menu and click Open

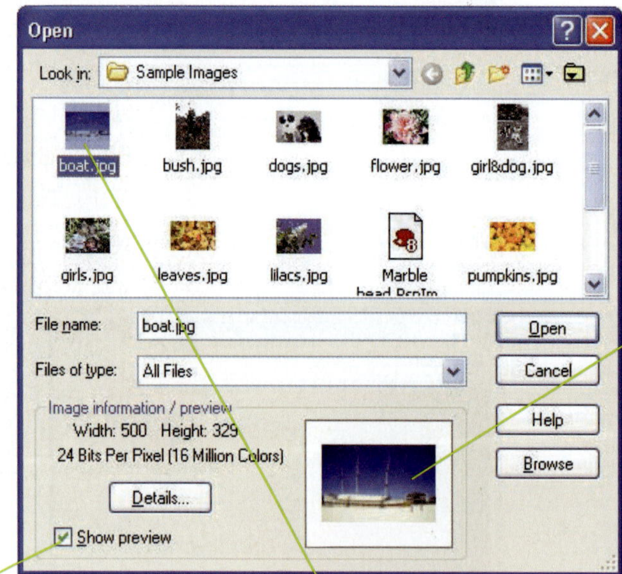

Image Preview

HOT TIP: Check Show preview to preview your image.

2 Use standard Windows techniques to locate a graphics file then double-click it. Complete any further dialog that launches

Opening images – the Browser route

Hit F5 to update thumbnails, Ctrl+F5 to update the folder tree.

1 Press Ctrl+B

2 Use the tree hierarchy to navigate to the folder that holds the image(s) you want to open

Working with lots of thumbnails? Use File, Sort to arrange them by specific characteristics (e.g. name or extension).

Image thumbnails

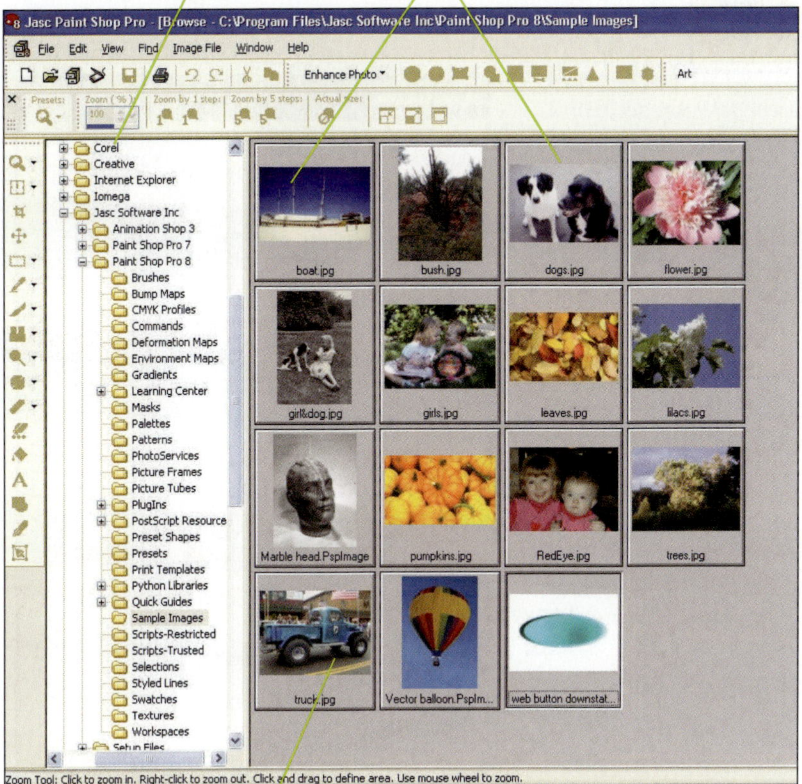

Want to customize thumbnail display? Right-click one and select Preferences.

3 Double-click an image

For brief image details, place the mouse pointer over a thumbnail for a few seconds – an explanatory box launches:

trees.jpg
1024 x 768 x 16 Million, 237.4 KB
JPEG - JFIF Compliant
18/04/2003 08:00:00

4 You can also use the Browser for file housekeeping e.g. copying/moving, renaming or deleting pictures. Right-click any thumbnail, select a command and complete any dialog that launches

New files

To duplicate the active image, click its Title bar (if you can't see it, hit Ctrl+W). Press Shift+D; Paint Shop Pro opens the copy in a new window.

Resolution is defined as the measurement (usually expressed in linear dpi – dots per inch) of image sharpness.

Re step 3 – use the following suggestions as guidelines as to the correct resolution:

- *Web pictures – use a resolution of 72 pixels per inch, and;*
- *other pictures – use the range 96–150 pixels per inch (a useful standard)*

Often, images will be "ready-made" for you in the form of clip art or scanned pictures. However, there will be times when you'll need to create an image from scratch. There are several stages, but Paint Shop Pro makes this easy.

Creating a new image

1 Hit Ctrl+N

2 Select a preset (e.g. 1024x748 or CD Insert)

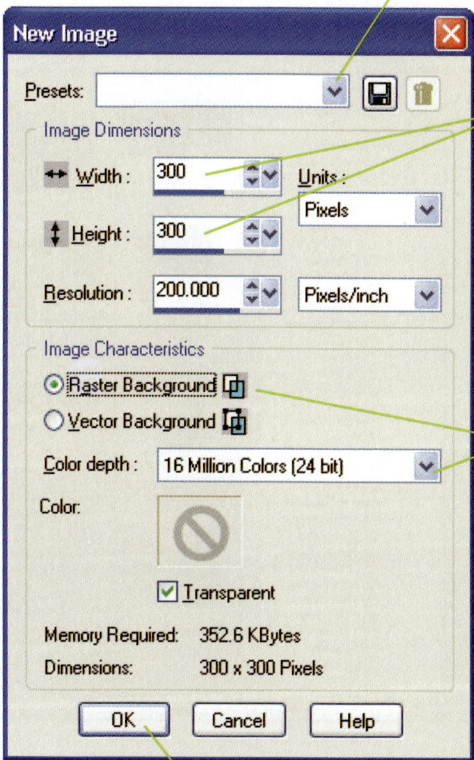

3 Or, if none of the 27 presets are suitable, enter your own dimensions and resolution

4 Select a background type then a color depth

5 Confirm the operation

6 The resulting new image is a blank canvas for your artistic efforts.

Resizing files

Pixels (a contraction of "picture element") are dots, the smallest element that can be displayed onscreen.

Bitmapped graphics consist of pixels; each is allocated a color (or grayscale).

Paint Shop Pro lets you resize an image. This is useful for a variety of reasons, but especially if digital photos you've taken aren't the right size. You can resize pictures in various ways.

Resizing an image

1 Pull down the Image menu and click Resize (or hit Shift+S)

2 Perform step 3, 4 OR 5 below. Finally, carry out step 6

4 Click here and select Percent or Pixels. Then amend the Width or Height fields

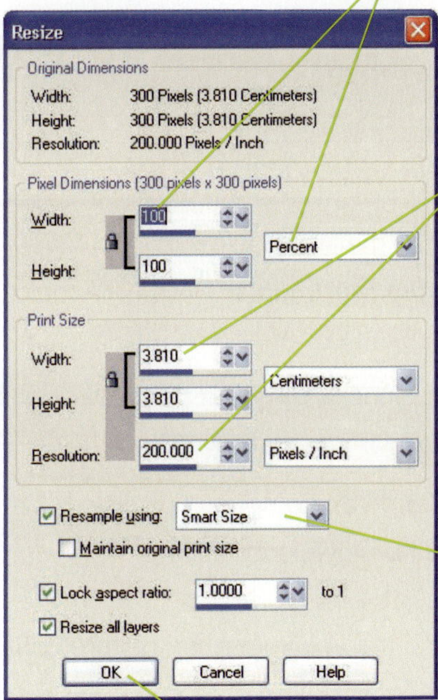

5 To change the size of the printed image, uncheck Resample using then specify new Width/Height values or enter a new resolution

3 Check Resample using and select a resample type (variable according to the image type)

6 Click here

Uncheck Lock aspect ratio to resize the Width or Height independently.

Re step 5 – increasing the resolution reduces the image size in pixels (and vice versa). This process is called "resampling".

Resizing bitmaps inevitably produces some level of distortion. The trick is to minimize this as far as possible. As a guide, don't enlarge a picture more than once and don't do so by more than 25%.

Importing files

Importing images from TWAIN-compliant scanners and digital cameras

1. With your scanner/camera connected to your PC and the relevant software installed, choose File, Import, TWAIN, Select Source and select your device in the dialog

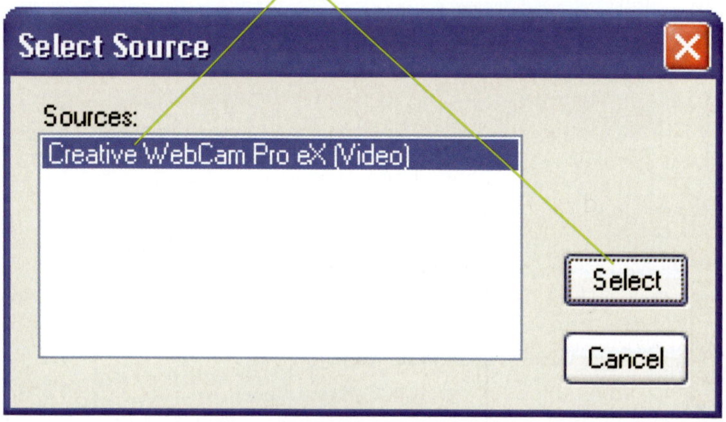

2. Choose File, Import, TWAIN, Acquire

3. For scanners, carry out the scan using the device's software

4. For cameras, complete the dialog that appears. Select pictures then hit Download

5. Refine the image (e.g. if a picture contains unwanted areas, crop it. Or remove red-eye)

Most scanners and digital cameras are TWAIN-compliant. However, Paint Shop Pro also supports importing images from WIA-compliant PCs using Windows Me and XP. Just select File, Import, From Scanner or Camera.

You can also import pictures from scanners or cameras that display as mounted drives. Just use standard Open techniques or Paint Shop Pro's Browser (see pages 16–17).

Saving files

See Chapter 7 for how to save pictures for the Web, and Chapter 8 for how to use Autosave.

When you're working on one or more images in Paint Shop Pro, it's important to save your work at frequent intervals, in order to avoid data loss in the event of a hardware fault or power interruption.

Saving a file for the first time

Pull down the File menu and click Save. Now do the following:

2 Navigate to the drive/folder you want to save to

Re step 1 – Paint Shop Pro has its own proprietary format (suffix: .pspimage) that retains layers, vectors, masks and selection data. Use the Paint Shop Pro format while you're working with an image; when it's complete, save it to a nonproprietary format.

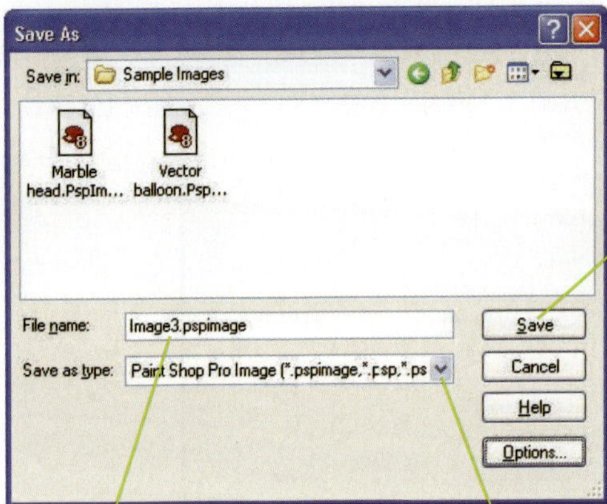

4 Click Save

3 Name the image

1 Click here; in the list, click a format to save to e.g. Photoshop or Encapsulated PostScript (for commercial printing)

Re step 1 – many image formats have sub-formats and/or compression options you can choose from.

If it's available, click the Options button immediately after step 1. In the resulting dialog, select the appropriate option(s). Click OK.

Saving previously saved files

Pull down the File menu and click Save. No dialog launches; instead, Paint Shop Pro saves the latest version of your file to disk, overwriting the previous.

Saving copies of images

You can also save a copy of the active picture (and leave the original intact).

Pull down the File menu and click Save Copy As. Now follow steps 1–4 above.

Enlarging an image's canvas

Enlarging an image's canvas (unlike resizing) does not expand the image itself.

As we've seen on page 18, when you create an image from scratch, you specify the width and height in pixels. When you do this, Paint Shop Pro automatically defines a "canvas" (the area on which the image lies) with the same dimensions. However, you can easily specify increased dimensions for the canvas (e.g. if you need to resize the image).

Increasing an image's canvas

1. Pull down the Image menu and click Canvas Size

Check Lock aspect ratio to resize the canvas proportionately.

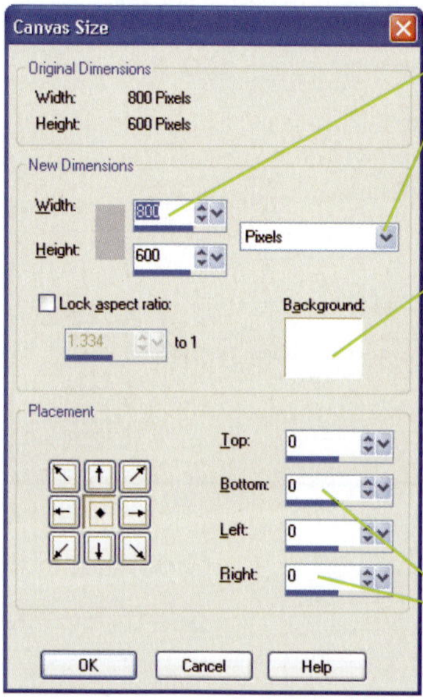

2. Choose a unit then complete the Width and/or Height fields

3. Click here and select a background color (white is the default)

4. Enter new placement dimensions

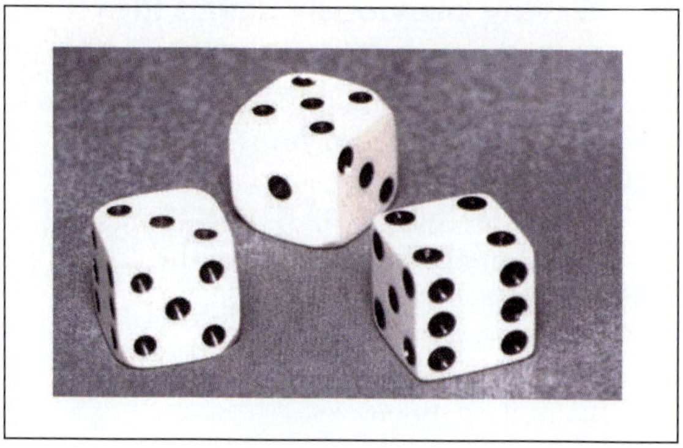

Here, the canvas has been enlarged vertically and horizontally (the background is white)

Zoom

The ability to "zoom in" (magnify) or "zoom out" (reduce magnification) is very important when you're working with images in Paint Shop Pro. When you zoom in or out, Paint Shop Pro increases or reduces the magnification by single increments.

When you zoom in or out, the picture's window resizes automatically to fit it. Don't want this? No problem: go to File, Preferences. Select the View tab. Uncheck one or both of the settings under Zooming.

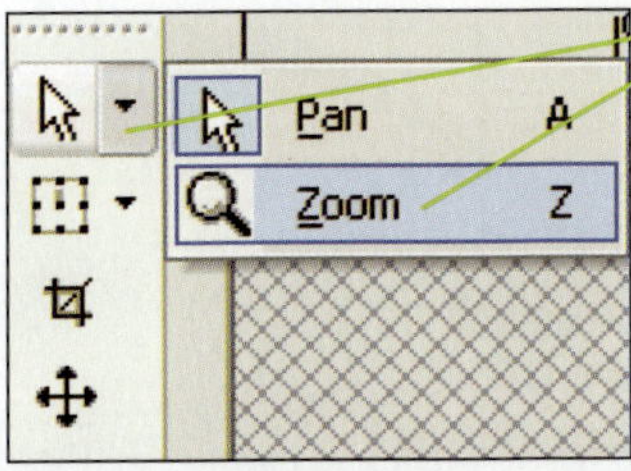

1 Click here in the Tool palette then click Zoom (or just hit Z)

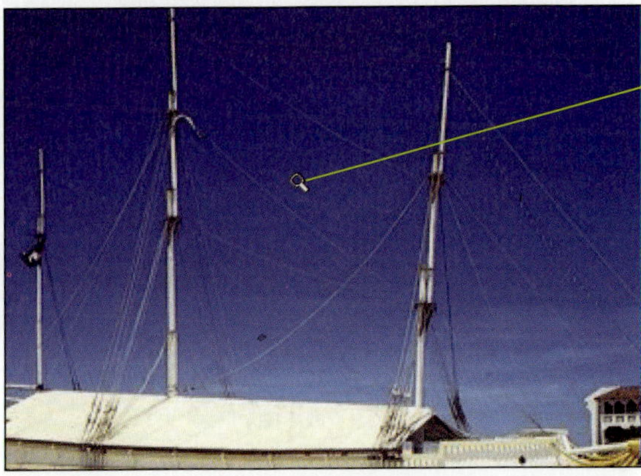

2 Position the mouse pointer where you want to zoom in/out

Re step 3 – you should repeat this as often as necessary.

3 Left-click to zoom in, OR right-click to zoom out

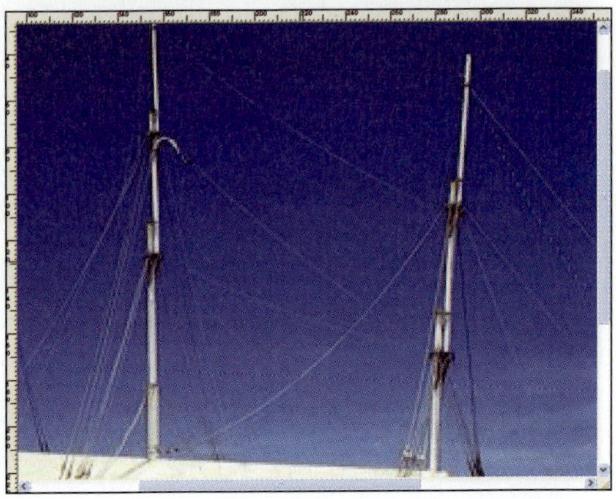

The result of zooming in several times

More zoom precision

1. Make sure the Zoom tool is active then drag out a box – the area inside the box is magnified

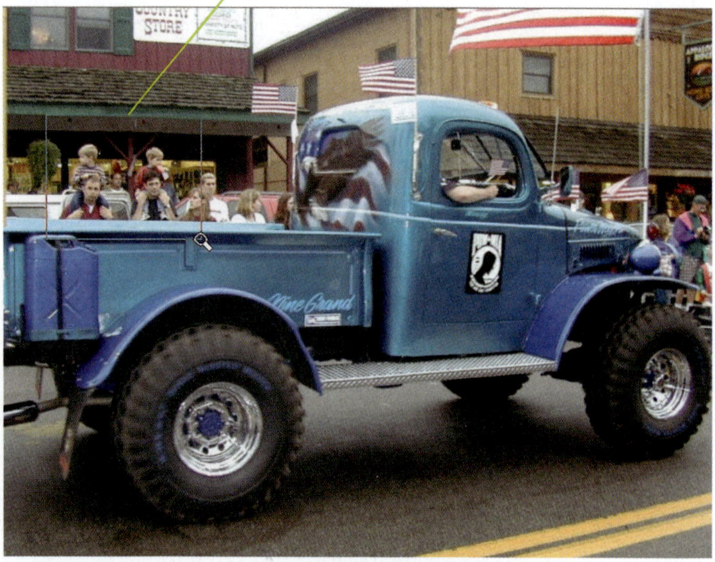

Paint Shop Pro now zooms in accurately to the area you specify – it doesn't (as before) just go to the nearest zoom setting.

Using the Magnifier

1. Hit Ctrl+Alt+M

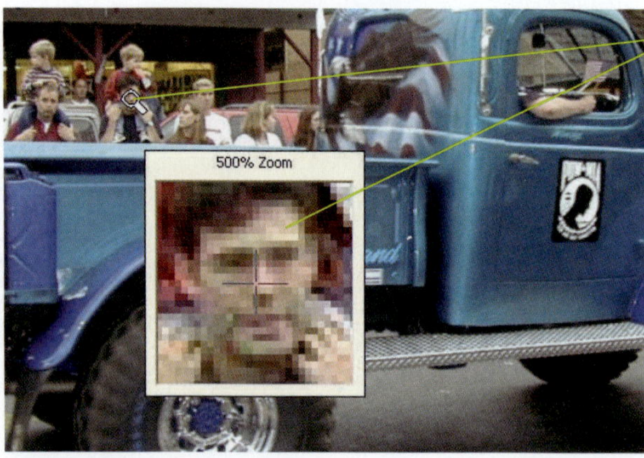

2. Place the cursor on the area you want magnified

The Magnifier enlarges to 500%, so the quality likely is less than perfect.

Using zoom presets

Many features in Paint Shop Pro 8 are supplied with extremely useful features called "presets". Presets are essentially scripts that define the way tools and dialogs operate. We'll look at scripts in more detail in Chapter 9 but in the meantime it's useful to examine how zoom presets work.

You can also use the Tools Options palette to apply standard zoom settings. For example, enter a percentage into the Zoom (%) box.

1 Follow step 1 on page 23

2 If the Tools Options palette isn't onscreen, hit F4

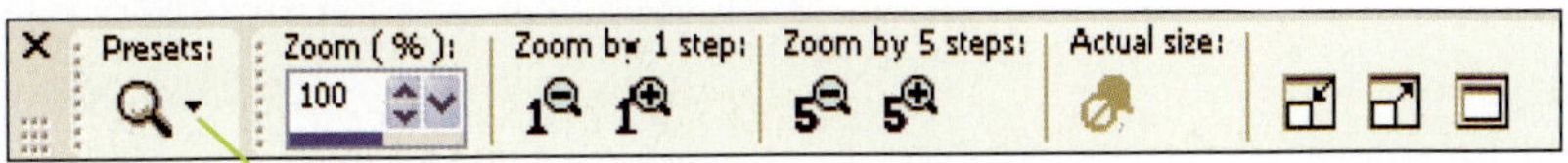

3 Click here

4 Select a preset zoom

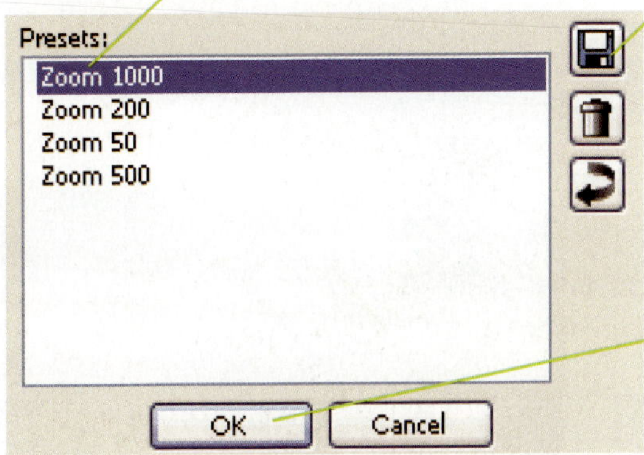

5 Or click here if you've already zoomed in and want to save this as a preset for future use

7 Click OK

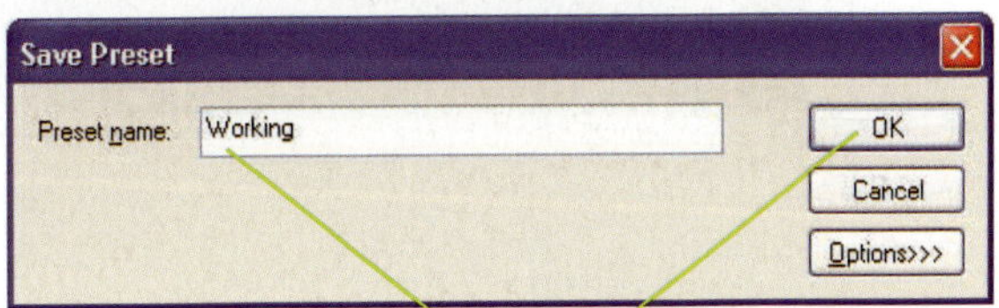

6 If you followed step 5, name the preset and hit OK

The Overview palette

When you've zoomed in on part of an image, Paint Shop Pro lets you view the entire image at the same time (in a way, this is the opposite of using the Magnifier). You do this by launching the Overview palette.

JASC, the manufacturers of Paint Shop Pro, have their own website: www.jasc.com. Use this to:

- *download a free, trial version of Paint Shop Pro*
- *upgrade existing installations of Paint Shop Pro*
- *download update patches to correct problems*
- *download other JASC software. These include WebDraw, the SVG (Scalable Vector Graphics) editor and Virtual Painter (turns your digital photos into paintings)*

Using the Overview palette

1 If the Overview palette isn't visible (by default, on the right of the screen), hit F9

2 If an image is being viewed at a high magnification and not all of it displays in its window, the Overview palette shows a rectangle representing the visible area. Drag this to view a new area in the main window

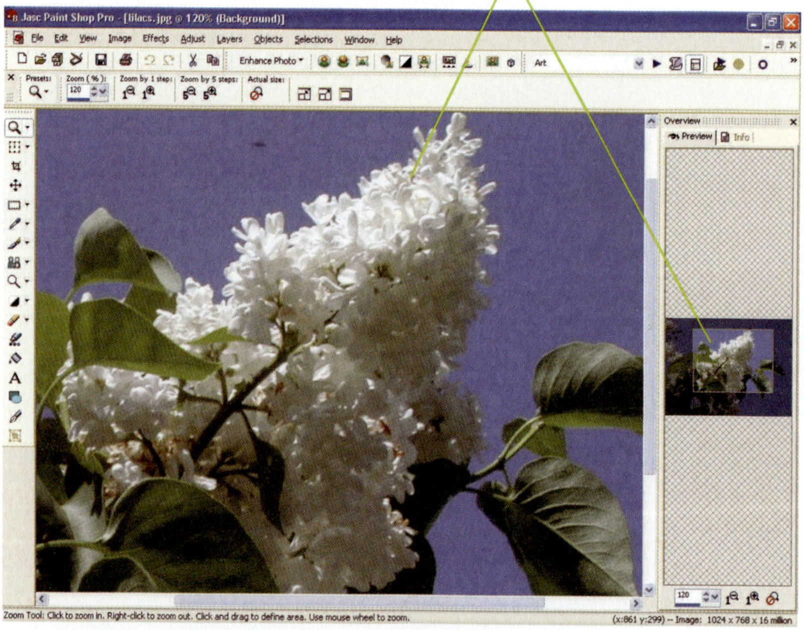

3 Select the Info tab for brief information about the picture

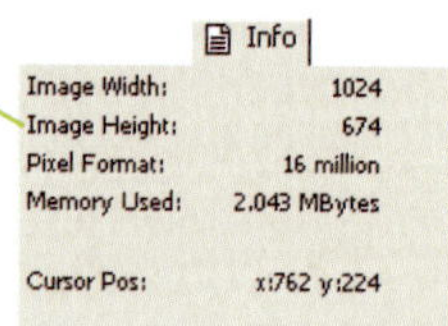

Special screen modes

Paint Shop Pro has two special screen modes that show more of the open picture and fewer extraneous screen components.

1. Hit Ctrl+Shift+A to enter Full Screen Preview mode (Esc to return to the normal screen):

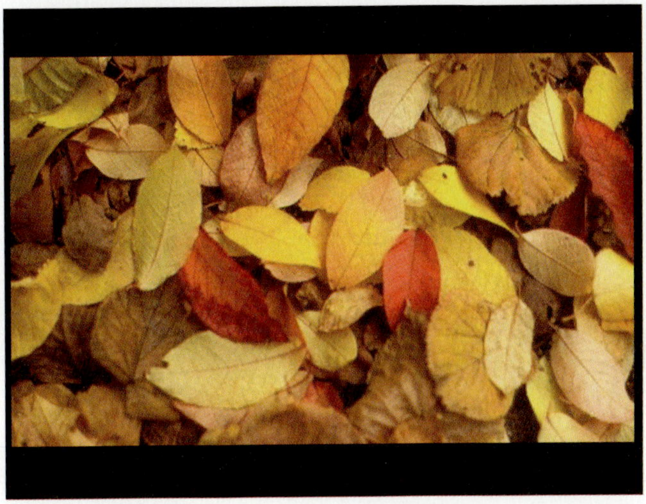

2. Press Shift+A to enter Full Screen Edit mode (repeat this to close):

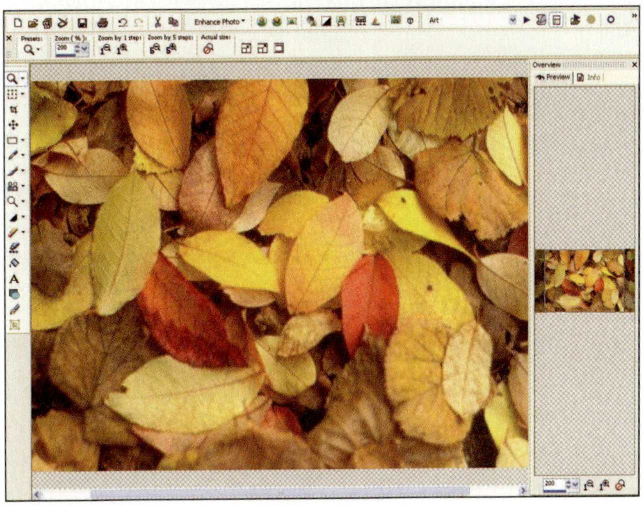

Full Screen Edit hides the Title, Menu and Status bars. Use this when you want to work with your picture.

Undo and Revert

Paint Shop Pro has two features that, effectively, allow you to revert to the way things were *before* you carried out one or more amendments to the active image.

You can turn off undos if you want. Pull down the File menu and click Preferences, General Program Preferences. Activate the Undo tab and uncheck Enable the undo system. Click OK.

Do the same for Enable the redo system to disable undos.

The Undo command

You can "undo" (i.e. reverse) the last editing action by issuing a menu command.

Pull down the Edit menu and do the following:

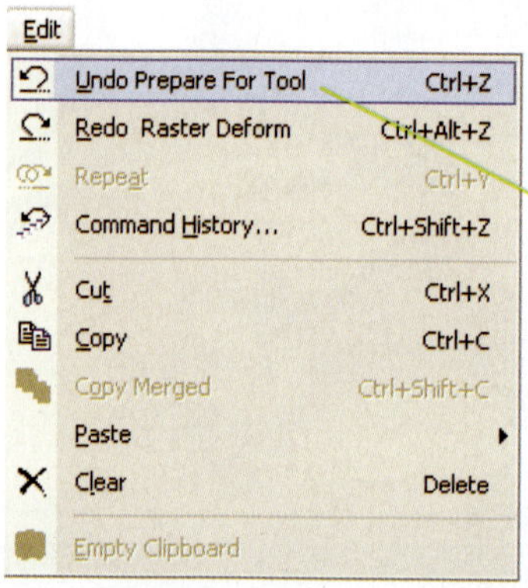

Click Undo . . .

The Revert command

You can – in a single command – undo all the editing changes made to an image since it was last saved. You do this by having Paint Shop Pro abandon the changes and reopen the last-saved version of the file.

1. Pull down the File menu and click Revert

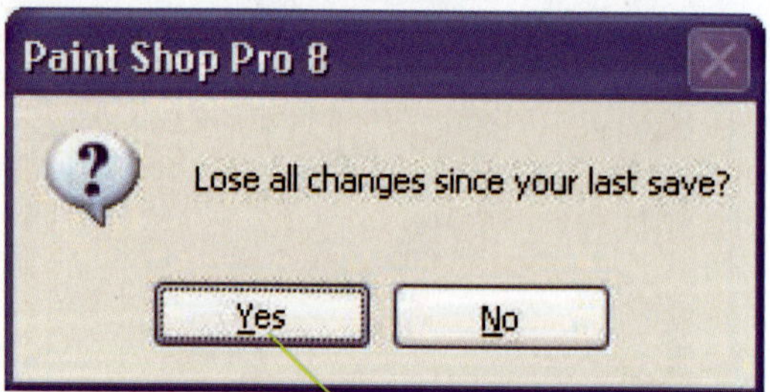

2. Click Yes

Redo

Paint Shop Pro also lets you undo undoes. This is called "redoing" an action.

The Redo command

Pull down the Edit menu and do the following:

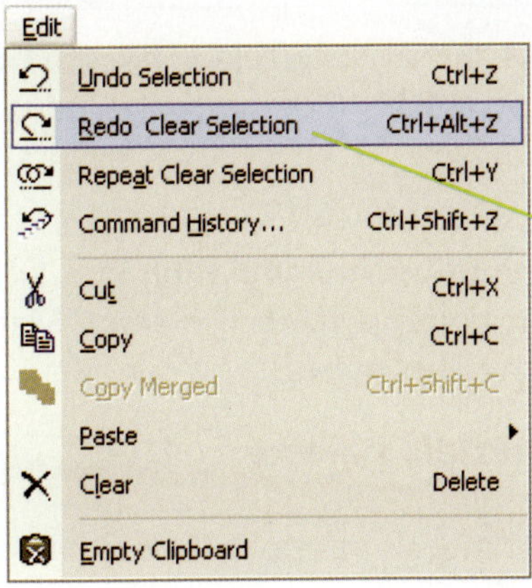

Click Redo . . .

Multiple undos and redos

1 You can undo or redo more than one action at a time. Hit Ctrl+Shift+Z

2 Click an undo or redo level, then click Undo or Redo (clicking a higher level automatically selects levels below it)

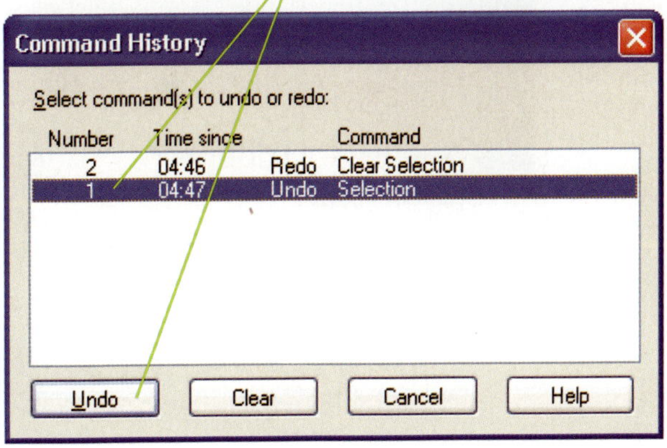

Background/foreground colors

If you're working with images with fewer than 16 million colors, Paint Shop Pro 8 only displays 256 colors in the Select Color panel. This means that when you select a color, Paint Shop Pro uses that color which is nearest to the one selected, so it may not be what you want...

For this reason, you may find it useful to have the Select Color panel only display the available 256 colors. To do this, pull down the File menu and click Preferences, General Program Preferences. In the dialog, select the Palettes tab. Activate Show document palette. Click OK.

Swatches are great timesavers. They're materials (i.e. colors or combinations of colors and gradients, patterns etc.) that you save for later reuse.

See page 32 for more on swatches.

Paint Shop Pro uses two broad color definitions – these are called "active" colors:

Foreground colors	These occupy image foregrounds and are invoked with the left mouse button
Background colors	These occupy image backgrounds and are invoked with the right mouse button

The way you work with foreground and background colors is crucial to your use of Paint Shop Pro. Fortunately, selecting the appropriate colors – via the onscreen Materials Palette – is very easy and straightforward.

The Materials palette

1. If the Materials palette isn't visible (by default, on the right of the screen), hit F6

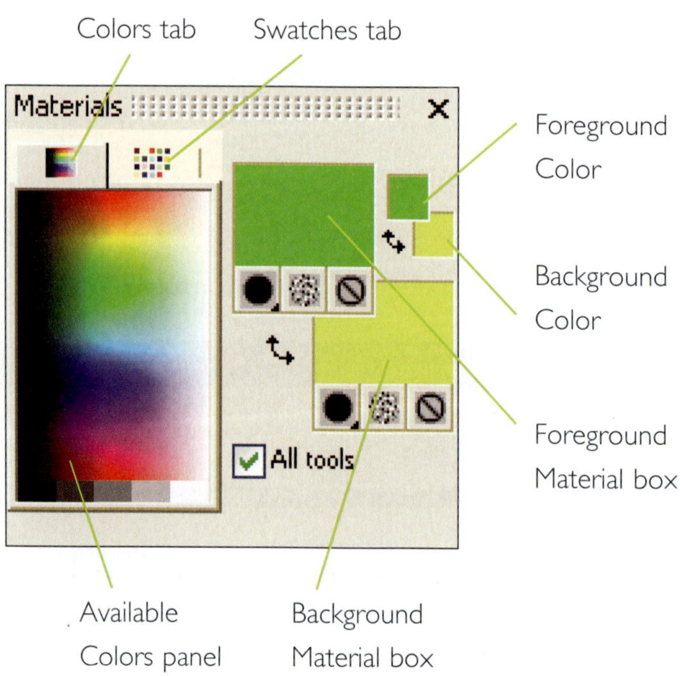

Using the Available Colors panel

1 Move the mouse pointer over any active area in the Select Color panel. The pointer changes to: 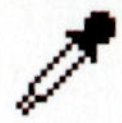

2 Move the pointer over the colors in the Select Color Panel; as you do so, Paint Shop Pro launches color details:

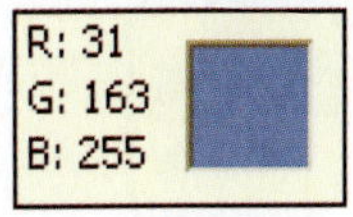

3 When you find the correct color, left-click once to select it as a foreground color (in the Foreground Color box)

4 Or right-click once to select it as a background color (in the Background Color box)

If you don't want to apply a gradient or pattern, click the Transparent icon in the Foreground or Background Material boxes.

You may be wondering, since they all display colors, why the Materials palette incorporates Foreground and Background Material boxes in addition to Foreground and Background Color boxes. The reasons are:

- the Foreground and Background Material boxes also display gradients and patterns:

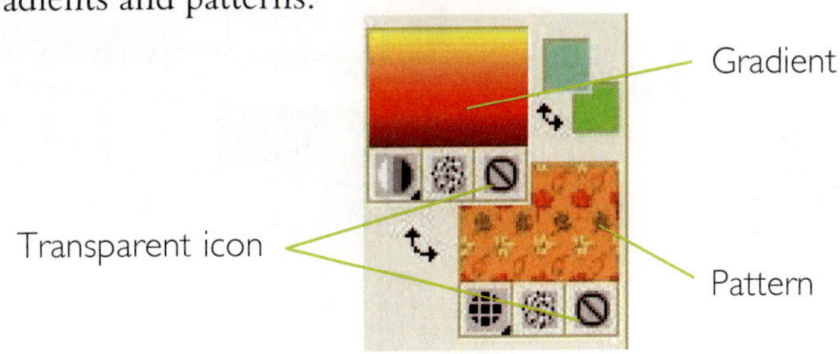

As a general rule, use the left mouse button to apply foreground effects and the right to apply background effects. (This does not apply to a few tools e.g. the Text tool.)

- even when the Material boxes display a gradient or pattern, you can use the Color boxes to apply new colors without changing the gradient or pattern

For more on how to apply gradients and patterns, see Chapter 3.

Using swatches

Save color/material combinations as swatches for later reuse.

You can also work the process in the opposite way. Create a color/material in the Material dialog then click the Add to swatches button. Name the swatch and hit OK.

Creating a swatch

1 In the Materials palette, select the Swatches tab

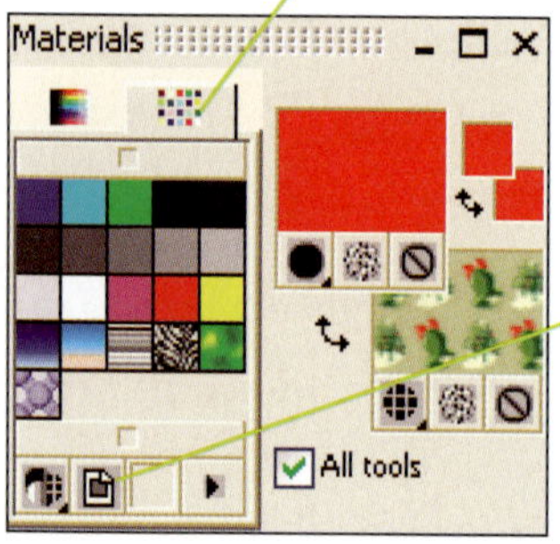

2 Click here then name the swatch and click OK

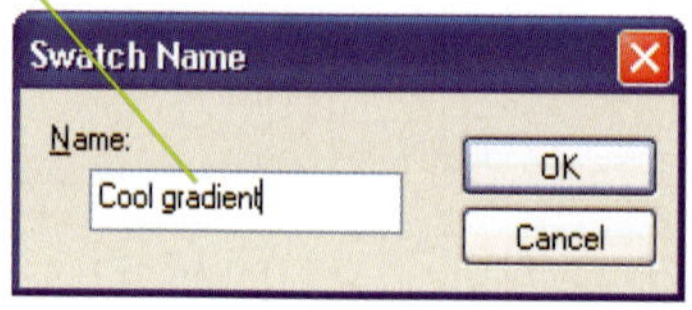

3 Complete the Material dialog – see pages 78 and 80–81

Using a swatch

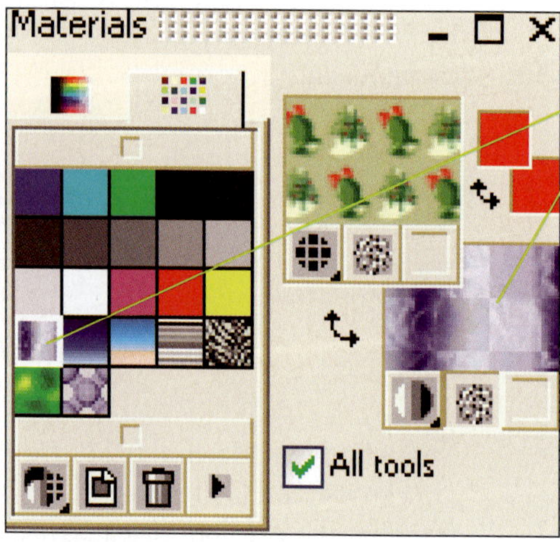

1 Left-click the new swatch to select it as the foreground material or right-click to select it as the background material

The Product Tour

Paint Shop Pro provides a handy Product Tour that you can use to get help on key program areas.

Launching the Product Tour

1 Pull down the Help menu and click Product Tour

2 After a few seconds, a Welcome screen launches:

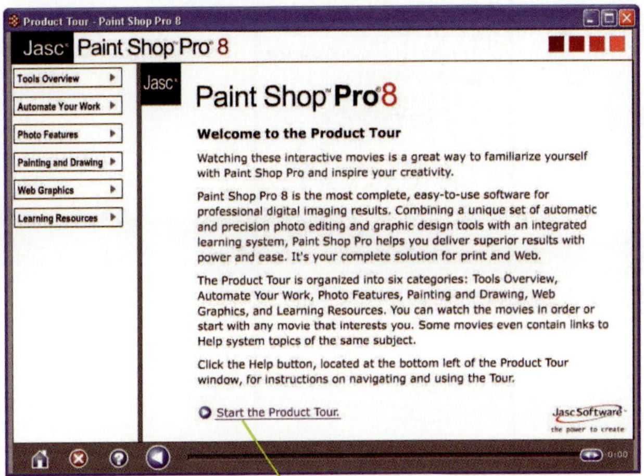

3 Click here to work through the tour (or select a specific topic on the left then carry out step 4)

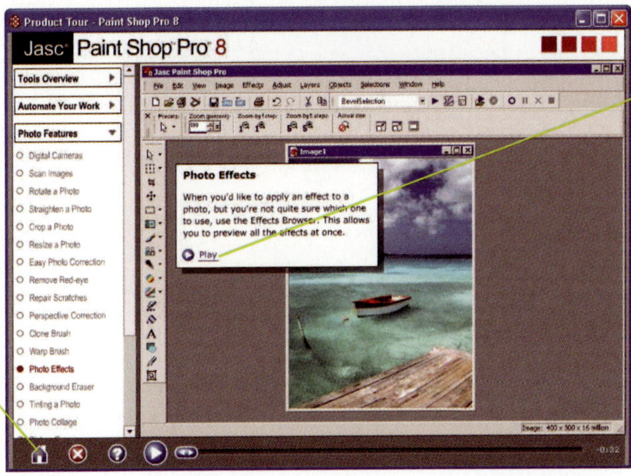

4 Click Play to view a helpful movie

HOT TIP *Click Home to return to the Welcome screen.*

Using Quick Guides

Paint Shop Pro provides a series of brief but useful tutorials. Use these when you're working with a picture or want to carry out a specific procedure but aren't sure how.

Launching Quick Guides

1 Hit F10 if the Learning Center palette isn't visible

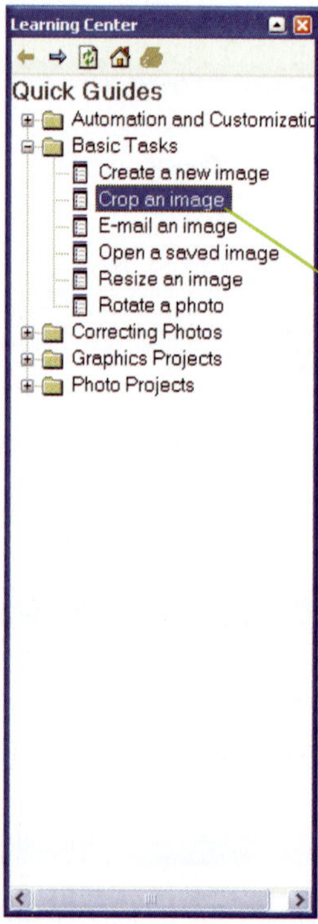

2 Drill down to the topic you need

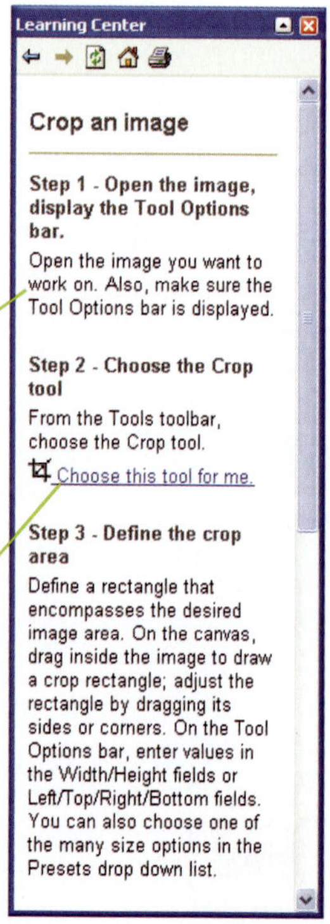

3 Take this on board. If you want Paint Shop Pro to perform a procedure, click its link

Making selections

Chapter Two

In this chapter, you'll define a wide variety of bitmap selections (even exotic ones like stars). You'll deselect, invert and move selections then amend feathering. You'll also select image areas by more advanced methods based on color and then manipulate them. You'll save selections to disk and as alpha channels then create multiple/subtractive selections. Finally, you'll select and group vectors.

Covers

Selections – an overview

Selecting all or part of a Paint Shop Pro image is the essential preliminary for performing any of its many editing operations.

You can make the following kinds of selections:

- rectangular, square, elliptical and circular
- triangular
- hexagonal/octagonal/polygonal
- star-shaped
- arrow-shaped
- freehand
- color-based
- additive and subtractive

Using combinations of the various types, you can create some truly unique selections (and have lots of fun at the same time).

Briefly, bitmaps consist of pixels (colored dots) while vectors are based on mathematical formulas. Care must be taken when resizing bitmaps that image quality isn't degraded.

Additionally, you can select an entire image (including vectors) in one go – just hit Ctrl+A.

You can also save image selections to disk as special files (and then reopen them at will within other images) and group/ungroup vector selections.

The selection types listed above are bitmap (raster) selections. However, you can also select vector objects you've created earlier – see opposite and pages 56–58.

Selected vector objects have broken borders interspersed with nodes (for how to use them, see pages 95–100)

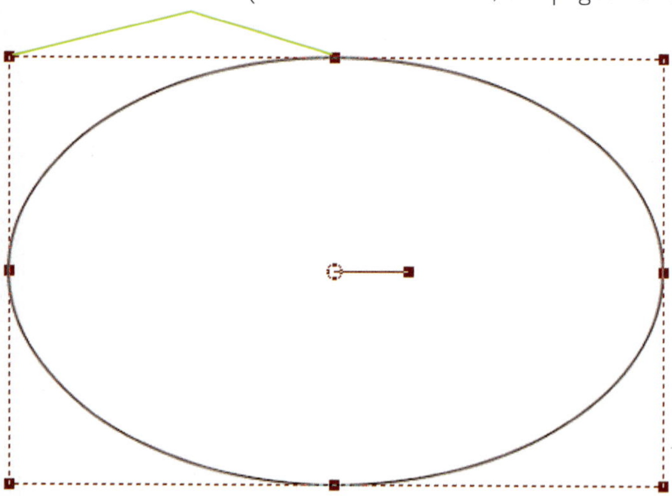

Selection borders

Generally, whenever you make a bitmap selection in Paint Shop Pro, you'll select *part* of an image. Whether you do this or select an image in its entirety, the portion you've selected is surrounded with a dotted line:

You can convert ("promote") raster and vector selections into raster layers (but note that the part of the new layer not containing the selection is transparent). Simply pull down the Selections menu and hit Ctrl+Shift+P.

For more information on layers, see Chapter 8.

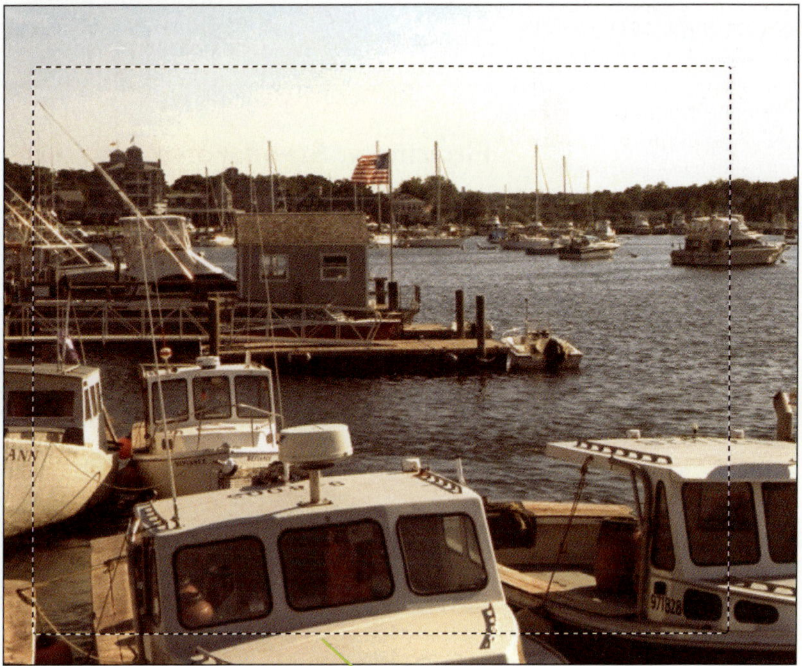

A rectangular selection

There are occasions when it's useful to hide raster selection marquees – for instance, when you've applied feathering and want to see the result more clearly. Note that hiding marquees does not cancel the selection; it's still there.

To hide the active selection's marquee, pull down the Selections menu and click Hide Marquee. Or hit Ctrl+Shift+M. (Repeat to reverse this.)

As with most programs, the selection border (sometimes called a "marquee" or "marching ants") moves and so is easy to locate.

Selection modes

A floated selection is temporarily raised above the host layer until you deselect it or create a new selection. At this point, it's either "defloated" to the nearest raster layer or promoted to a new one.

Mostly, Paint Shop Pro takes care of the distinction between standard and floating selections for you. Just bear in mind the main functional differences.

Floating/defloating does not apply to vector selections. However, if you float a raster selection on a vector layer (see Chapter 8 for more information on layers), it is rasterized.

Hold down Alt as you drag a Standard selection to float it automatically.

You can use two kinds of bitmap selection:

Standard	These form part of the original image. In other words, if you move a selection area, Paint Shop Pro fills the resultant gap with the background color
Floating	When a selection area is floating, the contents are deemed to be on top of (and distinct from) the original

Floating v. Standard selections:

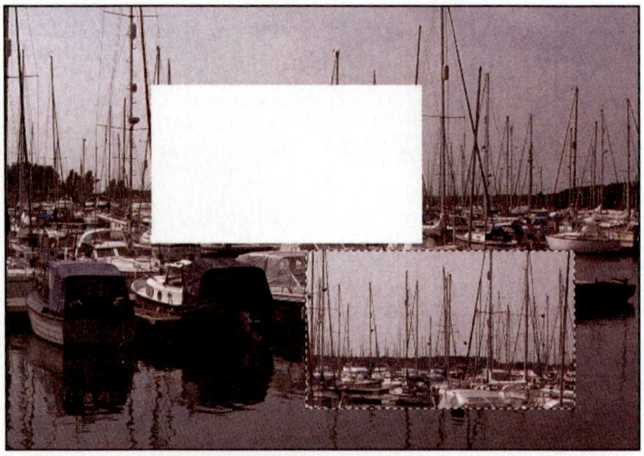

A Standard selection. The selection has been moved, filling the gap with the active background

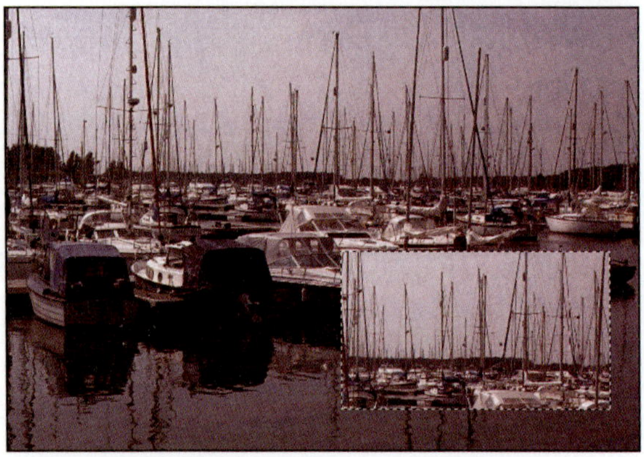

A Floating selection. As above, but the underlying image is unaffected

To float a selection, press Ctrl+F. To defloat a selection (return it to Standard), press Ctrl+Shift+F.

Creating rectangular selections

You can buy Xtras 1 and 2 (lots of cool selections, masks, frames, patterns, textures and picture tubes) for a small fee from ***www.digitalworkshop.com****. If you also have version 7 of Paint Shop Pro, you can install Xtras 1 and 2 into version 7 then download a small, free patch from Digital Workshop's website to make them work in Paint Shop Pro 8. If you don't have Paint Shop Pro 7, don't worry: version 8-specific Xtras 1 and 2 should be available by the time you read this.*

You can create rectangular bitmap selections in two ways:

- with the use of the mouse
- with the use of a special dialog

The mouse route

Ensure the Tool palette is onscreen (if it isn't, right-click any toolbar or palette – in the menu, select Toolbars, Tools). Then carry out the following steps:

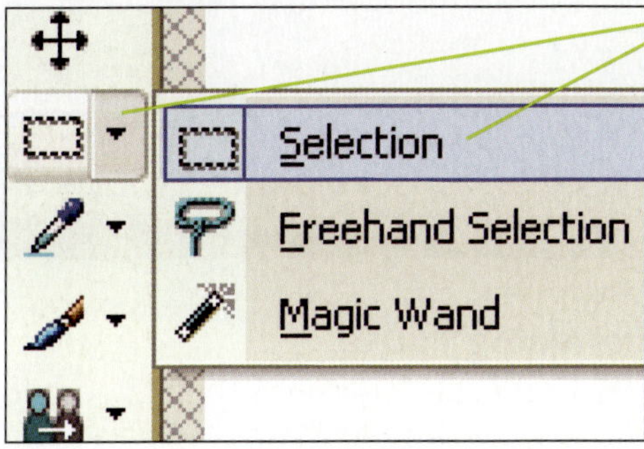

1 Click here in the Tool palette then click Selection (or just hit S)

To specify the amount of feathering (the sharpness of the selection), type in a value in the Feather field. The range is from 0 (maximum sharpness) to 200 (maximum softness).

2 If the Tool Options toolbar isn't onscreen, right-click the Tool Palette and select Palettes, Tool Options (or just hit F4)

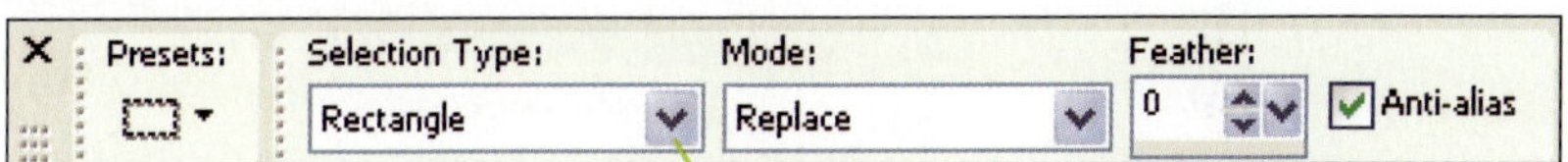

3 Click here and select Rectangle (or Rounded Rectangle to round off the corners)

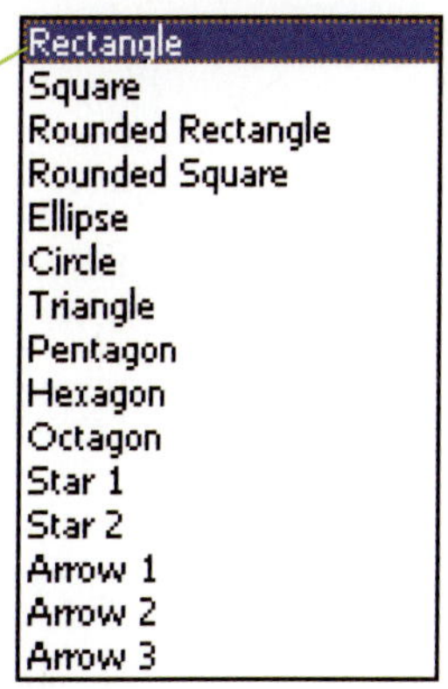

Less common is the need to create triangular, hexagonal, octagonal, polygonal, star- or arrow-shaped selections, but they can sometimes be useful. Just select any of these in the drop-down list then drag it out.

The Rectangle and Square selection cursor looks like this:

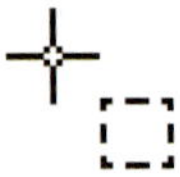

To create a square selection with the mouse, follow steps 1–2 on page 39. In step 3, select Square (or Rounded Square) instead.

4 Drag out the selection

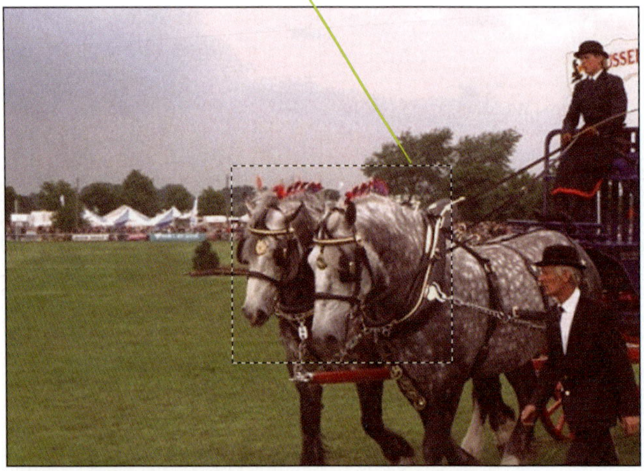

The dialog route

Refer to the Tool Options toolbar and do the following:

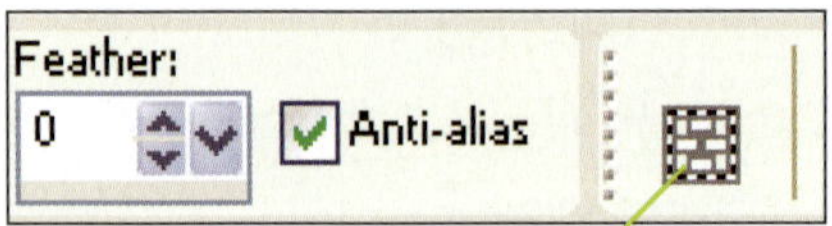

1 Click here

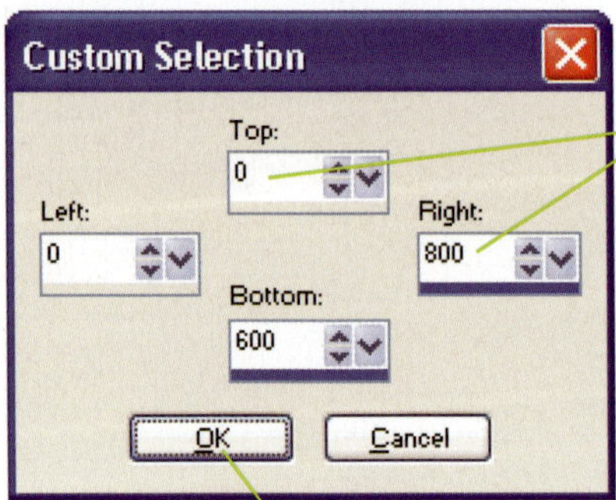

2 Type in the positions (in pixels) of the four corners (enter the same dimension four times to make a square)

3 Click here

Creating elliptical selections

1 Hit S

2 Carry out step 2 on page 39

3 In step 3 on page 39, select Ellipse

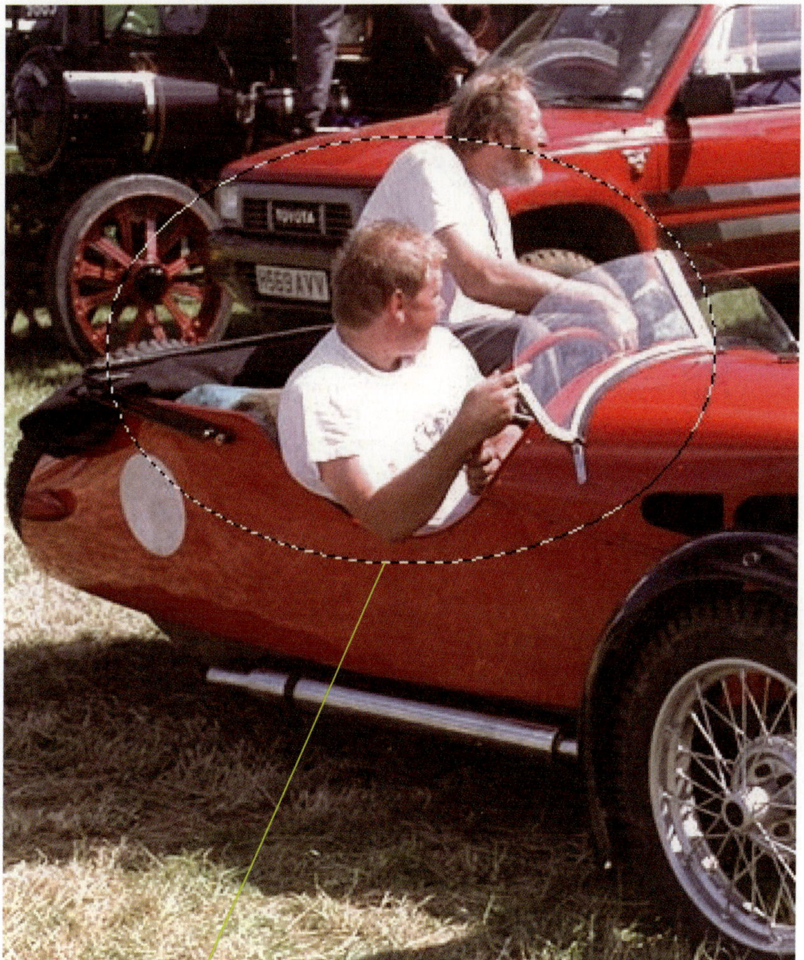

To create a circular selection, just select Circle in step 3.

4 Drag to define the selection

Irregular selections

You can use the Freehand tool to create selections by hand. This needs a steady hand and ideally a certain amount of artistic ability.

Creating freehand selections

Ensure the Tool Palette is onscreen (if it isn't, right-click any toolbar or palette and select Toolbars, Tools). Then do the following:

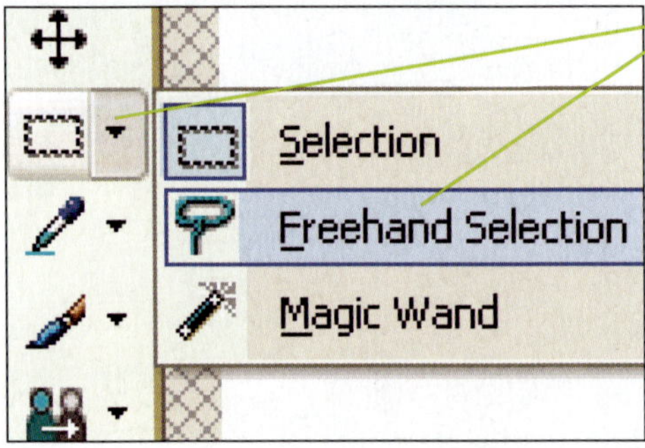

1 Click here in the Tool palette then click Freehand Selection

2 If you've saved any freehand presets earlier, click here and go to step 3

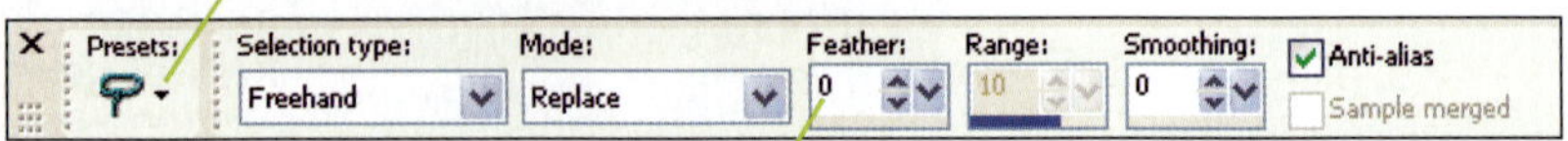

4 Complete any of the Tool Options toolbar settings. For example, type in a Feather setting (in the range: 0–200)

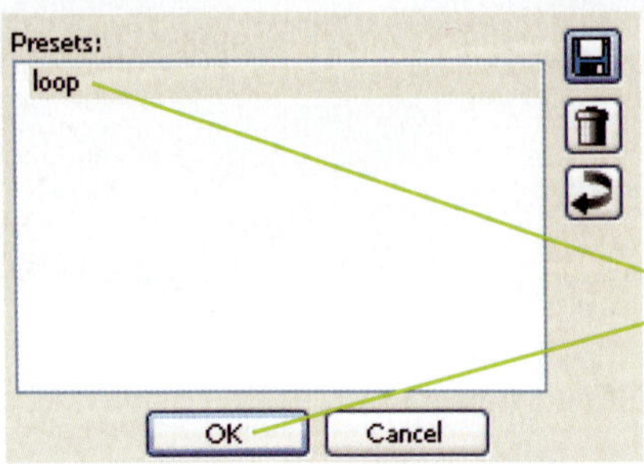

3 Select a preset and hit OK

You can refine freehand selections. To avoid the selection having irregular borders, click in the Selection type field and select one of these:

- *Point to point (the borders are straight)*
- *Smart Edge (the borders are defined between contrasting colors/light)*
- *Edge Seeker (Paint Shop Pro locates edges in areas with slight color/light changes)*

Consider unchecking Anti-alias if you're not working with text or merging pictures (antialising works like feathering to smooth image edges, but is more precise).

The Freehand cursor looks like this:

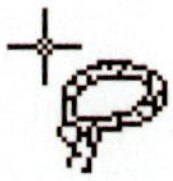

5 Drag to define the selection. Or, if you're using Point to point, Smart Edge or Edge Seeker, click around the area you want to select then double-click when you've finished

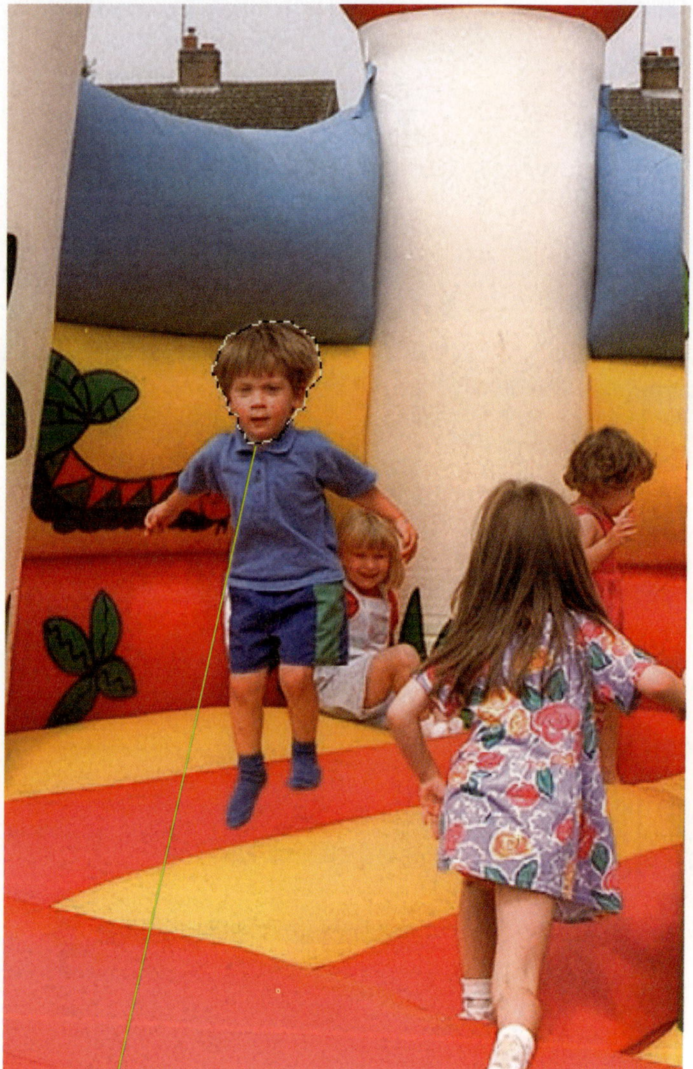

6 This is Edge Seeker in action – experiment with the Tool Options toolbar settings until you get the precision you need

Selections based on color

You can use another Paint Shop Pro tool – the Magic Wand – to select portions of the active image which share a specific color.

Creating color-based selections

Ensure the Tool Palette is onscreen (if it isn't, right-click any toolbar or palette and select Toolbars, Tools). Then do the following:

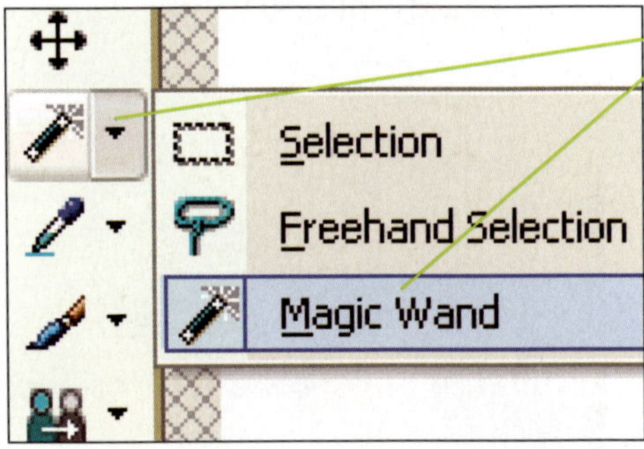

1 Click here in the Tool palette then click Magic Wand

2 If you've saved any freehand presets earlier, click here and go to step 3

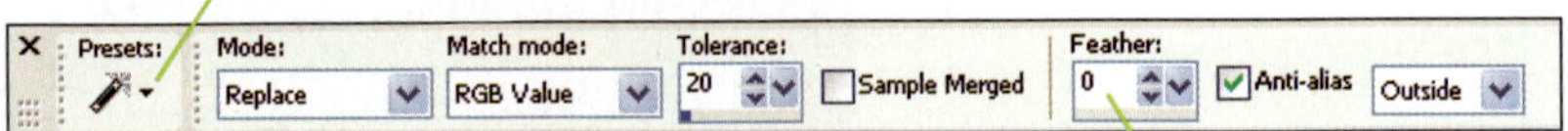

4 Complete any of the Tool Options toolbar settings. For example, type in a Feather setting (in the range: 0–200)

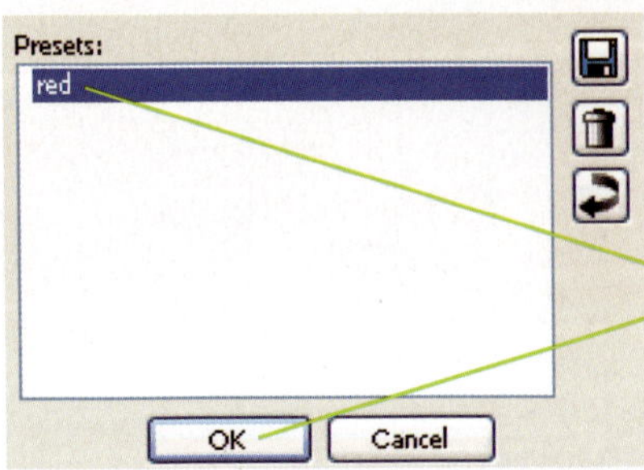

3 Select a preset and hit OK

HOT TIP: *Type in a value in the Tolerance field. (Tolerance is the degree to which image pixels must approach the chosen one to activate selection.) Use this range:*

- *0 – only exact matches result in selection*
- *200 – all pixels are selected*

DON'T FORGET: *Check Sample Merged to make a selection based on all (not just the active) layers.*

The Magic Wand cursor looks like this:

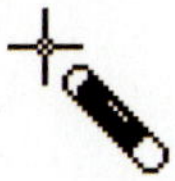

5 Place the mouse pointer over the area you want to select and left-click once

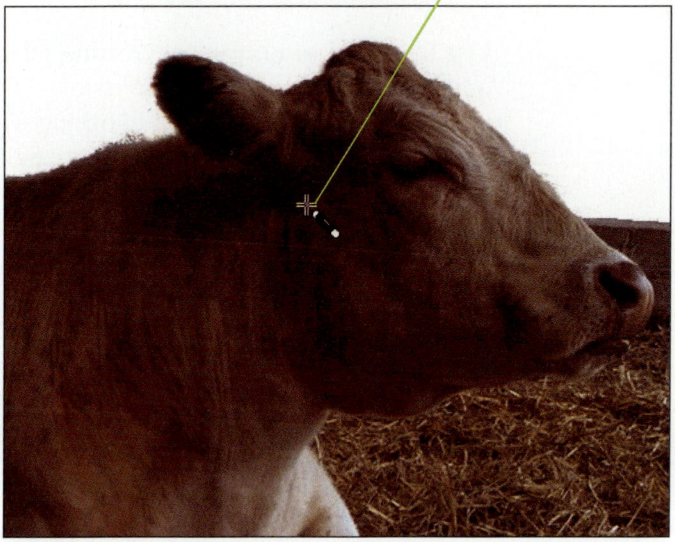

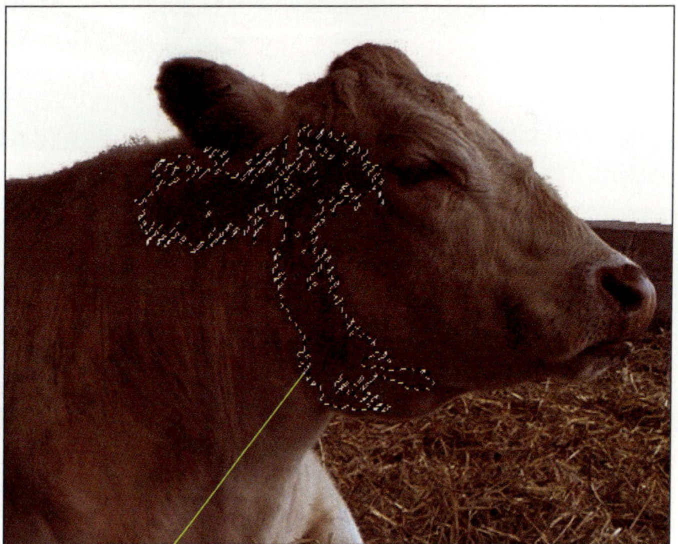

6 The new selection area

To remove a specific color from an existing selection, follow steps 1–4 on the facing page. Now hold down Ctrl as you click the color.

Inverting raster selections

When you've selected a portion of a bitmap, you can have Paint Shop Pro deselect the selected area AND select the external area which was previously unselected, all in one operation. Paint Shop Pro calls this "inverting a selection".

Use inversion as a means of creating selections which would otherwise be difficult – or impossible – to achieve. Inversion is especially useful when you're working with photographs of people set against a single-color background. Select the background and then invert it as a really useful way to select the person. Much easier and quicker than using the Freehand tool.

Inverting a selection

1. Make a normal selection then hit Ctrl+Shift+I

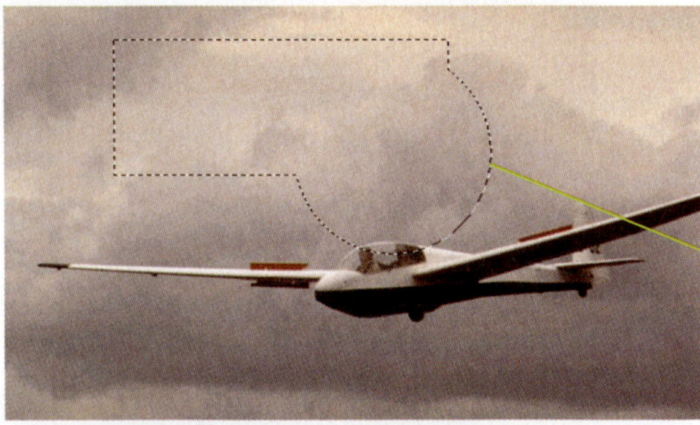

Before – an additive selection (see page 52)

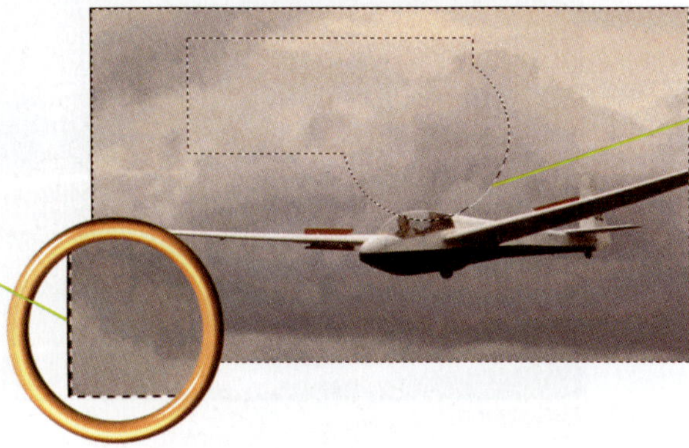

After – the marquee now encloses the *unselected* area

In the "After" illustration, Paint Shop Pro has also surrounded the selected area (here, the image minus the additive selection) with a dotted border, magnified for effect:

Moving raster selections

Paint Shop Pro lets you move bitmap selections (by detaching them from the host layer). You can move just the frame which defines the selection area or the frame AND the contents.

Moving selection frames only

1 Ensure the selection you want to move isn't floating (if it is, press Ctrl+Shift+F)

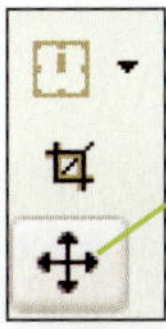

2 Click the Move tool in the Tool palette

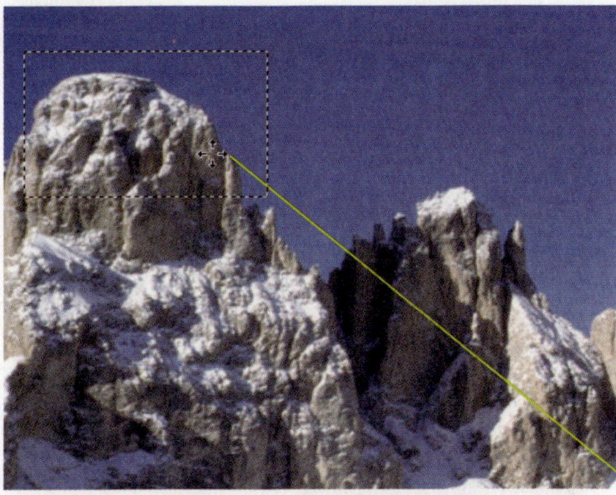

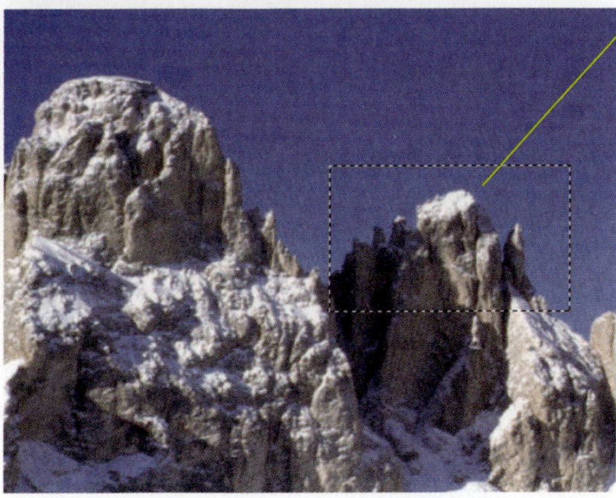

3 Right-click inside the selection area then drag it to a new location

If you perform this technique on floating images (Ctrl+F) you'll move the frame AND contents.

To move just a marquee, you must use the Move tool. If you right-click in it with the original Selection tool, you'll deselect it instead. If you left-click and drag with the original tool, you'll move the selection content as well as the marquee.

You can also move selections and their contents with the keyboard. Ensure the relevant selection tool is active. Hold down Shift. Now press and hold down any of the cursor keys.

(Hold down Ctrl and Shift to increase the move speed.)

Moving bitmap selection frames and contents

First, ensure that the selection area is Standard or Floating, according to the effect you want to achieve. (See page 38 for a description of the two possible effects). Then:

1. In the Tool palette, activate the tool which was used to create the selection
2. Drag the selection to a new location

The procedures in the above tip also apply to selected vector objects (except that the underlying image is unaffected).

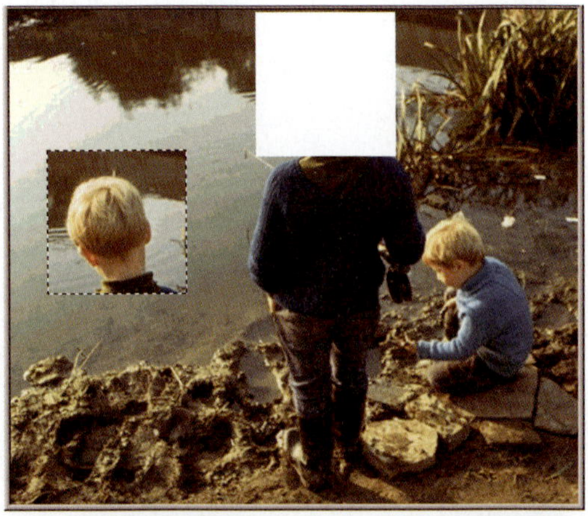

Moving the contents of a Standard selection (the original area is filled with the active background color)

Hold down Ctrl and Alt while pressing any of the arrow keys to simultaneously copy the selection (leaving the original unaffected) AND move it one pixel at a time.

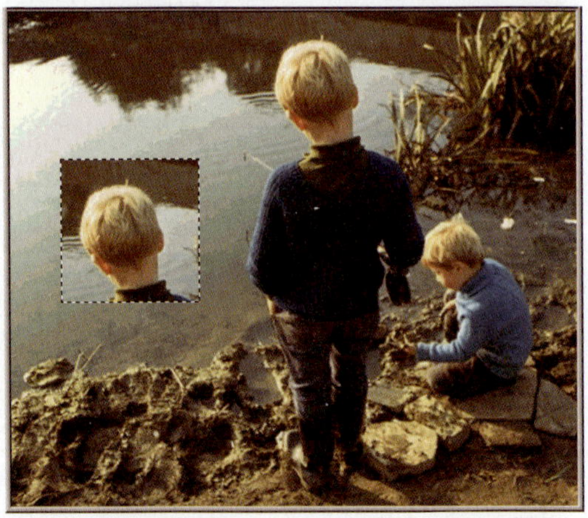

Moving the contents of a Floating selection

Amending selection feathering

When you define a selection, you can feather it. You can also do this *after* the selection has been created.

If you've previously saved a feather preset, click in the Presets field and select it. Or hit the Save icon to create a preset based on the step 2 setting.

Imposing a new feathering

1 Define a selection then hit Ctrl+H

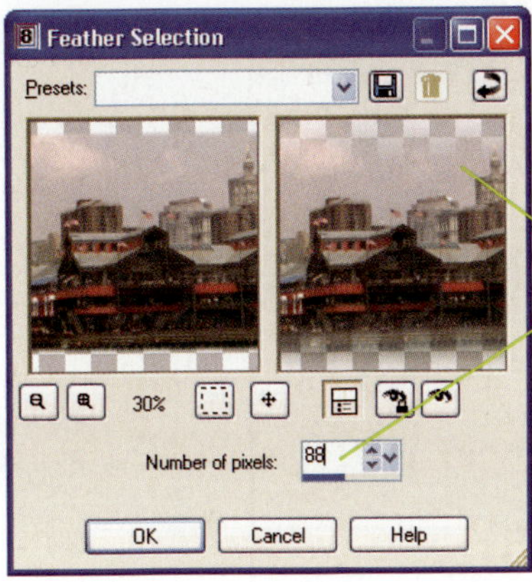

2 Enter a feathering value in the range 0–200 (the preview on the right is updated)

Feathering is useful: it helps a selection blend into the area around it. However, moving selections can leave some of the surrounding pixels attached to the selection border. Fortunately, Paint Shop Pro has an easy solution: matting.

If the selection is on a black or white background, choose Selections, Matting, Remove Black Matte or Selections, Matting, Remove White Matte. If it's a colored background, however, select Matting, Defringe.

Magnified view of the feathered selection edge – this selection has been dragged to the right

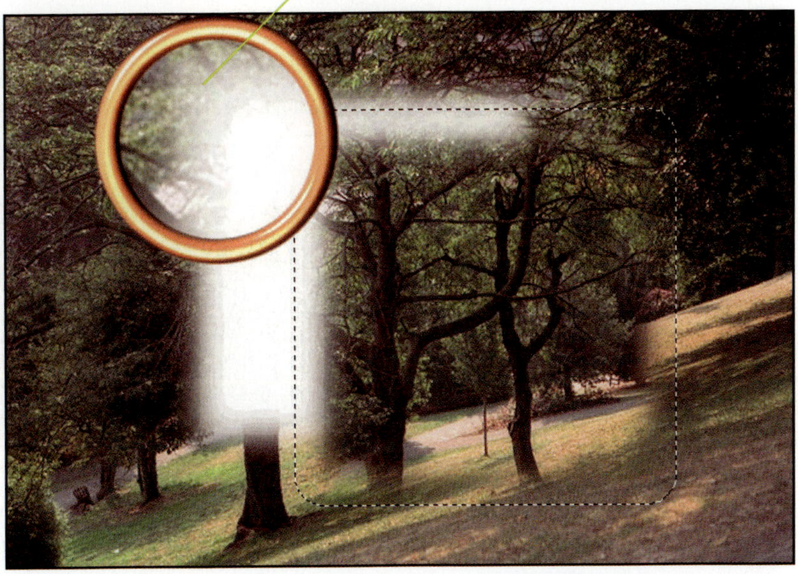

Matting also cleans up layers created from selections.

Selecting a color range

You can specify a color and tell Paint Shop Pro to add it to (or take it away from) a selection.

Selecting a color

You can create and use your own range presets here:

1 Define a selection then pull down the Selections menu and click Modify, Select Color Range

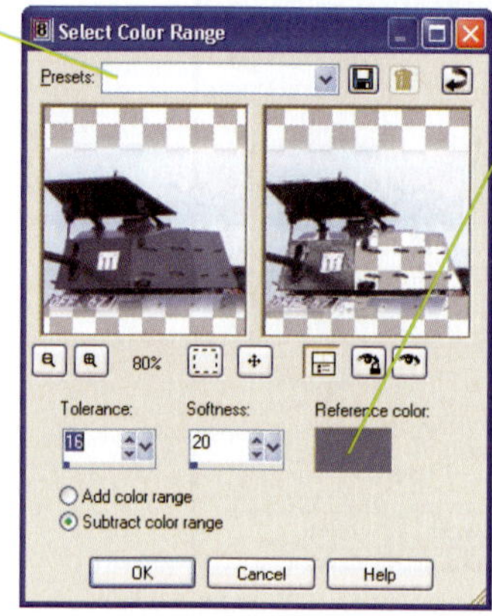

2 Click the Reference color field. Select a color in the dialog or close it then (as here) click in the image to select the color you want to add or subtract

3 Select Add color range or Subtract color range then specify Tolerance and Smoothness settings. Click OK

Tolerance is the degree to which image pixels must approach the chosen one to activate selection. Use the range 0 (only exact matches result in selection) to 256 (all pixels are selected).

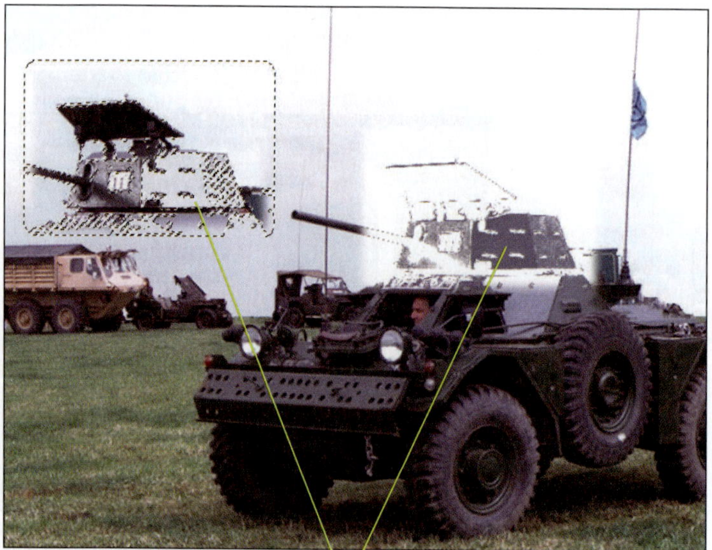

Moving this selection illustrates color range selection – see the DON'T FORGET tip

In this example, a rectangular selection was made around the turret, then one of the turret colors was selected (with a low tolerance) in step 2. When the frame was moved to the left, all colors apart from the selected one were moved.

Reusing selections

Paint Shop Pro lets you save a selection area (but not the contents) to disk as a special file. You can then load it into the same or a new image. This is a convenient way to reuse complex selections.

You can also save selections as "alpha channels", secret areas within pictures that you can use to store some items you'll need later.

Choose Selections, Load/Save Selection, Save Selection to Alpha Channel. In the dialog, name the channel, select the open picture you want it added to and hit Save.

Saving a selection

1 To save a selection to disk (with the extension: .PspSelection), choose Selections, Load/Save Selection, Save Selection to Disk

2 Name the selection

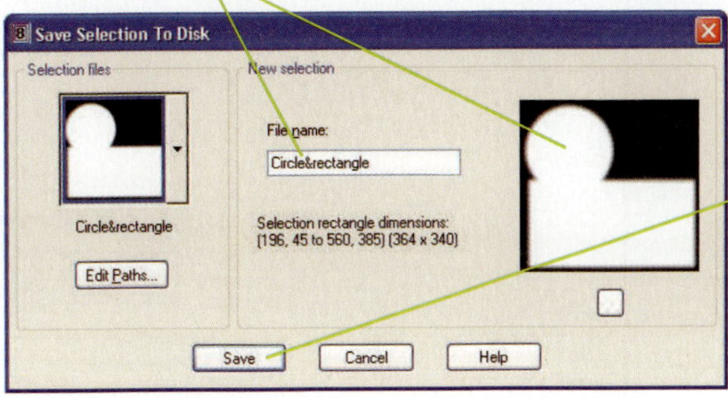

3 Hit Save

To open an alpha channel selection, choose Selections, Load/Save Selection, Load Selection From Alpha Channel. Complete the dialog.

Loading a selection

1 To reopen the selection into the same or a new image, choose Selections, Load/Save Selection, Load Selection From Disk

2 Select a selection

3 Choose how the selection is added

You can also specify what the selection is created from, though Source luminance is probably the most faithful to the original:

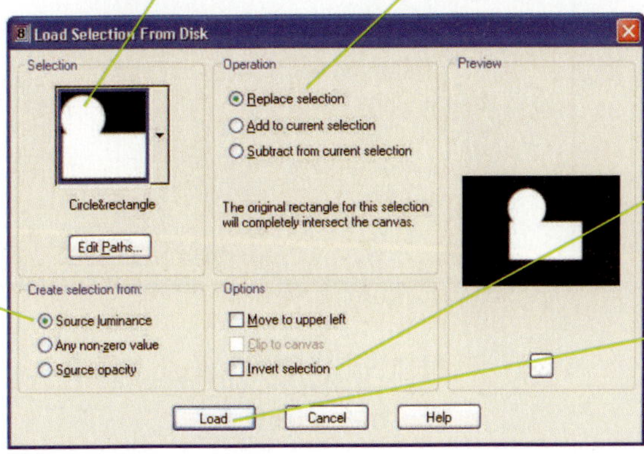

4 You can invert the selection, if you want

5 Click Load

Selection additions/subtractions

When you create multiple selections, a plus sign is added to the cursor for the relevant tool. For example, the Rectangle selector looks like this:

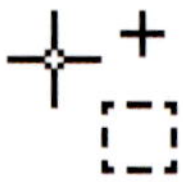

You can define multiple (additive) selections. This is a very useful technique that enables you to create spectacular effects. You can also create selections subtractively, where Paint Shop Pro decreases the size of a selection in line with further contiguous selections you define.

Creating multiple (additive) selections

1. Define the first selection, using any of the techniques previously discussed:

If you define the second selection so that it does not touch the first, this creates two separate selections.

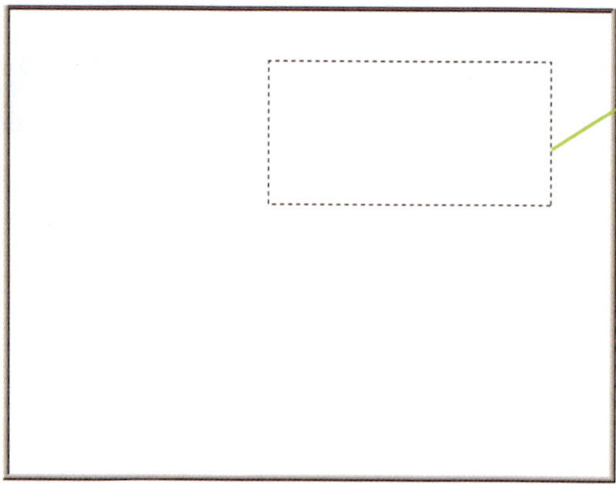

Here, a rectangular selection has been created

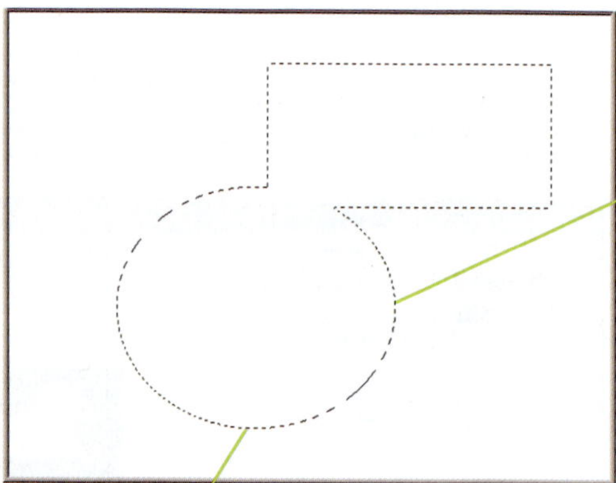

A further elliptical selection has been defined (forming one unusual selection)

2. Hold down Shift, then define another selection

Re step 2 – if you're using the Magic Wand to create multiple selections, simply hold down Shift as you click the area you want to add.

Creating subtractive selections

When you perform selection subtractions, Paint Shop Pro adds a minus sign to the cursor for the relevant selection tool. For example, the Rectangle selector looks like this:

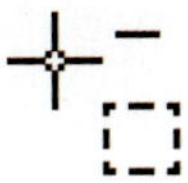

1 Define the first selection, using any of the techniques previously discussed:

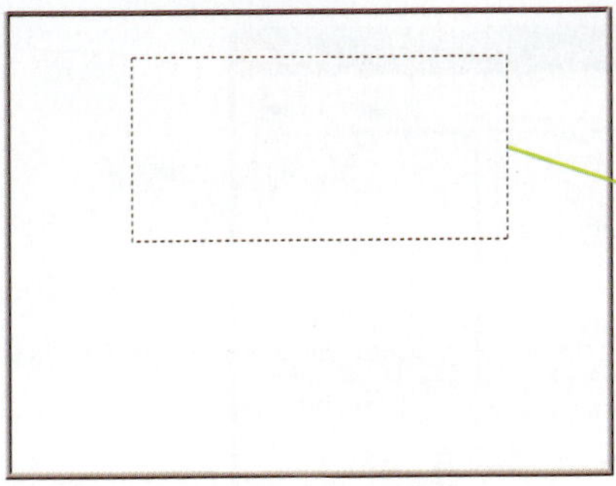

The first selection

If you're using the Magic Wand tool, simply hold down Ctrl as you click within the first selection area – Paint Shop Pro subtracts the second selection from the first.

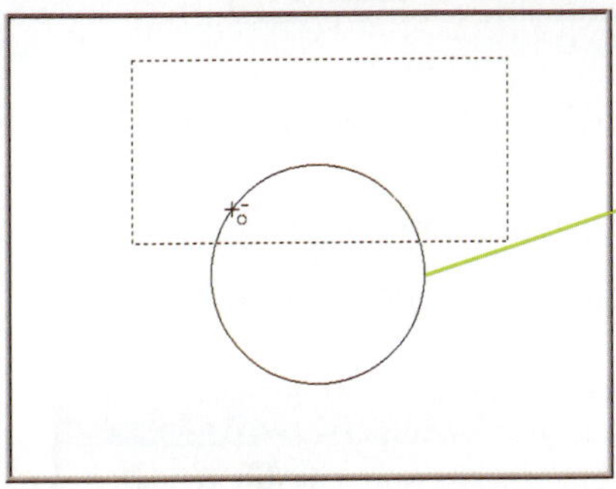

2 Hold down Ctrl as you define another contiguous selection

3 Release the mouse button

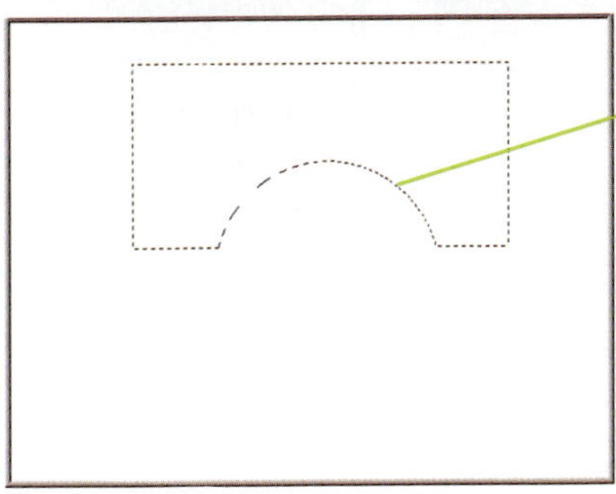

Paint Shop Pro has "subtracted" the second selection from the first

Advanced selection operations

Expanding/contracting selections by specific pixels

Remember you can create and use your own expansion and contraction presets here:

1 To contract or expand bitmap selections uniformly, choose Selections, Modify, Contract or Selections, Modify, Expand

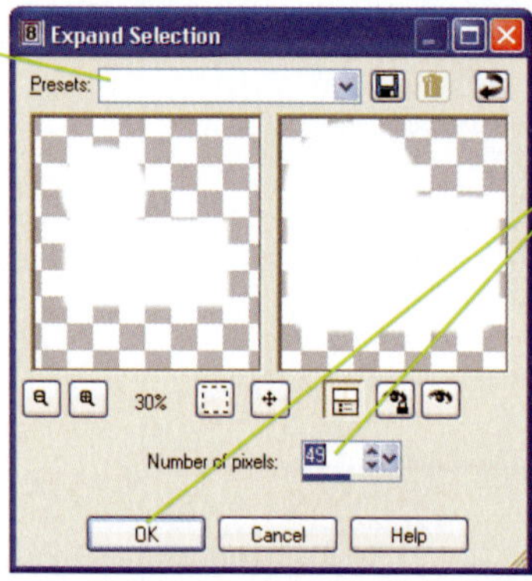

2 In the Number of pixels: field, type in the extent of the contraction or expansion (in the range: 0–100 pixels). Click OK.

Expanding selections by color values

This can be an extremely useful technique. Here, selecting a small area in the body of the helicopter (the left screen) has resulted in nearly all of it being selected on the right. Customize the Tolerance value until you get exactly the result you want.

If the dialog doesn't look like this for you, hit the Toggle Selection button under the left image:

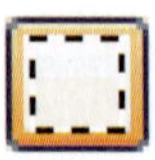

1 To expand bitmap selections based on color values, choose Selections, Modify, Select Similar

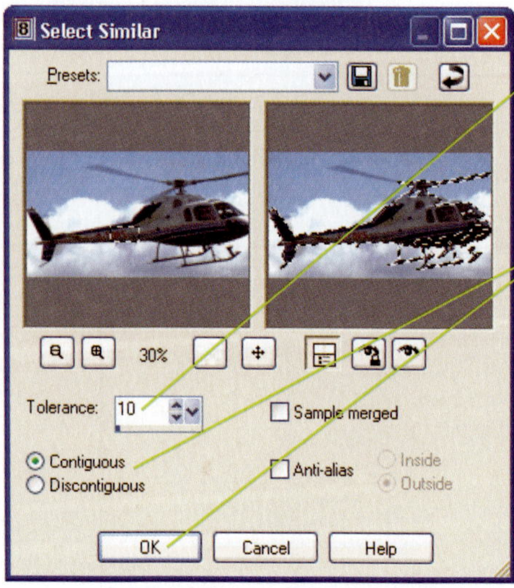

2 Enter a Tolerance setting (in the range: 0–100)

3 Select Contiguous (for adjacent matches) or Discontiguous (for matches anywhere in the image) then click OK

Imposing borders on selections

It's sometimes useful to smooth out selection edges. Choose Selections, Modify, Smooth then experiment with the Smoothing amount and Corner scale settings till you get the effect you want. (Don't forget you can save your settings as a preset for later reuse.)

Drawn a selection and want to fill it with the Flood Fill tool, or maybe apply an effect to it? There's a way to do this:

1 Choose Selections, Modify, Select Selection Borders

2 Choose a placement

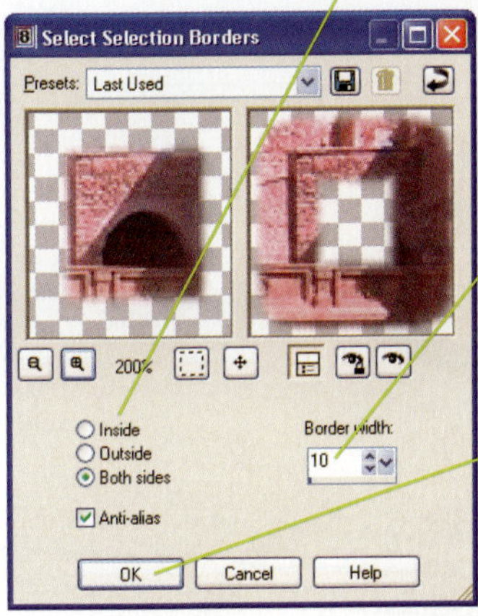

3 Tinker with the Border width setting till you get the effect you need

4 Click OK

The bordered selection, ready for filling

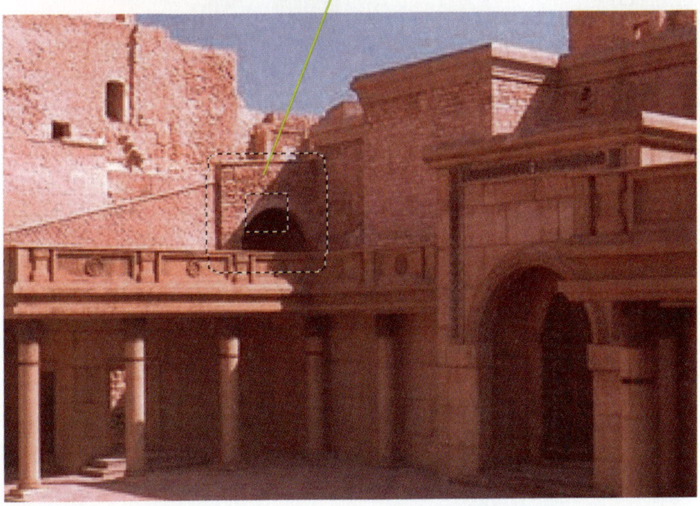

Vector selections

To select vector objects you've already created, carry out the following procedure.

Selecting vector objects via the mouse

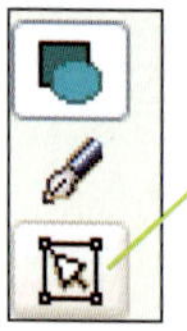

1 Click the Object Selection tool in the Tool palette

See pages 92–93 for how to create vector objects.

To deselect all selections you've already made, hit Ctrl+D.

You can also use the Object Selection tool to move vector objects. Click the object's outline (not its bounding box). Keep the pointer on the outline until it becomes a four-pronged arrow. Drag the object to a new location.

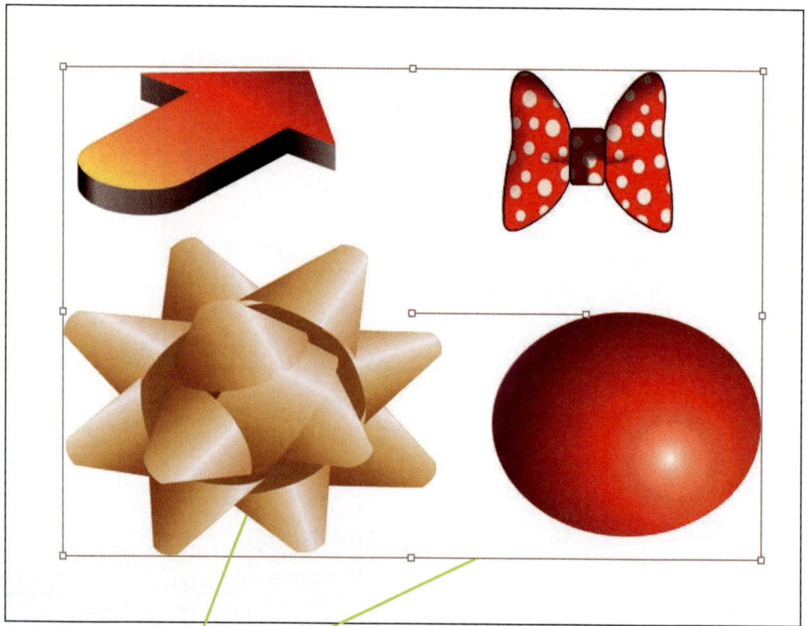

2 Click a single vector object (or its outline) or drag out a marquee around multiple objects

3 For multiple selections, you can also hold down Shift as you left-click on successive objects

4 To remove a vector object from a selection group, hold down Ctrl as you left-click it

Selecting vector objects via the Layer palette

1 If the Layer palette isn't docked on the right of the screen, hit F8

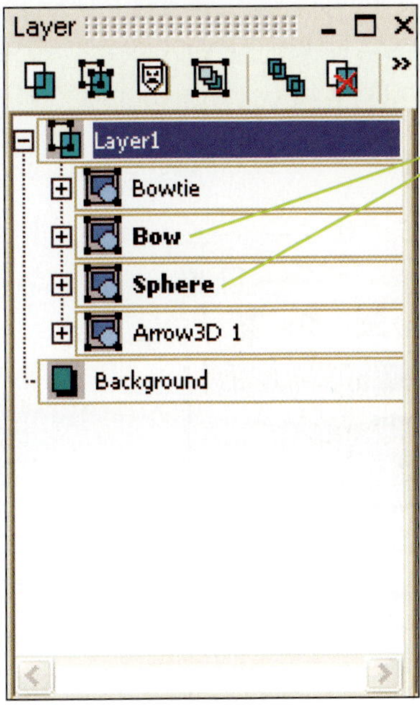

2 Hold down Shift and click each object's layer name button

Layers are an extremely powerful editing tool which can take your use of Paint Shop Pro to a much higher level. See Chapter 8 for more information on layers.

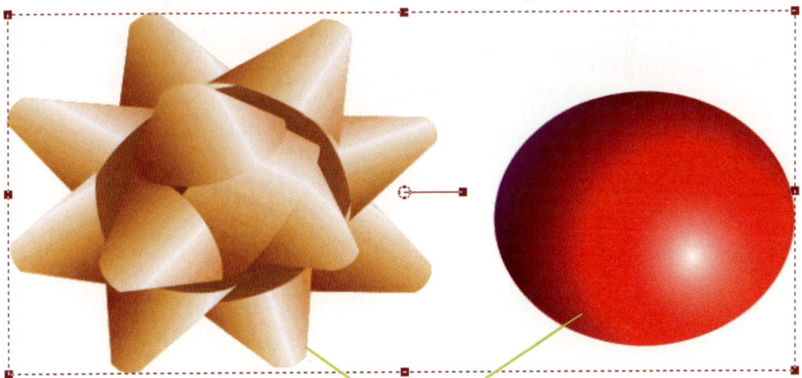

3 Here, step 2 has resulted in just the bow and sphere being selected

Grouping/ungrouping

Paint Shop Pro lets you organize vector objects into "groups". When grouped, objects can be manipulated jointly in the normal way (for instance, you can save/load them.)

Grouping vector objects

1 First select all the relevant vector objects (see pages 56–57 for how to do this)

2 Pull down the Objects menu and click Group

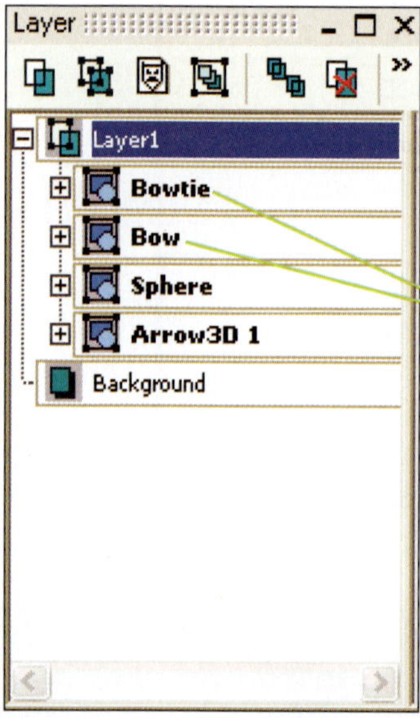

3 Or refer to the Layer palette. Hold down Shift and click the objects you want to group. Then right-click one and select Group in the menu

Ungrouping vector objects

1 Select the group

2 Pull down the Objects menu and click Ungroup

3 Or, in the Layer palette, right-click the group name layer and select Ungroup

HOT TIP: *Grouping vectors automatically moves them to the same layer.*

HOT TIP: *You can have groups within groups (up to 100 levels). This is called "nesting".*

DON'T FORGET: *To remove just one vector object from a group, drag its entry in the palette to a new layer or group.*

Painting and drawing

Chapter Three

In this chapter, you'll use paint/draw techniques with scanned-in images or photographs captured via digital cameras. You'll perform freehand painting; copy colors; carry out color substitutions; select specific colors for foreground/background use; retouch images; spray-paint; fill images with colors, patterns, images, gradients and textures; and paint with object collections (picture tubes). You'll also create your own brush tips and get rid of backgrounds with the Background Eraser.

Finally, you'll format and insert text; create lines and preset shapes; then reshape them by moving their nodes/contours.

Covers

Painting with the Paint Brush tool

Creating a painting

You can paint with the Warp brush, too, for some really cool effects – see pages 127–128.

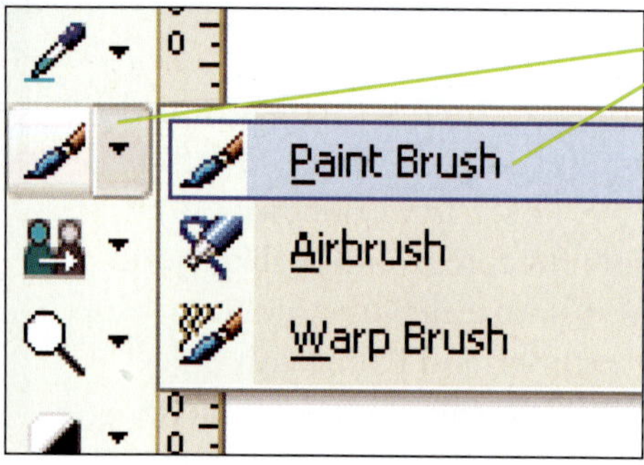

1 Click here in the Tool palette then click Paint Brush (or just hit B)

If your Tool Options palette is floating, it'll likely look rather different. This book uses both docked and floating examples.

2 If the Tool Options palette isn't onscreen, right-click the Tool Palette and select Palettes, Tool Options (or just hit F4)

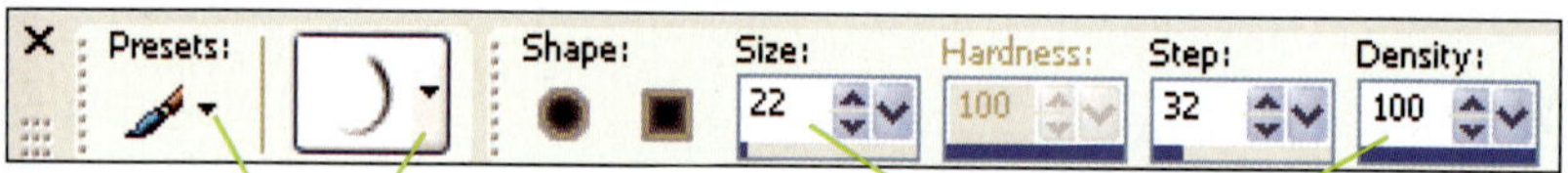

3 Consider selecting a brush preset and/or brush tip – there are some really cool ones

4 Complete these additional fields – see the Hot Tip

Use the following guidelines just before you begin painting in Paint Shop Pro:

- *Shape – select a shape (Square or Round)*
- *Size – select a brush size in pixels in the range 1–500*
- *Hardness – select a % in the range 0–100*
- *Opacity – select a % in the range 1–100*
- *Step (mimics brush contact) – range 1–200*
- *Density – range 1–100*

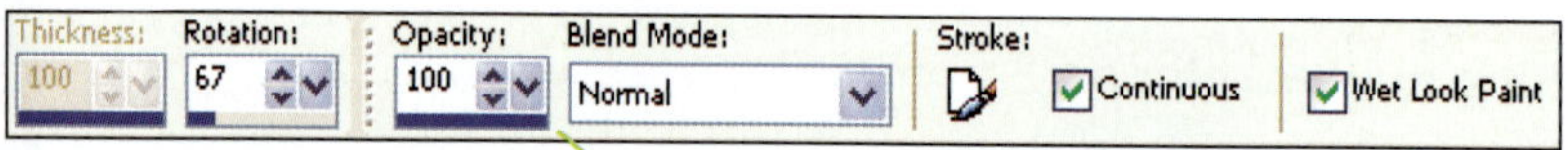

5 Complete the remaining settings, as appropriate – the Wet Look Paint one is really neat

6 Drag with the left mouse button to paint with the active foreground color/materials or with the right mouse button to paint with the active background color/materials

You can also draw with the Paint Brush tool. Just left- or right-click where you want to start drawing. Hold down Shift then click again to create a new line segment. Go on doing this till you're through.

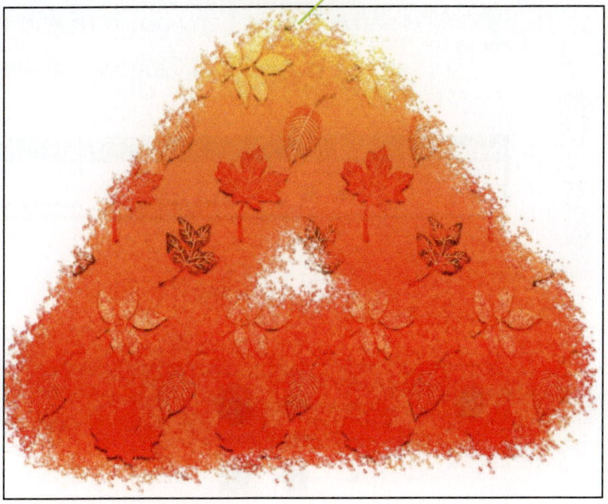

The *Animal fur2* preset with the *Marble2* brush tip and a texture

With many of the operations in this chapter, you can restrict the effect to specific image parts by using selection areas or masks.

Using the Brush Variance palette

Once you've set brush options in steps 3–5 on page 60, you can customize painting even further with an extra palette.

Don't overuse the Brush Variance palette: the standard brush settings work pretty well as they stand!

1 Hit F11

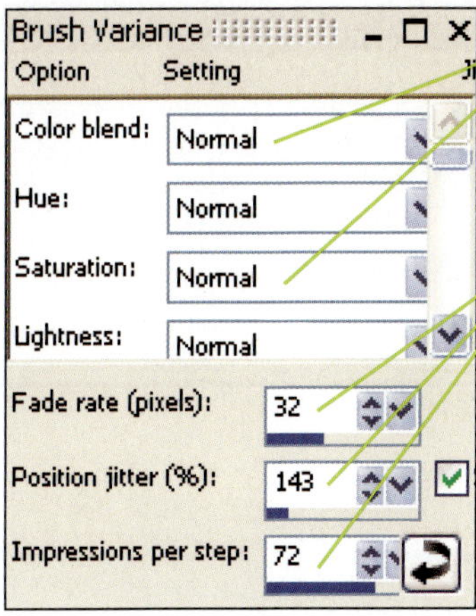

2 Click in each field and make a choice

3 Experiment with these, especially Position jitter (it randomizes brush output)

4 Begin painting

Customized brush tips

You can create you own brush tips for later reuse:

1 Want to convert an image area into a brush tip? Just select it

2 Alternatively, select any brush tool in the Tool palette then adjust its settings in the Tool Options palette

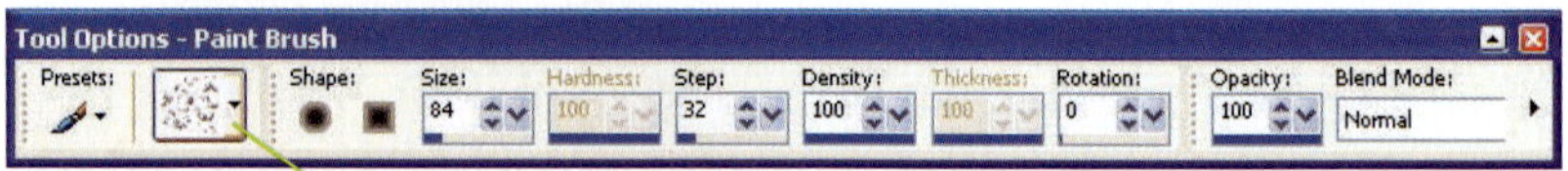

3 Click here

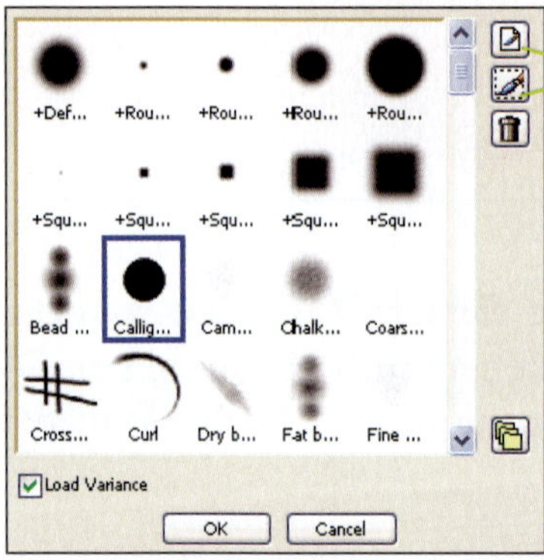

4 Select Create brush tip or Create brush tip from selection, as appropriate

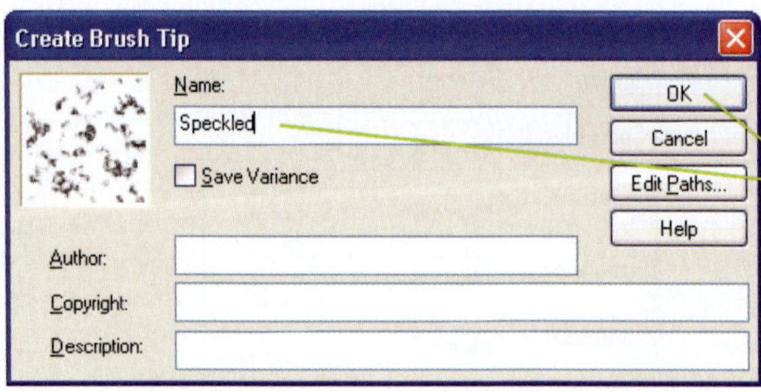

5 Complete the dialog then hit OK

Bet you're wondering, why save brush tips when you can already save brush presets?

Good question. The answer is that you can use brush tips with any brush tool (obviously, this includes the Paint and Airbrush tools, but also less obvious ones like the Retouch tools and the Background Eraser) while presets are tool-specific.

Copying with the Clone brush

Cloning is extremely useful when you're working with photographs: use it to replace unwanted colors with colors that are desirable.

Cloning is the copying of color from one location within an image to another (or to another image which has the same number of colors). To clone colors, you use the Clone brush.

Cloning

Refer to the Tool palette and do the following:

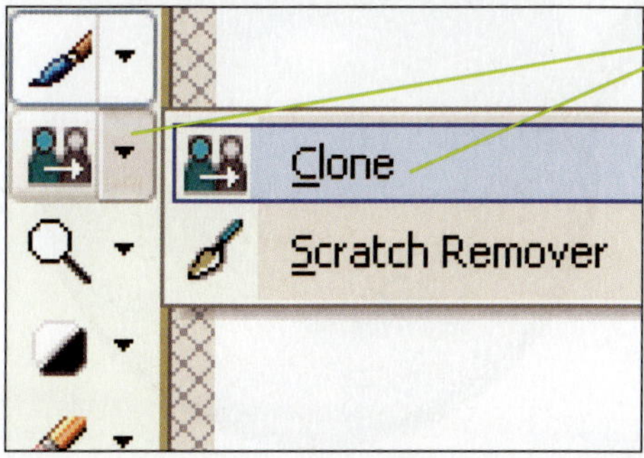

1 Click here in the Tool palette then click Clone (or just hit C)

Remember you can save Clone presets for reuse later – click here to access the Presets dialog:

2 If the Tool Options palette isn't onscreen, right-click the Tool Palette and select Palettes, Tool Options (or just hit F4)

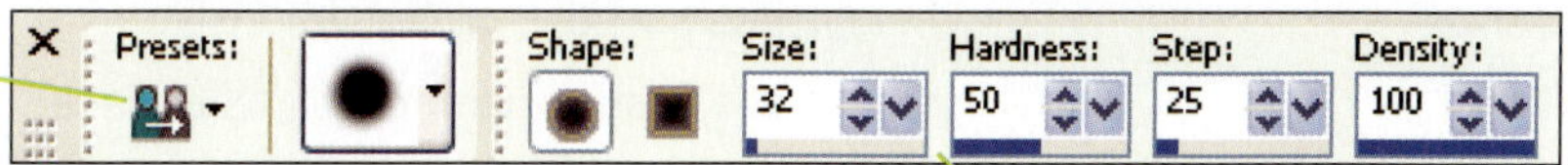

3 Customize your clone operation

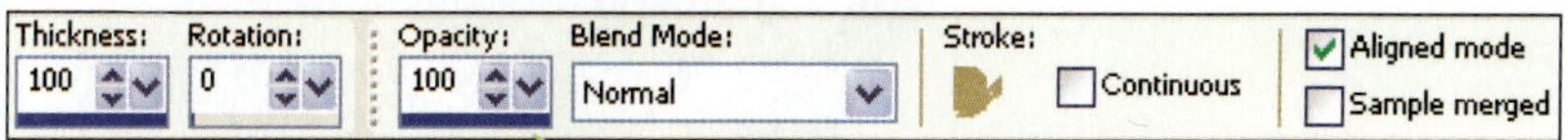

4 Complete the remaining settings, too, as appropriate

5 Place the mouse pointer over the image section you want to copy

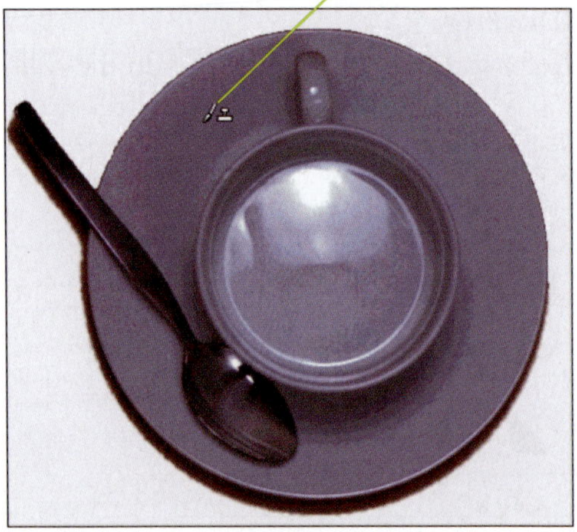

6 Right-click once

7 Position the cursor where you want the paste operation to take place, then drag repeatedly

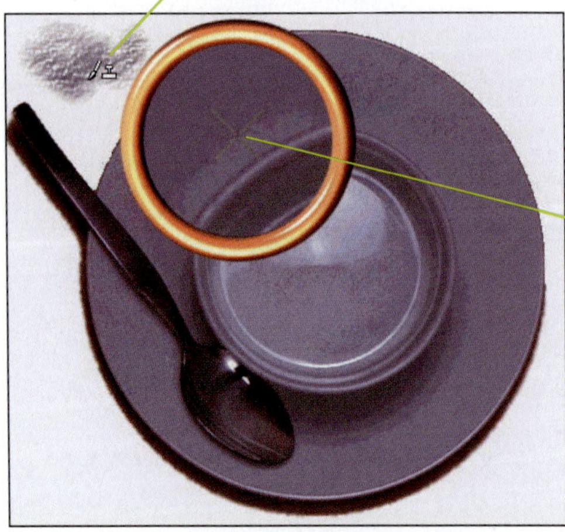

Crosshairs – these indicate the pixel which is currently being copied. As you drag in step 7, the crosshairs move, so you can select (on-the-fly) the area being copied

Replacing colors globally

You can have Paint Shop Pro replace a specified color with another. You do this by nominating the color you want to replace as the foreground color, then selecting the new color as the background color. (Or vice versa).

You can replace colors globally (within an image or selection area) or manually (by using the Color Replacer tool as a brush).

Carrying out a global substitution

1 Optional – if you want to limit the color exchange to a selected area, define a selection area

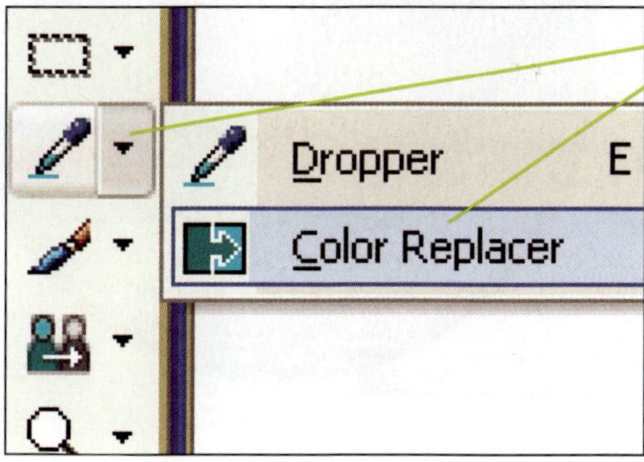

2 Click here in the Tool palette then click Color Replacer

3 If the Tool Options palette isn't onscreen, right-click the Tool Palette and select Palettes, Tool Options (or just hit F4)

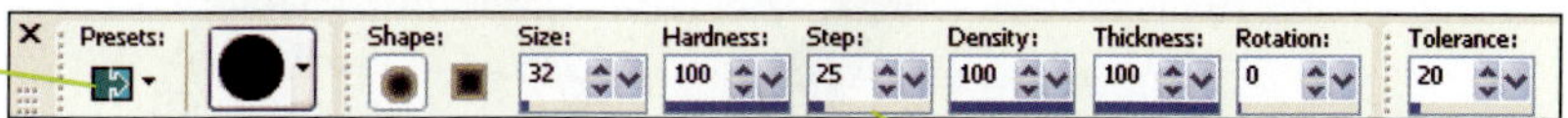

4 Customize your color replace operation

Remember you can save replace presets for reuse later – click here to access the Presets dialog:

Tolerance settings are especially important with the Color Replacer. Low settings ensure that only pixels whose color is very similar will be changed. Increase the Tolerance settings to broaden the effect.

5 Double-click the left mouse button to replace the background with the foreground color

6 Alternatively, double-click the right mouse button to replace the foreground with the background color

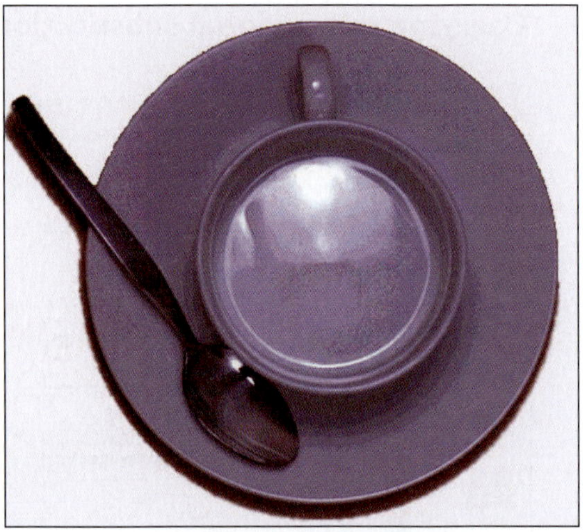

Before . . .

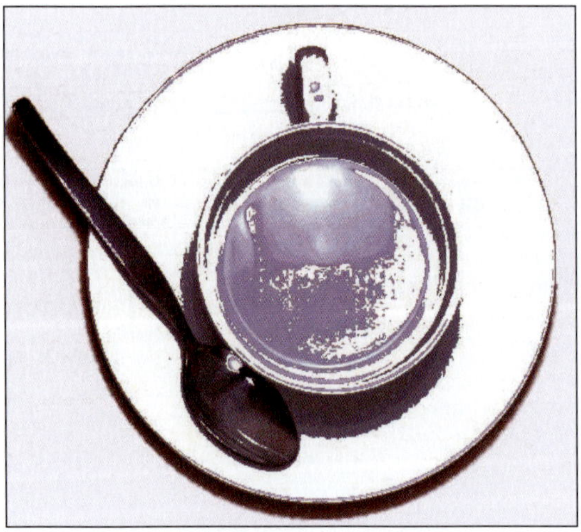

After – the color in the saucer (and part of the cup) has been replaced with white

Replacing colors manually

Carrying out a manual substitution

1. Create a selection area if you want to limit the replacement

2. Fire up the Color Replacer tool – see step 2 on page 65

3. Customize the Color Replacer tool till it works exactly the way you want it to – see steps 3–4 on page 65

4. Drag with the left mouse button to replace the background with the foreground color or with the right to replace the foreground with the background color

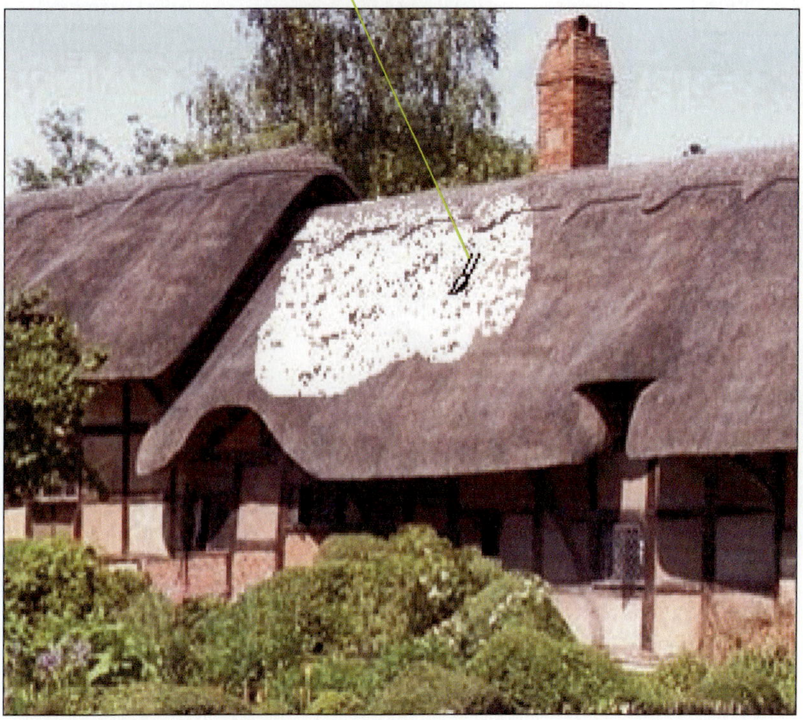

More expensive programs like Adobe Photoshop have a color replacement feature but Paint Shop Pro's is arguably a lot easier to use.

You can also use the Color Replacer to substitute colors as you create lines. Just left- or right-click (as appropriate) where you want the line to begin then hold down Shift and click somewhere else. Repeat as often as required.

Using the Color Replacer manually, it's especially important to get the right brush. Experiment and have fun!

Using the Dropper tool

The Dropper is an extremely useful tool which you can use to:

1. select a color in the active image
2. nominate this as the active foreground or background color

Using the Dropper

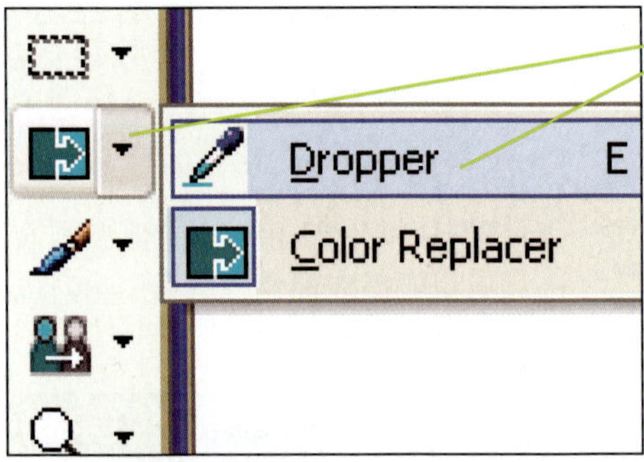

1 Click here in the Tool palette then click Dropper. Or just press E (why not D? Easy – that's the Deform tool)

A great timesaver – you can activate the Dropper within most paint tools by holding down Ctrl.

The makeup of the color selected in step 2 displays in a fly-out:

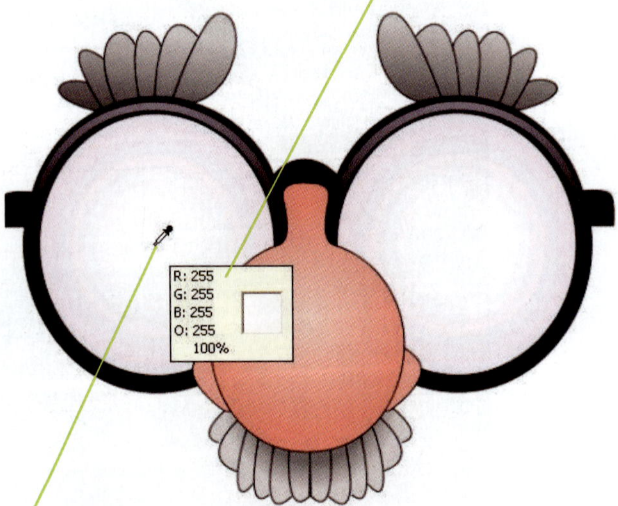

After step 2, the selected color appears in the Materials palette.

2 Click with the left mouse button to nominate the selected color as the foreground or with the right to nominate it as the background

Retouching – an overview

You can use the various Retouch tools to perform photo-retouching operations on images (or selected areas). These operations include:

Soften	Mutes the image or selection and diminishes contrast
Sharpen	Emphasizes edges and accentuates contrast
Emboss	Produces a raised (stamped) effect where the foreground is emphasized in relation to the background
Smudge	Produces a stained, blurred effect
Push	Like Smudge but no color is picked up
Dodge	Lightens image shadow
Burn	Darkens images

All the above tools (excluding Dodge and Burn) work with images which are 24 bit (16 million colors) or grayscale; the remainder work only with 24 bit images.

As a rule, you can't perform retouching operations globally. However, there are three exceptions to this:

- Embossing
- Softening
- Sharpening

You achieve these effects with filters/effects.

Retouching images manually

Carrying out a manual retouch operation

You can also use the Retouch tools to retouch images by defining lines. Just left-click where you want the line to begin then hold down Shift and click somewhere else. Repeat as often as required.

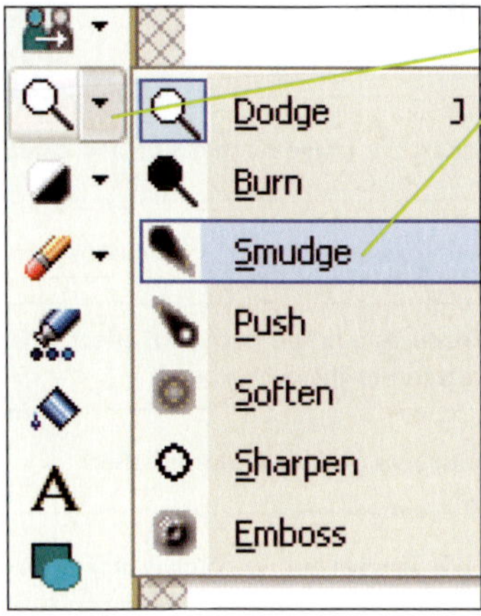

1 Click here in the Tool palette then select a retouch tool

Different retouch tools have different options in the Tool Options palette. Try them all out.

2 In the Tool Options palette (F4), customize your retouch operation e.g. select a preset if you've saved any and/or specify Size, Hardness, Density, Thickness and Opacity settings

3 Using a light touch, hold down the left mouse button and drag over the relevant area

Here, an Emboss retouching operation is being carried out.

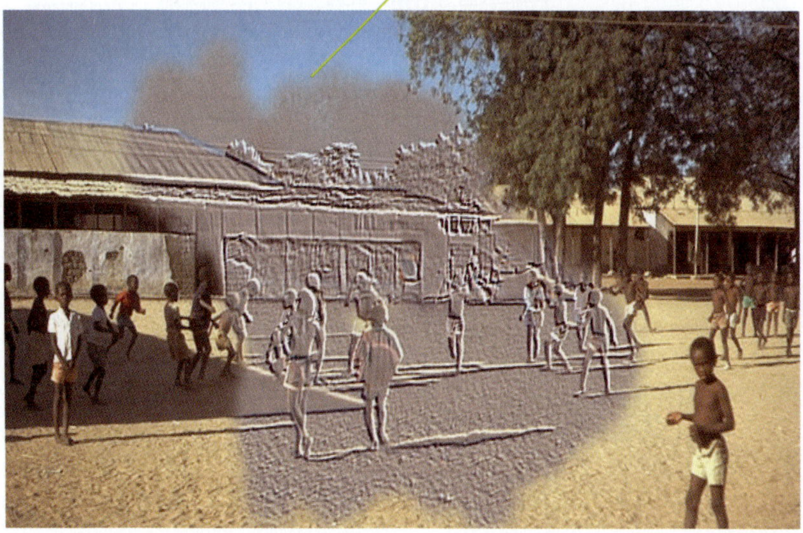

Using the Background Eraser

The new Background Eraser tool is a great way to get rid of image backgrounds while isolating the element of the picture you want to keep (often a person).

1 If the background you want to erase is on the Background layer, hit Layers, Promote Background Layer

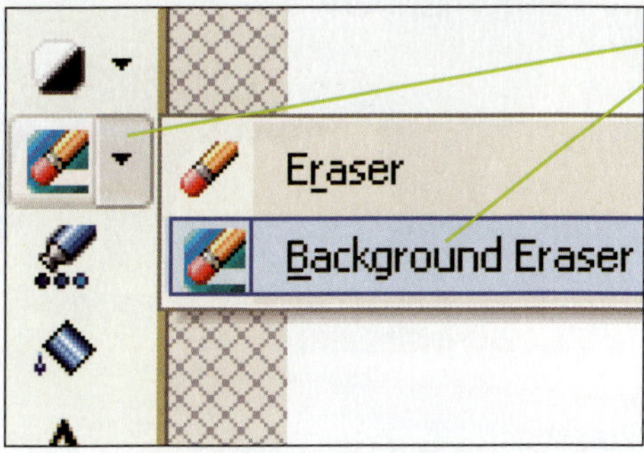

2 Click here in the Tool palette then Background Eraser

You can save Background Eraser presets for reuse later – click here to access the Presets dialog:

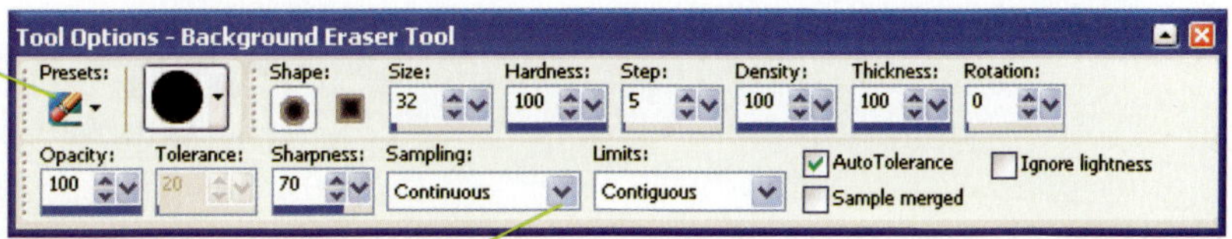

3 Customize your output in the Tool Options palette (F4) e.g.:

- Leave AutoTolerance checked initially. Later, uncheck it and enter a manual Tolerance setting – this may produce a better effect
- If you want to replace the background with the foreground or background color/materials, select BackSwatch or ForeSwatch in the Sampling box
- Try reducing the Step size when you increase the Size setting – this can increase the rate at which the background is replaced

Because it intelligently senses where edges are, the Background Eraser tool does a lot of the work for you. However, you'll still have to spend some time making sure it hasn't missed any background.

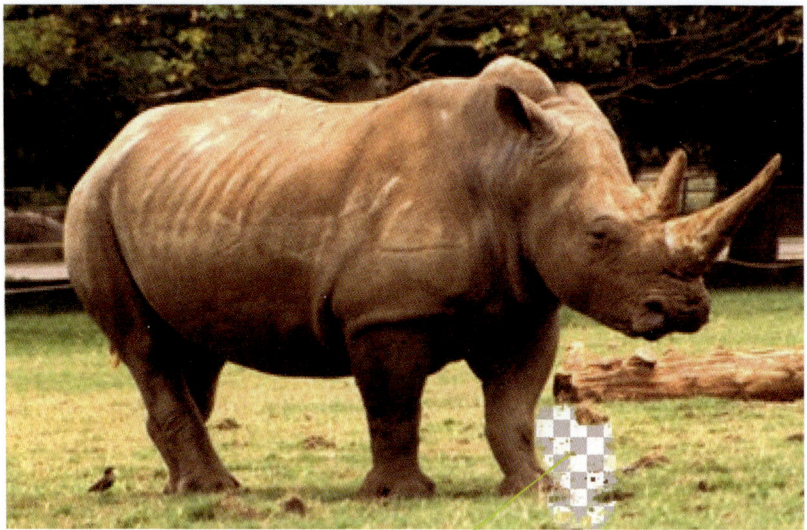

4 Drag with the left mouse button near the picture's edge

Zoom in with a small Size setting to tidy up around image edges. Then "mop up" the remainder of the background by zooming out, using a larger Size setting and holding down the Spacebar as you drag.

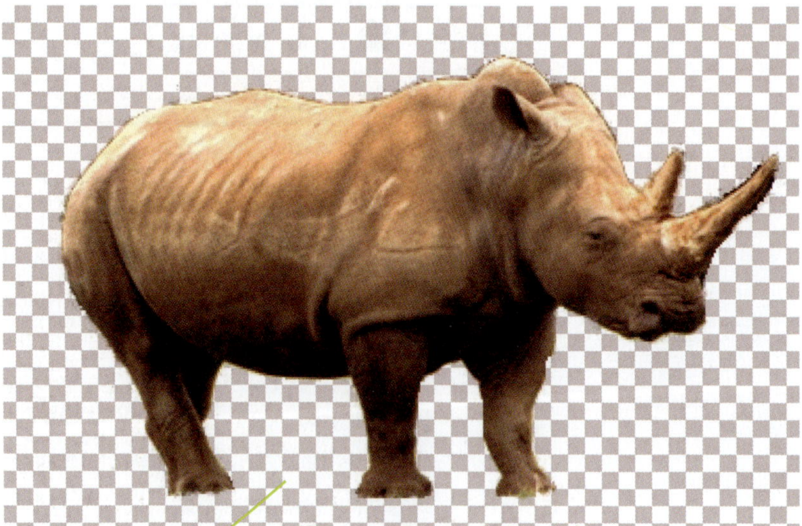

5 The picture now has a transparent background

Using the Airbrush tool

You can use the Airbrush tool to simulate painting with a spray can. You can do this in two ways.

Using the Airbrush as a brush

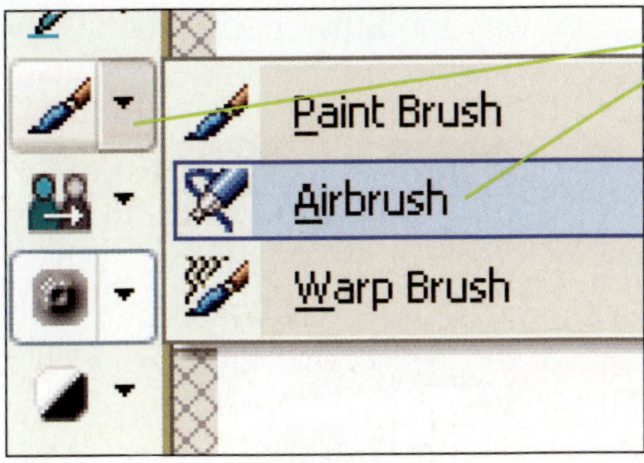

1 Click here in the Tool palette then select Airbrush

Remember you can save Airbrush presets for reuse later – click here to access the Presets dialog:

2 If the Tool Options palette isn't onscreen, right-click the Tool Palette and select Palettes, Tool Options (or just hit F4)

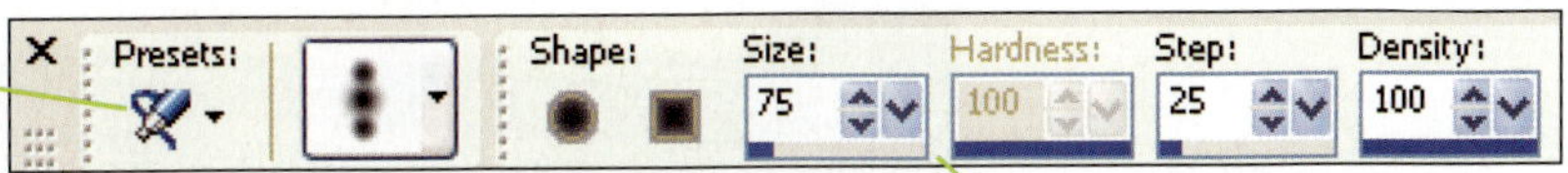

3 Complete all these additional fields, as appropriate

The Rate box is especially important for the Airbrush tool because it determines the rate at which paint is applied (range: 0–50). 0 applies an even quantity of paint while higher values apply more when you drag slowly or pause.

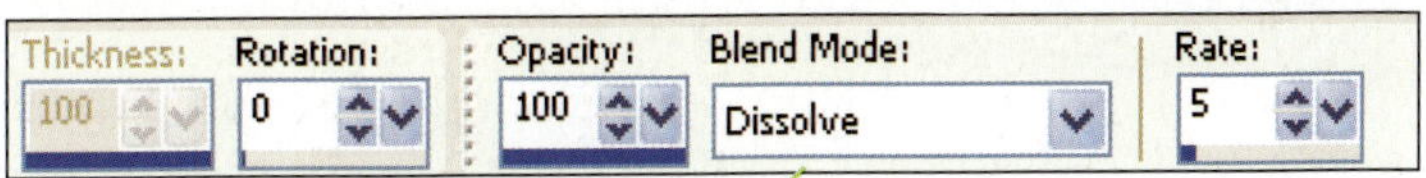

4 Complete the remaining settings, too, as appropriate

5 Hold down the left mouse button then drag to paint with the active foreground color/materials

6 Alternatively, hold down the right mouse button then drag to paint with the active background color/materials

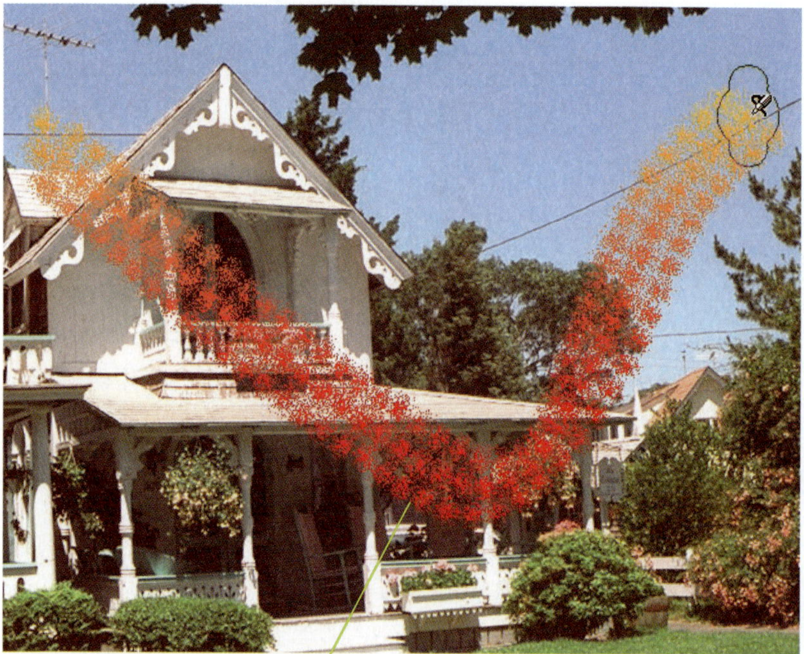

This Airbrush uses the *Bead* brush tip with the Rate setting at 5 and the Blend Mode setting at *Dissolve* – the color/materials incorporate the *Red-orange-yellow* linear gradient

Using the Airbrush to draw lines

1. Fire up the Airbrush tool – see step 1 on page 73

2. Customize the Airbrush tool till it works exactly the way you want it to – see steps 2–4 on page 73

3. Click where you want the Airbrush operation to begin

4. Hold down Shift and click where you want the line segment to end

Repeat Step 4 for as many extra line segments as you want to insert.

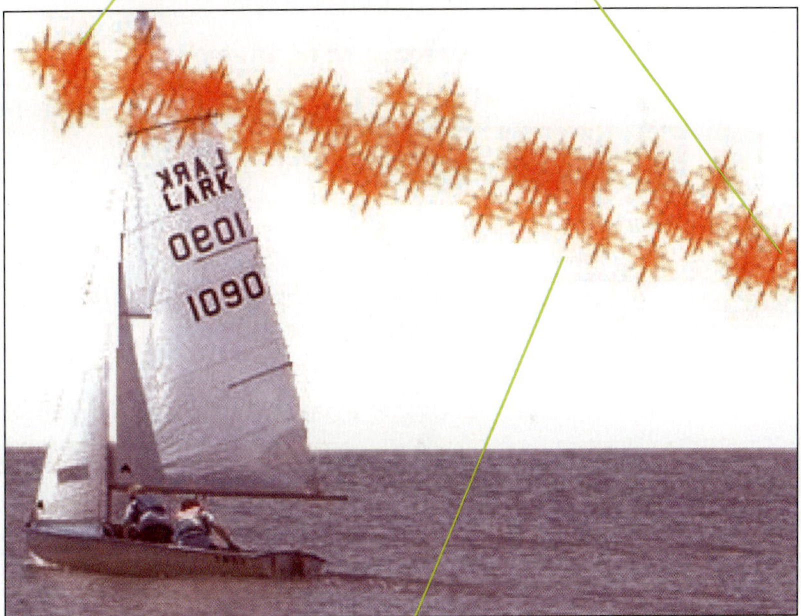

This Airbrush uses the *Surreal* brush tip with the Rate setting at 43 and the Blend Mode setting at *Multiply* – the color is simply red. The line is uneven because the Brush Variance Position jitter setting is greater than the default

Filling with colors

You can use the Flood Fill tool to fill a selection or image layer with color/materials (e.g. gradients). You can also fill with a specific image you've already opened into an additional window – this can produce some unique and fun effects.

Filling images with a color

1 If you want to limit the effect of your fill, select part of the picture

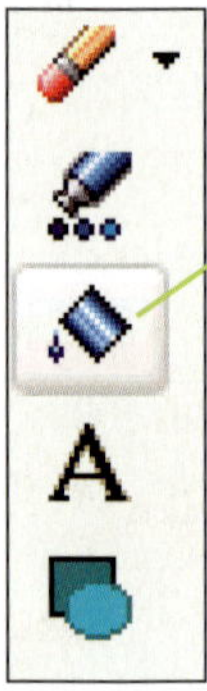

2 Click the Flood Fill tool in the Tool palette

Remember you can save Flood Fill tool presets for reuse later – click here to access the Presets dialog:

3 If the Tool Options palette isn't onscreen, right-click the Tool Palette and select Palettes, Tool Options (or just hit F4)

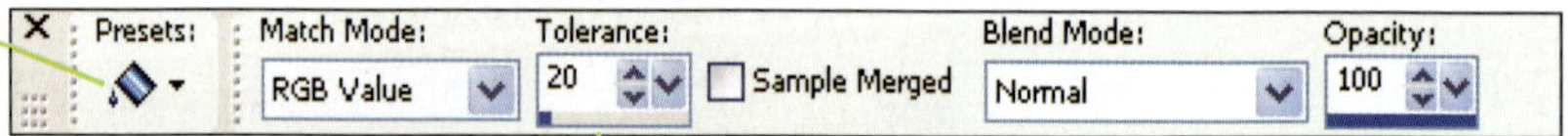

4 Customize your flood fill operation e.g.:

- Blend mode – all options except Normal ensure that the fill is affected by the underlying image colors
- Match Mode – determine how Paint Shop Pro decides which pixels are covered (None covers all pixels)
- Opacity (range: 1–100)
- Tolerance – enter a value in this range: 0 (only exact matches are filled) to 200 (every pixel is filled)

5 Left-click to insert the foreground color OR right-click to insert the background color

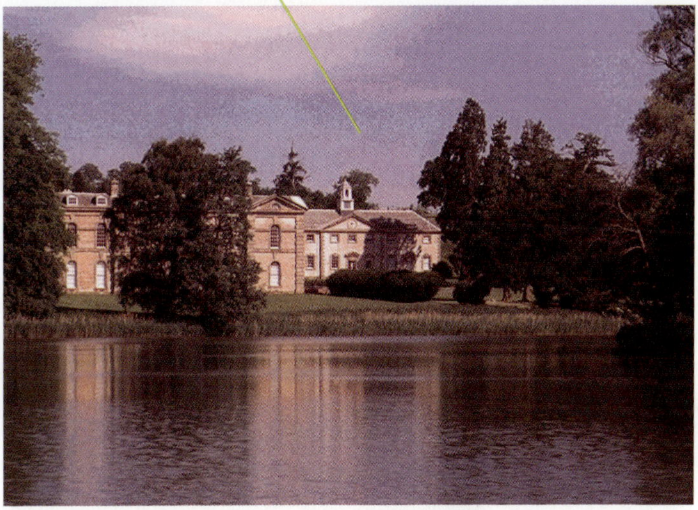

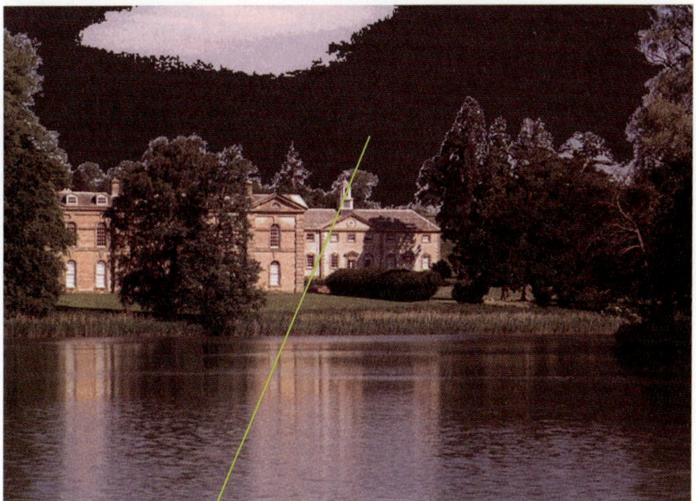

A completed color fill

In effect, because they both target pixels that fulfill specific color criteria, the Flood Fill tool is similar to the Color Replacer tool. The main difference, however, is that Flood Fill operations affect contiguous pixels whereas color replacement operations generally target pixels in the whole layer.

Filling with images

You can use the Materials palette to apply images to other images.

Filling an image with another

1. Open the 16-million-color or grayscale image you want to insert
2. Open the 16-million-color or grayscale image you want to insert it into
3. Activate the Flood Fill tool and customize it (2–4 on page 76)

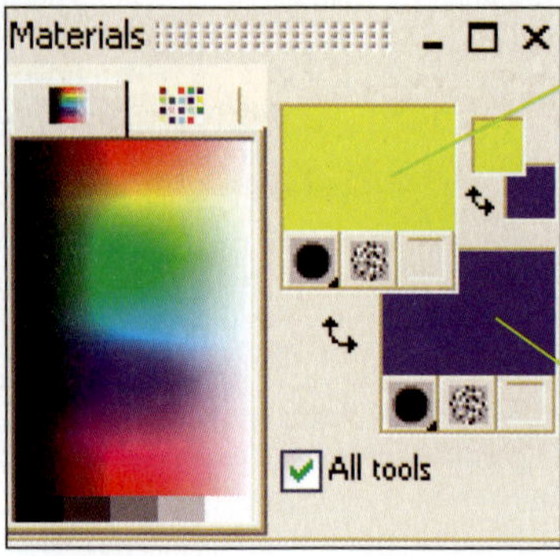

4. In the destination image, click here (for a foreground fill)
5. Or here for a background fill
6. Select the Pattern tab

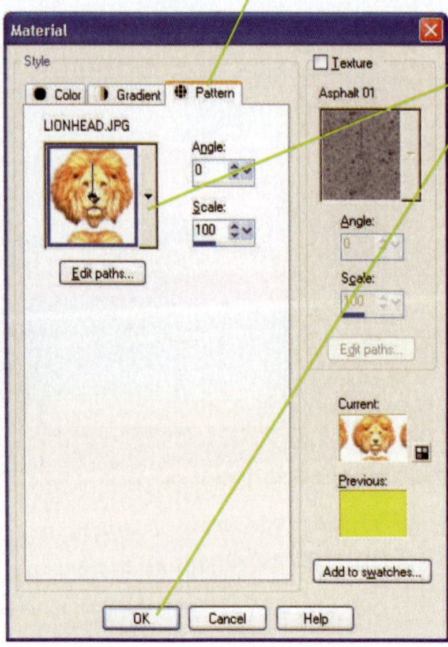

7. Click here and select the fill image. Then click OK
8. In the destination image, left-click to insert the foreground color/materials or right-click to insert the background color/materials

HOT TIP: Want to add a texture to colors, gradients or patterns? Check Texture on the right of the dialog then click in the box below and select a texture. Customize the texture till you get it the way you want.

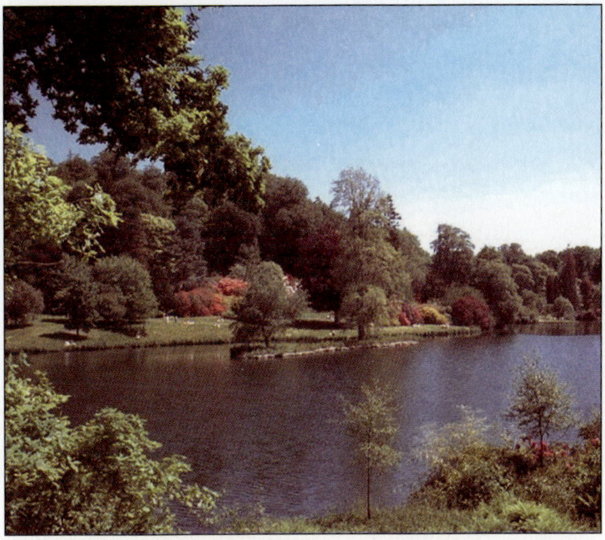

The original image

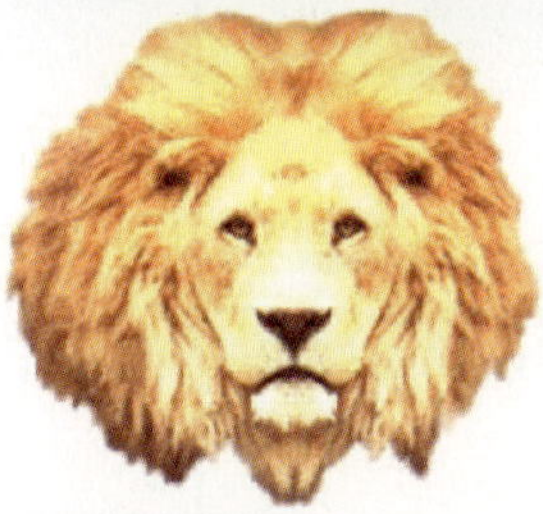

The image to be inserted

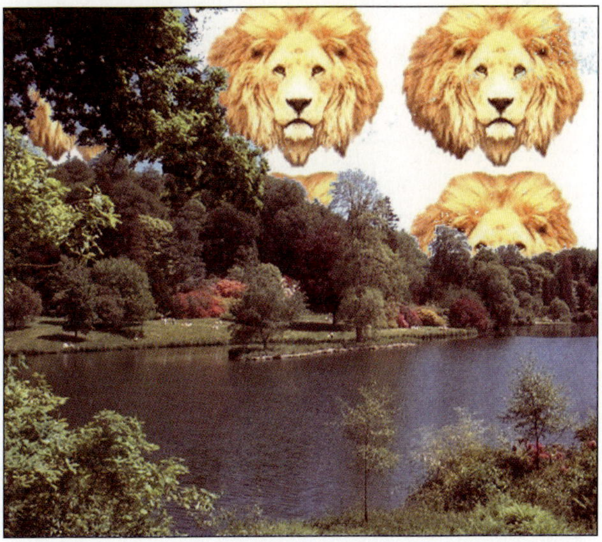

The end result

Filling with gradients

Gradient fills can look spectacularly effective.

Select image areas before applying the gradient to limit its effect.

1 Open the 16-million-color or grayscale image you want to fill

2 Carry out steps 3–5 on page 78

3 Select the Gradient tab

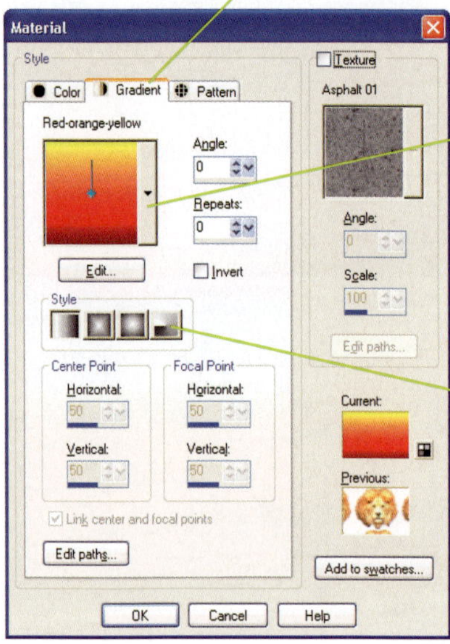

4 Click here and select a gradient

5 The preset gradients are great but you can customize your own. Experiment with the settings – especially, try changing the gradient type

Additional tools with which you can apply gradients include the following:

- *Paint Brush*
- *Clone*
- *Color Replacer*
- *Airbrush*

6 Left- or right-click repeatedly in the image to insert the gradient

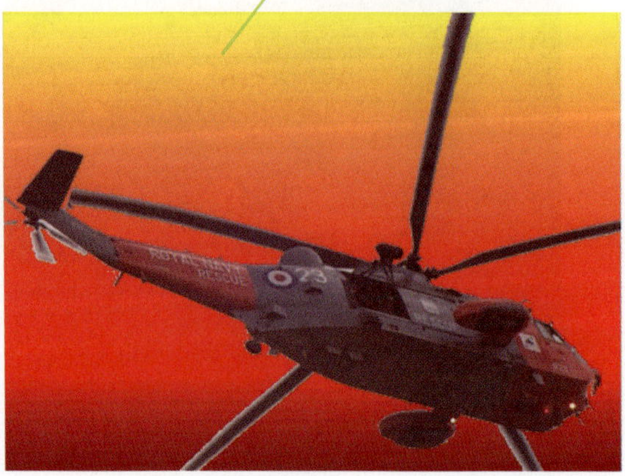

Inserting patterns

1 Open the 16-million-color or grayscale image you want to fill

2 Carry out steps 3–5 on page 78

3 Select the Pattern tab

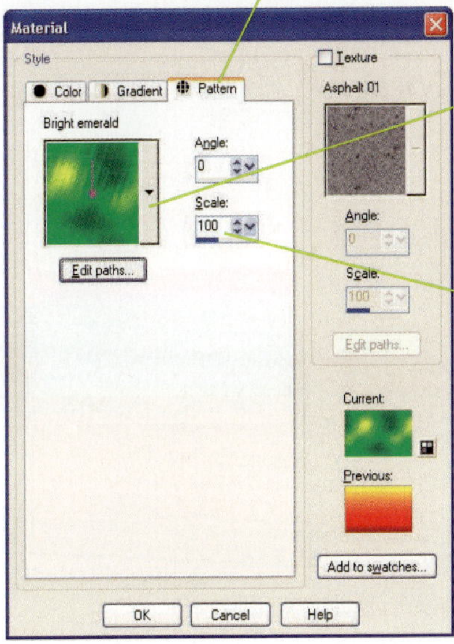

4 Click here and select a pattern

5 Customize the Angle and Scale settings

6 Left- or right-click repeatedly in the image to insert the pattern

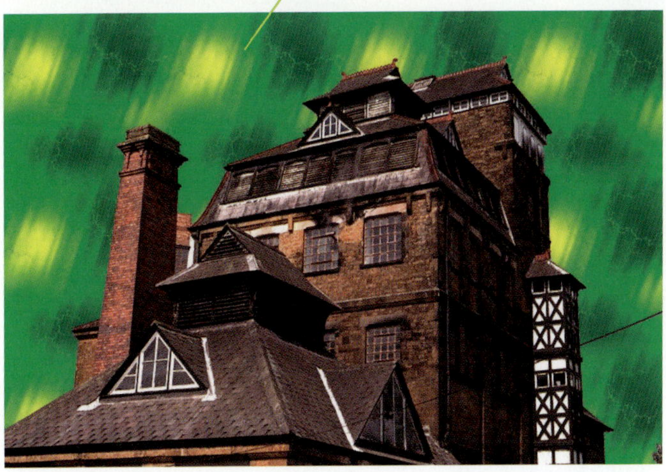

Inserting text with the Text tool

Use vector text mostly. Why? Because it's the only text where you can edit the content and typeface etc. later. Use the other text types when you're certain you won't need to change the text and you want to apply special effects/fills.

You can insert three principal types of text:

- Vector text – can only be created on a vector layer. Vector text is actually a vector object and can thus be edited, moved and deformed. (It can also be added to paths.)
- Floating (raster) text – appears above the current layer
- Selection – an empty, transparent selection that can be filled

Inserting text

Here's a neat tip. Create selection text over a picture then hit Ctrl+X. Hit Ctrl+V and you get text (in a new image) that was cut out of the original picture:

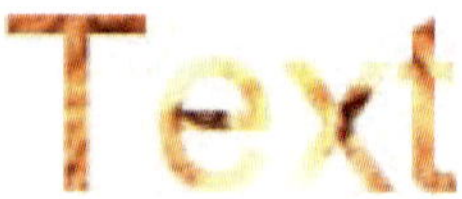

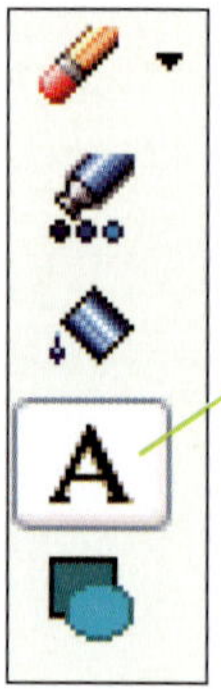

1 Click the Text tool in the Tool palette (or just hit T)

2 Use the Materials palette to select a background color (for the text fill)

3 If the Tool Options palette isn't onscreen, right-click the Tool Palette and select Palettes, Tool Options (or just hit F4)

You can save Text presets for reuse later – click here to access the Presets dialog:

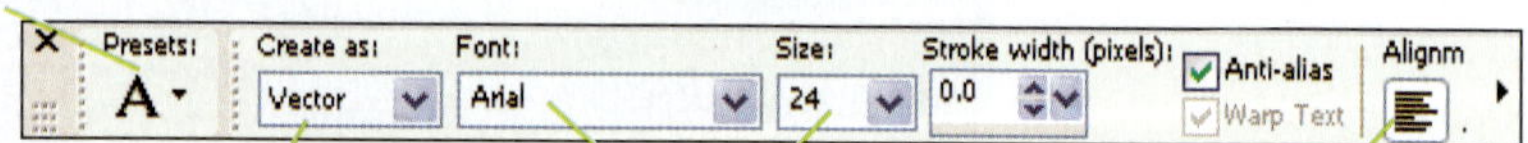

4 Select a text type

5 Select a font and type size

6 Select an alignment

Anti-alias removes jagged distortions; it makes text look and print smoother but generally isn't so effective with very small point sizes.

...cont'd

Auto kern adjusts the gaps between letters, so text looks better. Leading is the gap between lines.

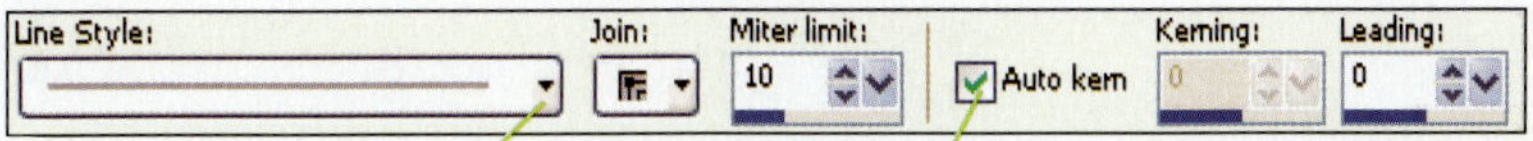

7 Select one of the many line styles

8 Complete the remaining fields – e.g. check Auto kern or specify a leading

Want text with a colored border? Use the Materials palette to select a foreground color before you create the text, then enter a Stroke width value in the Tool Options palette.

9 Click where you want the text inserted

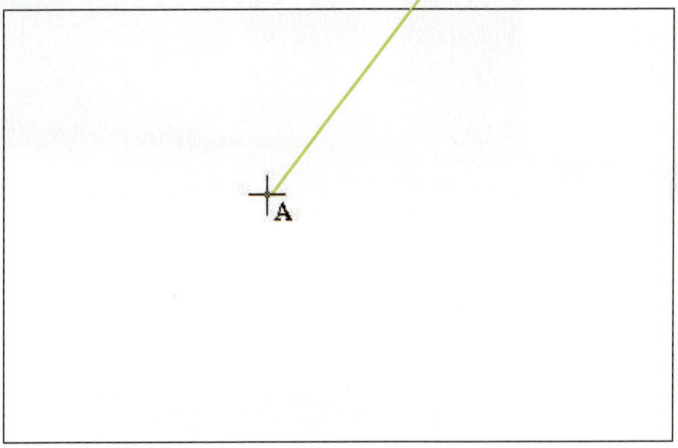

10 Enter your text and watch it appear onscreen. (Need a line break? Just hit Enter)

You can use the dialog on the right to apply text formatting. Just highlight text then make changes in the Tool Options palette – however, the changes don't show up in the dialog, just onscreen.

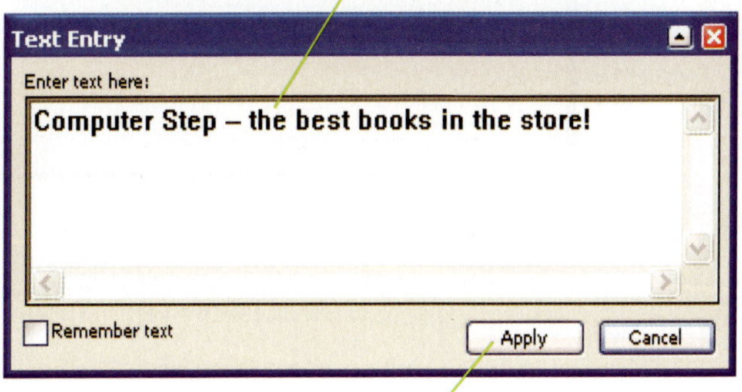

11 Click here

Editing text

1 To edit inserted vector text, place the Text tool mouse pointer over the text and left-click

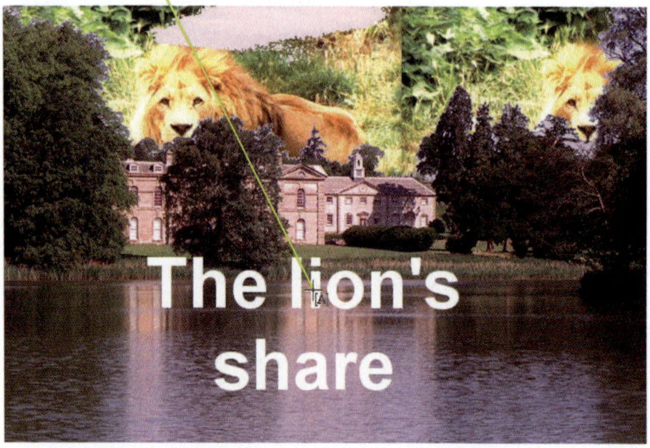

To resize, rotate or distort vector text, you can use the Object Selection tool.

2 Change and/or reformat the text in the Text Entry dialog

3 Alternatively, you can use the Layer palette. Hit F8 if it isn't visible

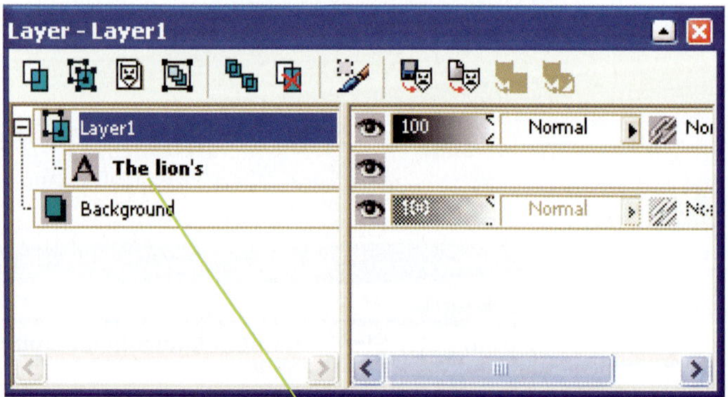

4 Double-click the relevant text layer (shown by "A" to the left) to launch the Text Entry dialog

Advanced text use

Text and vectors

1. You can insert vector text onto vector object outlines or open paths (open paths have start and end points)

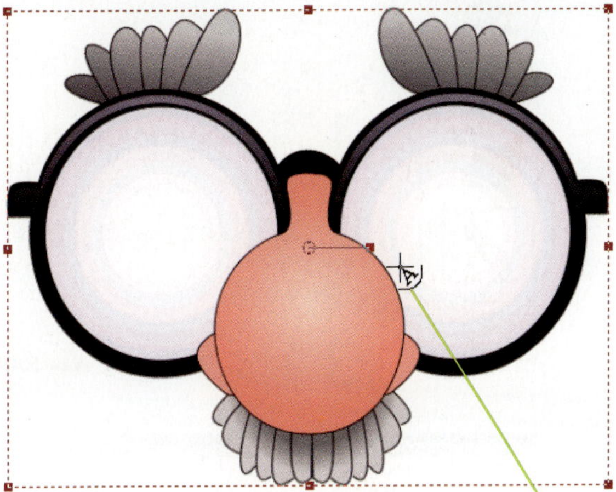

3. Ensure you've selected Vector (and an alignment) in the Tool Options palette

Another advantage vector text has is that you can convert it to curves. This means it's now a vector object not text, and so you can't edit the font or type size any more. However, you can edit the text nodes (see pages 95–99). This can produce unique effects.

Select the text. Choose Object, Convert Text to Curves, As Single Shape (the entire text is one object) or Object, Convert Text to Curves, As Character Shapes (each letter is a separate vector in its own right).

2. With the Text tool active, move the mouse pointer over the relevant vector object (as here) or path until the cursor changes

4. Click the outline or path then complete the Text Entry dialog

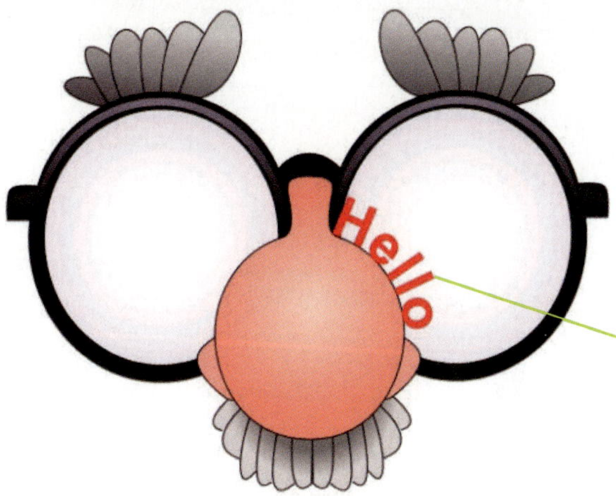

5. Click Apply in the dialog to confirm

Drawing with the Pen tool

Paint Shop Pro has a separate tool which you can use to create more detailed lines/curves.

Drawing single lines

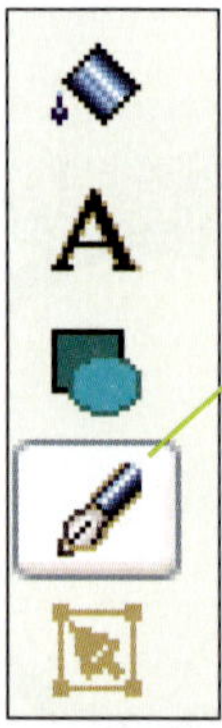

1 Click the Pen tool in the Tool palette. Or just hit V (not P – that's the Preset Shapes tool)

3 Select this

4 Select this

You can save Pen presets for reuse later – click here to access the Presets dialog:

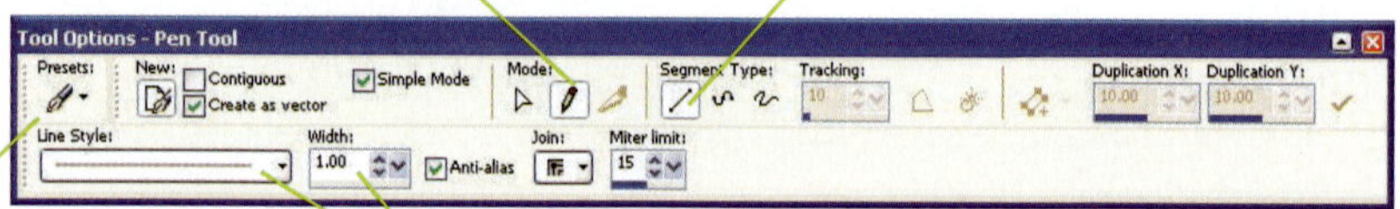

2 Customize your output in the Tool Options palette (F4). For example, click in the Line Style field and select a style. Enter a line width in the Width: field (range: 1–255). Select Create as vector (for a fully editable line)

The line is drawn with the current foreground color/materials, so make sure these are right in the Materials palette before you start.

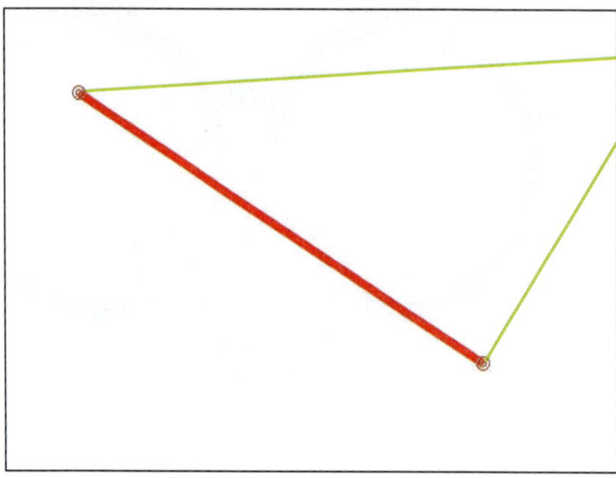

5 Drag with the left mouse button to draw the line

Drawing single lines with multiple segments

1 Follow step 1 on the facing page

3 Select this

4 Select this

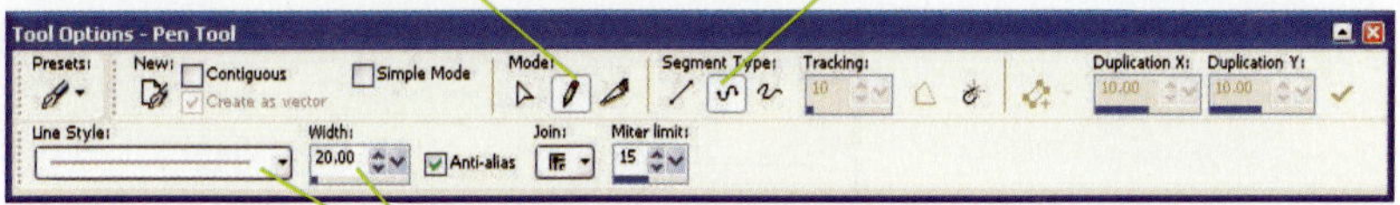

2 Customize your output in the Tool Options palette (F4) – see the facing page for suggestions

5 Left-click to start then click elsewhere to start new line segments

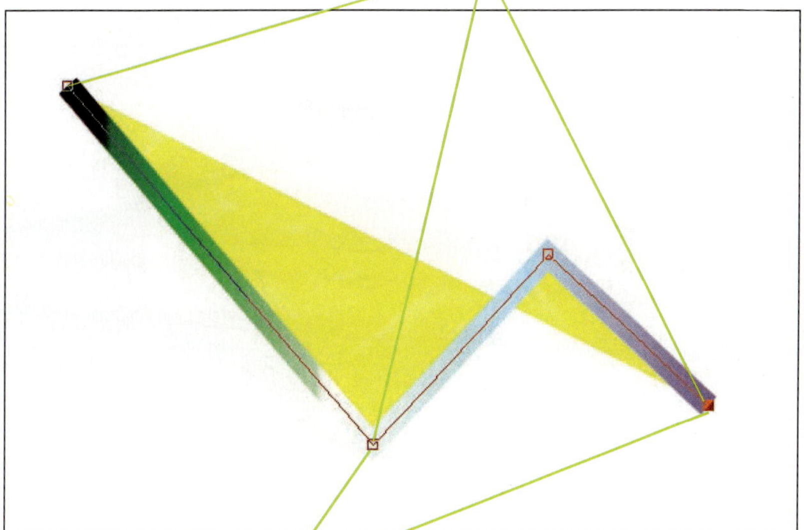

Nodes

If you create three nodes without clicking the New Shape button in the Tool Options palette:

Paint Shop Pro treats the new lines as a single object and fills it (as here) with the background color/materials.

Drawing Freehand lines

1 Follow step 1 on page 86

3 Select this

4 Select this

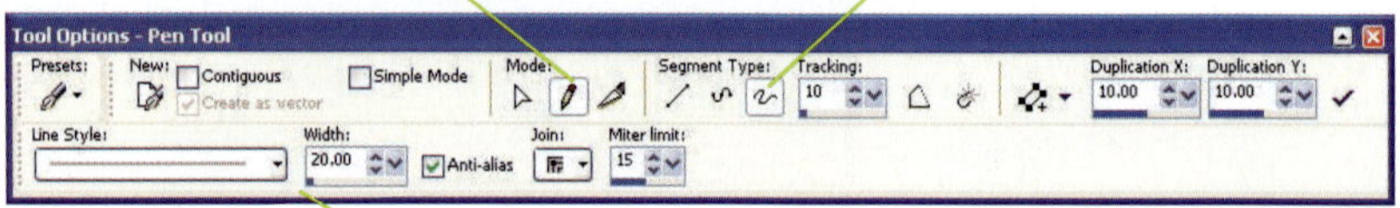

2 Customize your line in the Tool Options palette (F4) – see page 86 for suggestions

5 Drag with the left mouse button to draw with the foreground color/materials

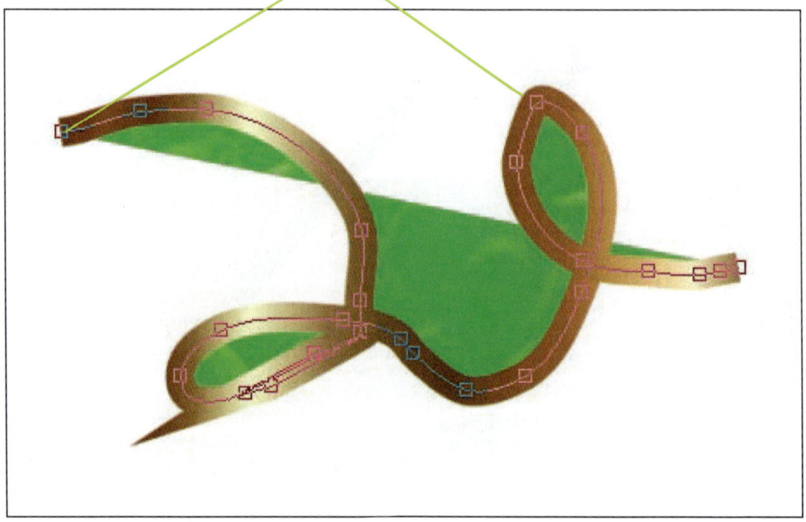

Drawing Bézier curves

1. Follow steps 1–4 on page 86

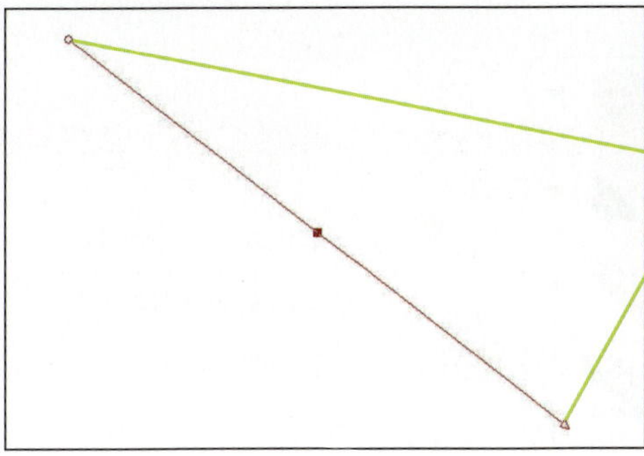

2. Drag with the left mouse button to define the curve's length then release the button

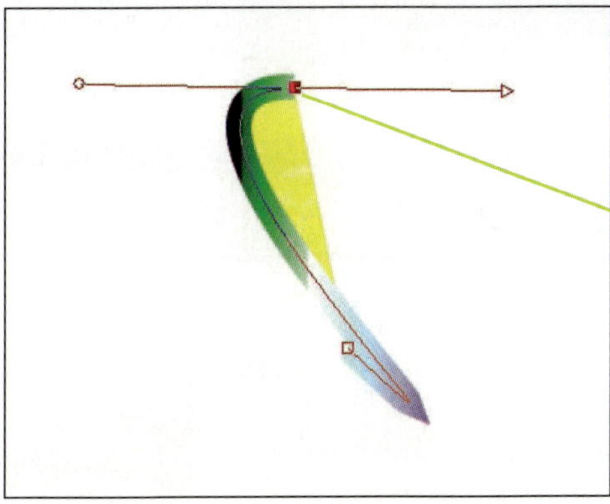

3. Drag elsewhere to create a curve then release the button

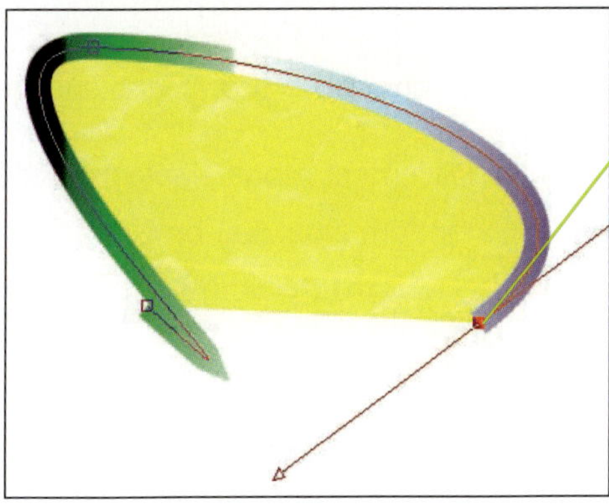

4. Repeat for as many curves as you need

Using the Picture Tube tool

You can also paint using object collections called "picture tubes". When you do this, Paint Shop Pro automatically inserts a variety of related objects.

Picture Tubes only work with raster layers. Also, images must be grayscale or 16-million colors.

Painting with the Picture Tube tool

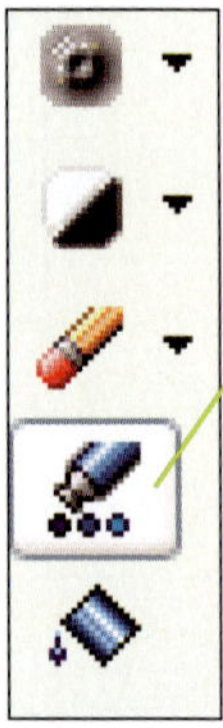

1 Click the Picture Tube tool in the Tool palette. Or just hit I (don't ask why – it's likely the only letter Jasc had left)

You can save Picture Tube presets for reuse later – click here to access the Presets dialog:

3 Select a tube

4 Click this

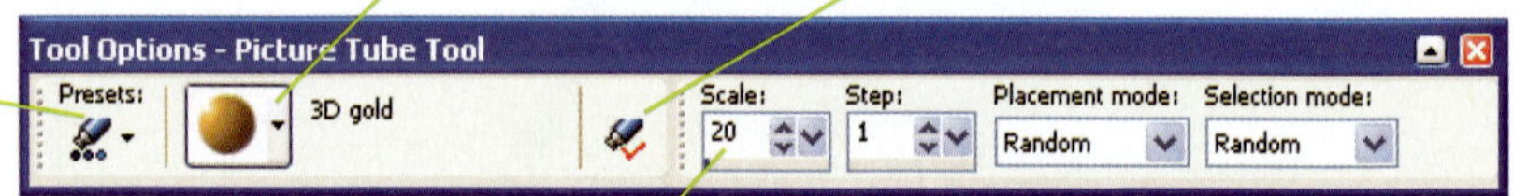

2 Customize your output in the Tool Options palette (F4) e.g.:

- set the tube size in the Scale field (range: 10%–250%)
- increase the Step setting to give less contact between the brush tip and the image surface (this makes the tube's outline more prominent, and the stroke less dense)
- Placement mode – select Random (objects appear at random intervals) or Continuous (equal intervals)
- Selection mode – select Random (objects are chosen haphazardly); Incremental (objects are inserted one at a time); Angular (objects appear according to painting direction); or Velocity (objects appear according to painting speed)

...cont'd

Want more picture tubes? You can get them free at: ***www.jasc.com/tubes/tubedl.asp?***

Version 7 tubes will work with Paint Shop Pro 8. Just copy them to your version 8 Picture Tubes folder.

You can get your version 5 and 6 tubes to work with Paint Shop Pro 8 but you need a special converter. Go to ***www4.jasc.com/pub/tubcnvrt.exe***

Adjust the various settings to vary the impact – the effect can be quite marked.

5 You optionally can customize cell arrangement details

6 Click OK

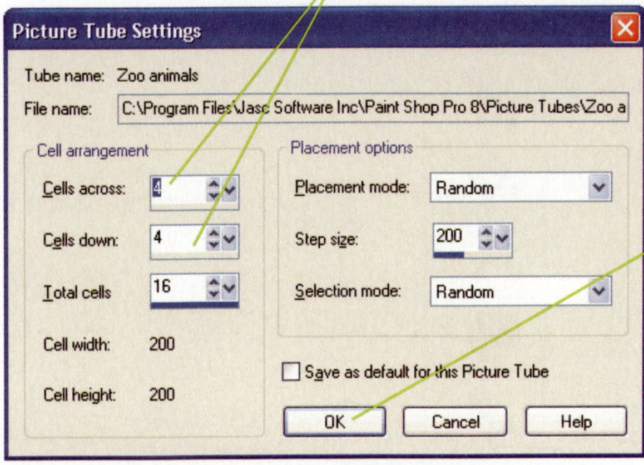

7 Drag with the left mouse button and/or click repeatedly

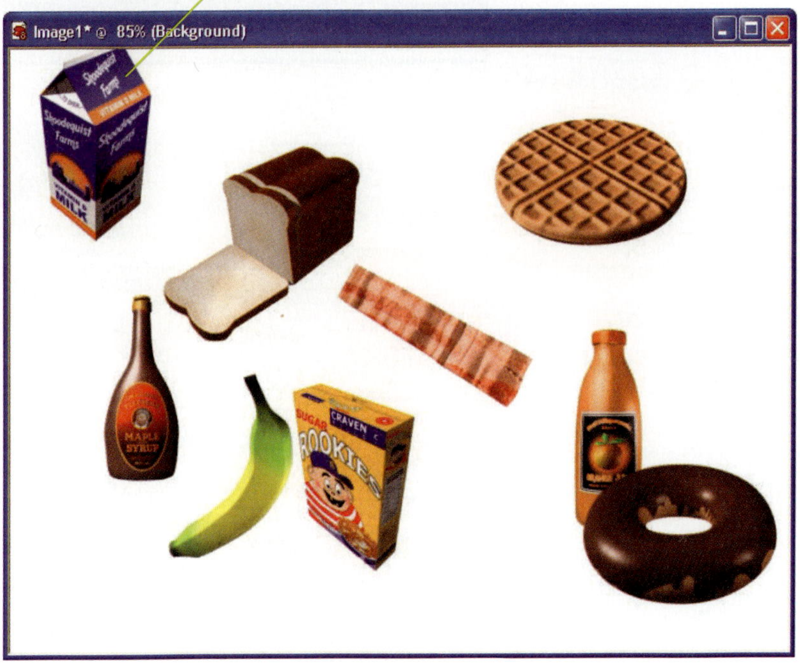

Drawing via the Preset Shapes tool

You can create shapes e.g. complex vectors like buttons, callouts or 3D spheres, or symbol-based vectors like arrows, circles and stars.

Using the Preset Shapes tool

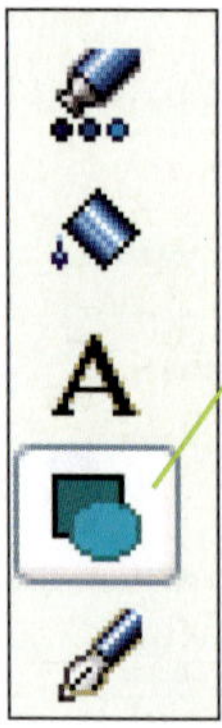

1 Click the Preset Shape tool in the Tool palette. Or just hit P

You can save Preset Shape presets for reuse later – click here to access the Presets dialog:

3 Click here

5 Select Create as vector for optimal editability

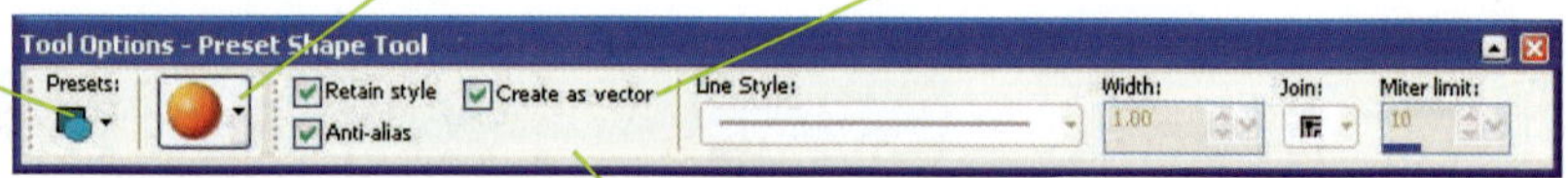

2 Customize your output in the Tool Options palette (F4)

Select Create as vector to define a vector shape, or deselect this to create a raster one instead.

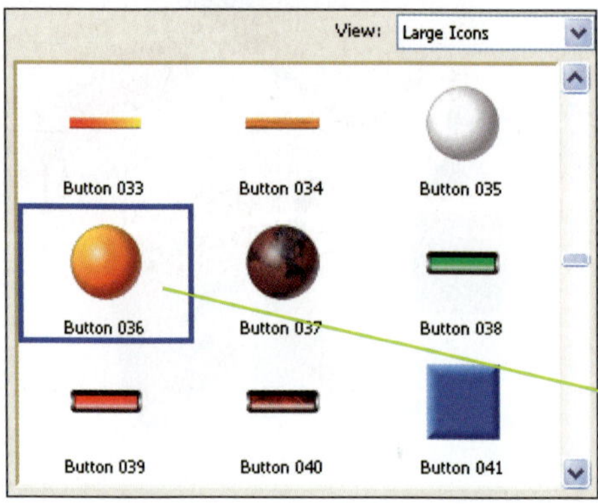

4 Select a shape

6 Drag with the left mouse button to draw the shape

To draw from the center outwards, drag with the right mouse button. To draw proportionately, hold down Shift.

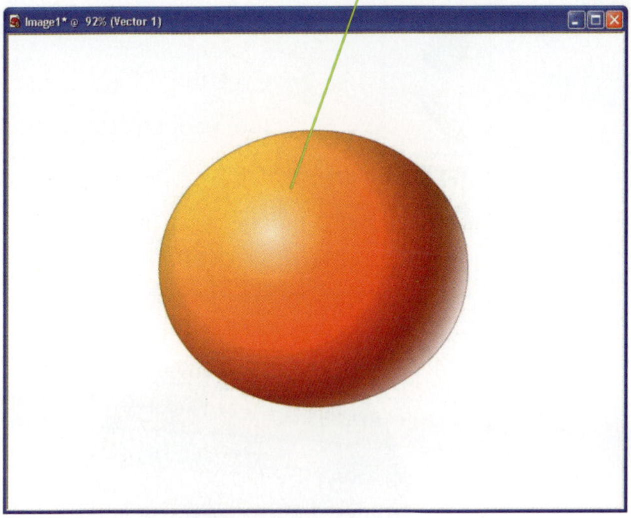

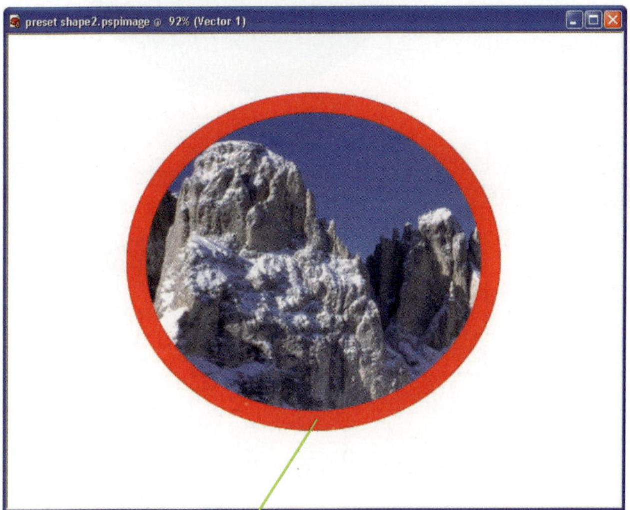

7 Uncheck Retain style in the Tool Options palette if you want the shape's line to follow the foreground color/materials, or its fill to follow the background color/materials

Editing preset shapes

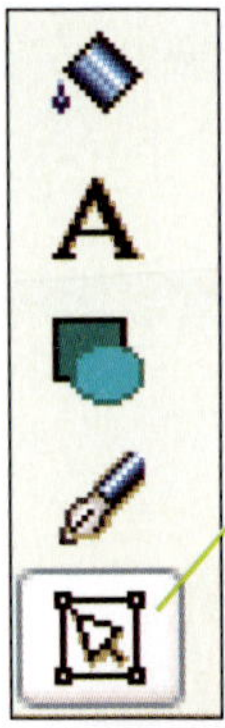

1 Click the Object Selection tool in the Tool palette. Or just hit O

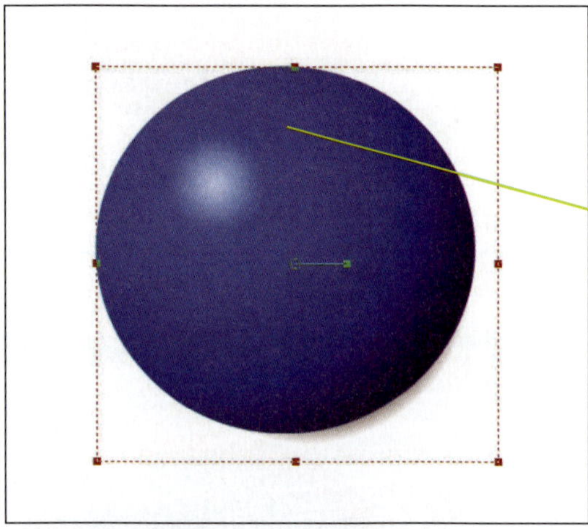

2 Right-click the selected vector and hit Properties

You can also customize vector placement, alignment and distribution in the Tool Options palette.

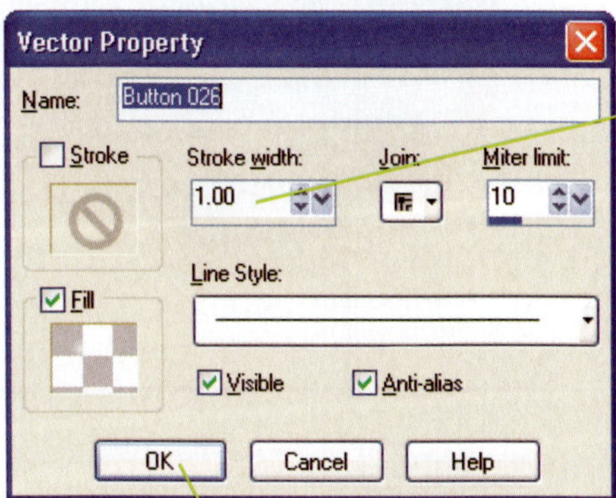

3 Complete the dialog fields (e.g. to amend the shape width, enter a new entry in the Stroke width field)

4 Click here

To apply a new fill, make sure Fill is checked then click in the box below.

Node editing – an overview

Vector objects use a hierarchy. Each object contains one path. Each path consists of at least one contour. Each contour has at least one straight or curved segment and two or more nodes (they determine object shape) and can be open or – as here – closed.

The ability to edit nodes in Paint Shop Pro 8 means you can produce some unique effects.

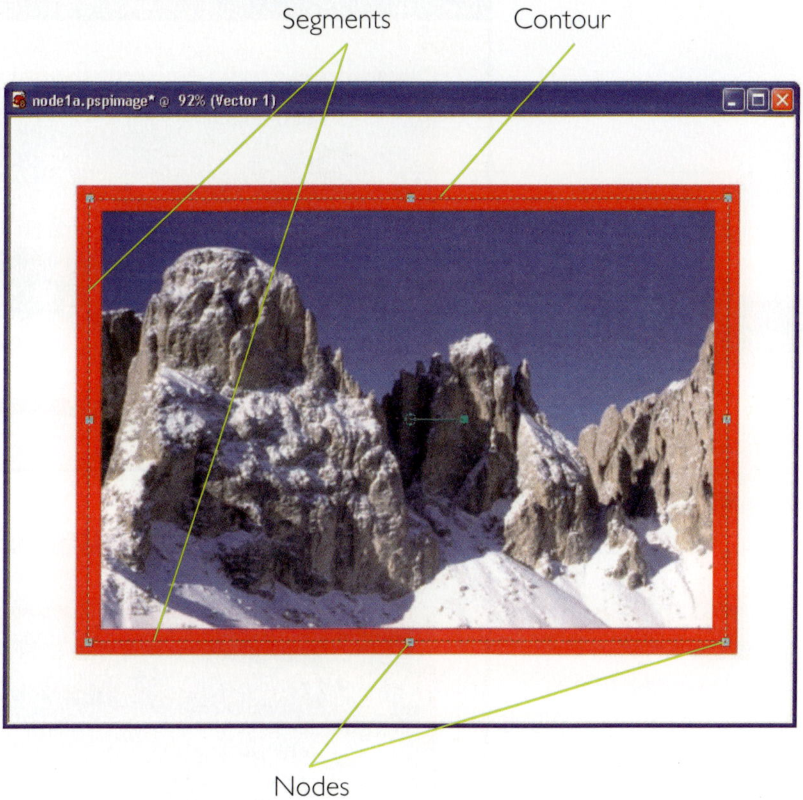

Editing (manipulating) nodes is carried out in a special mode called Edit Mode. This

- displays the vector's path
- does not accurately reflect the vector's true appearance

Only one path can be edited at once, but you can use nodes to reshape vector objects in an almost infinite number of ways.

Selecting nodes

1. If the Pen tool isn't active, hit V
2. In the Tool Options palette, select the Edit Mode icon: 
3. Select a node for editing

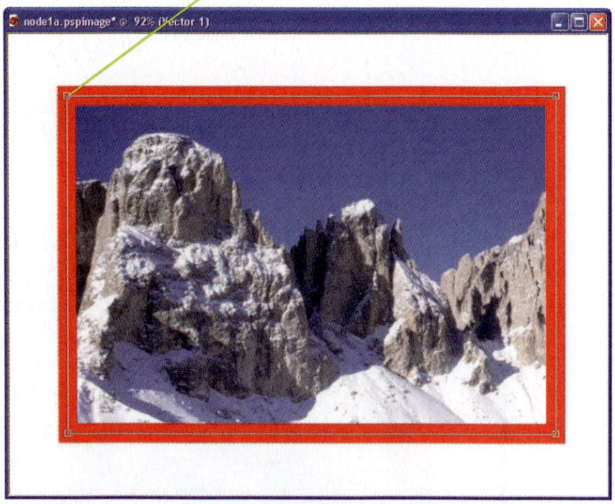

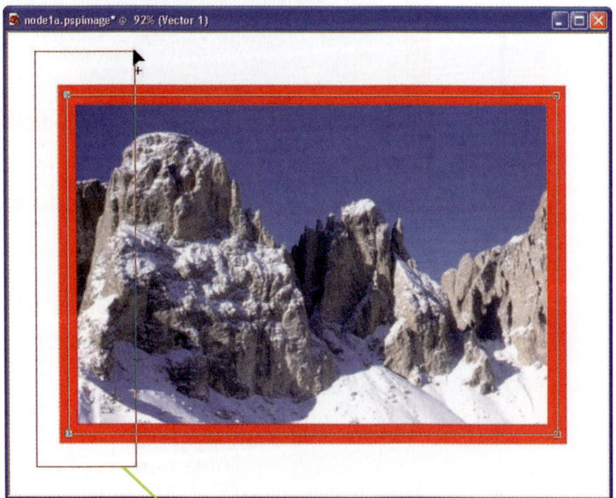

4. Or drag out a marquee to select multiple nodes

Node operations

Adding new nodes

Follow steps 1–2 on the facing page then:

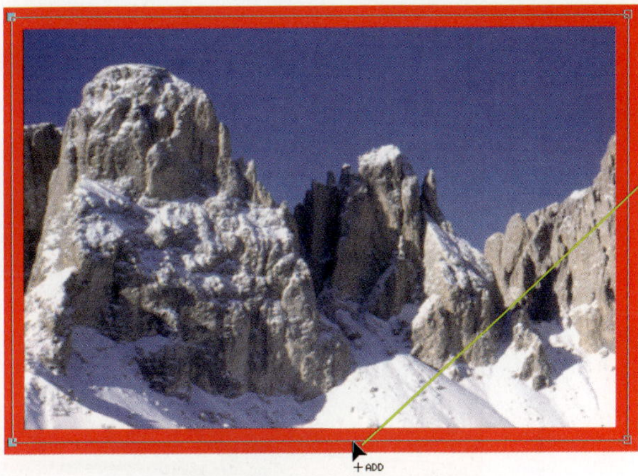

1 Hold down Ctrl as you left-click a contour

Moving nodes

Follow steps 1–2 on the facing page then:

1 Select one or more nodes

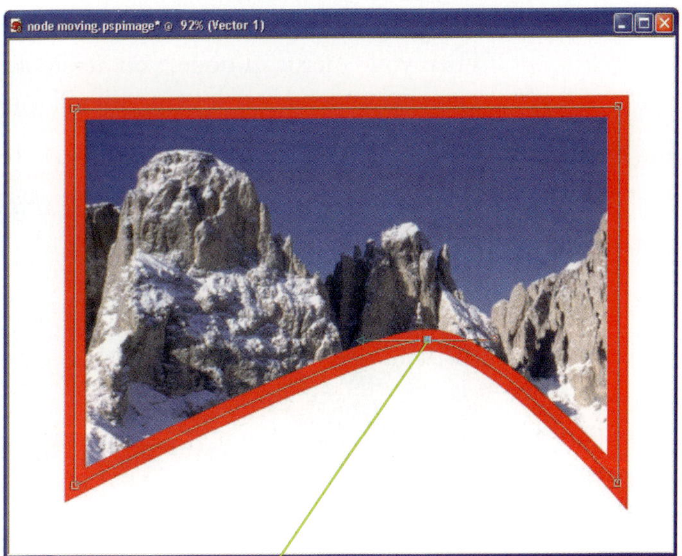

2 Drag the node(s) to a new location

The effect of moving a node depends on its type – see page 98 for more information.

Dragging a segment rather than a node moves the entire contour.

Changing a node's type

Applying a new type to a node has an impact on the segments which enter and leave it.

You should note that Paint Shop Pro has the following node types:

- *Smooth – allows curves and lines to blend smoothly*
- *Cusp – produces marked directional changes*
- *Symmetric and Asymmetric – both give a smooth flow through the node but in Symmetric the result is more harmonious*

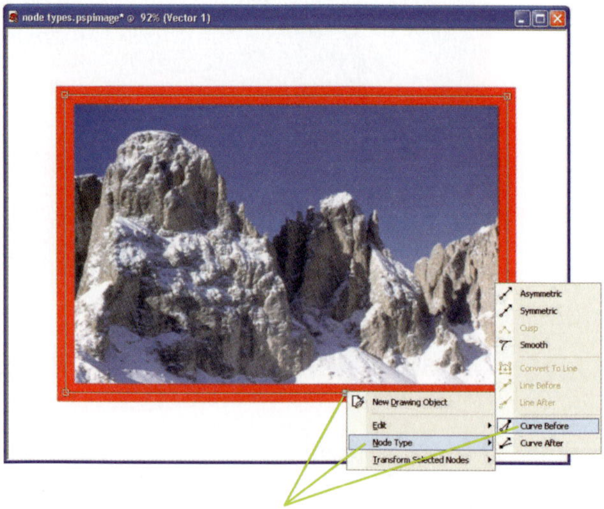

In Node Edit mode, right-click a node. Select Node Type then click a type

Merging nodes

When you "merge" a node, you delete it. This results in the two segments which enter it being united into one.

Nodes have handles – you can use these in Edit Mode to customize the shape of contours:

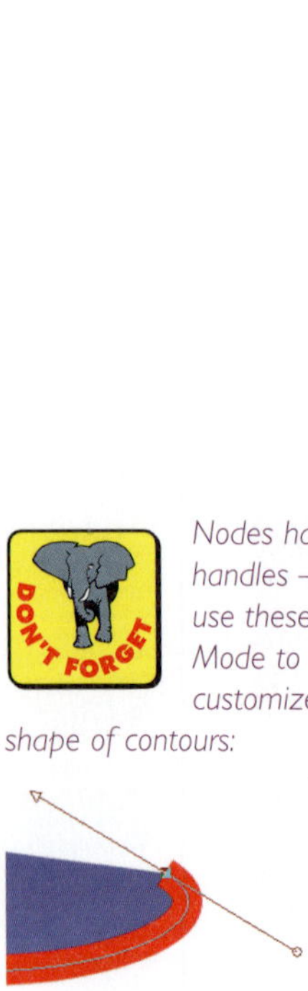

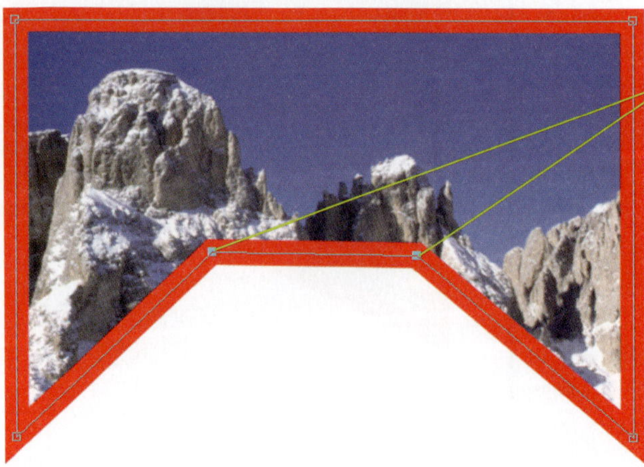

In Edit Mode, select 1 or more nodes

Merging every node within a contour deletes the contour.

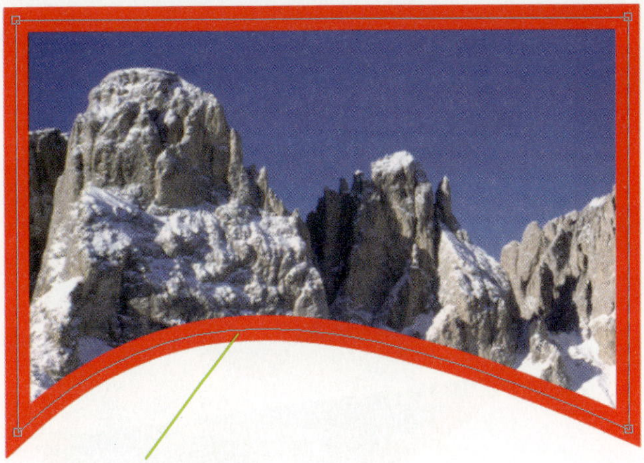

2 Hit Ctrl+M – the result can be unexpected

Breaking nodes

You can "break" nodes. This means that the contour in which the node is situated is split into two separate contours (if the original was open) or opened out (if the original contour was closed).

1 In Node Edit mode, left-click a node

2 Press Ctrl+K then drag the nodes apart

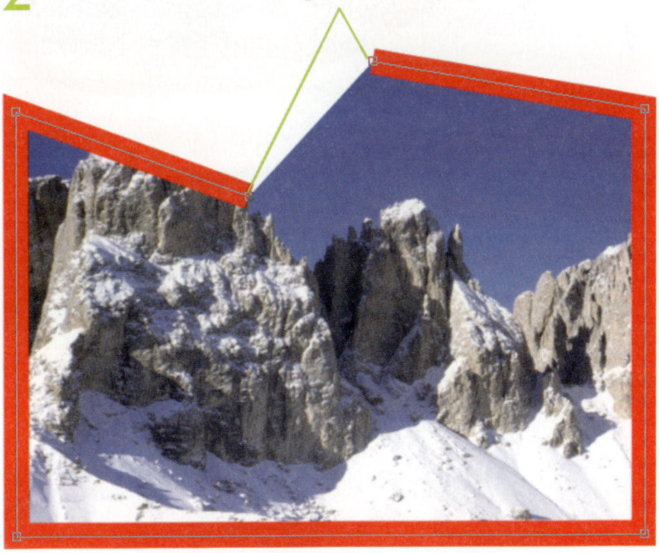

Working with contours

1. Ensure the Pen tool is active and you're in Edit Mode

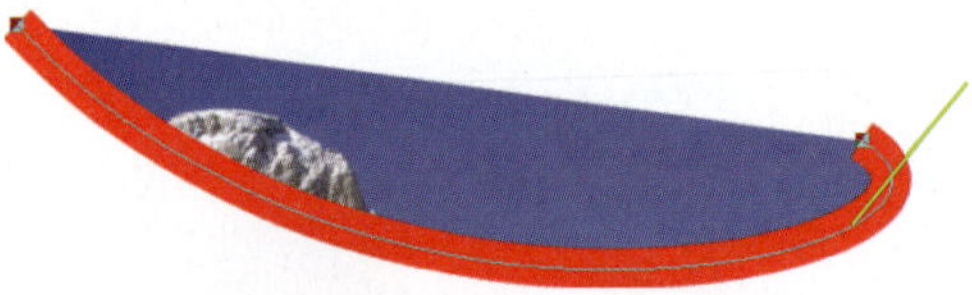

2. To add a new contour, click the object . . .

To delete a contour, click it then press Delete.

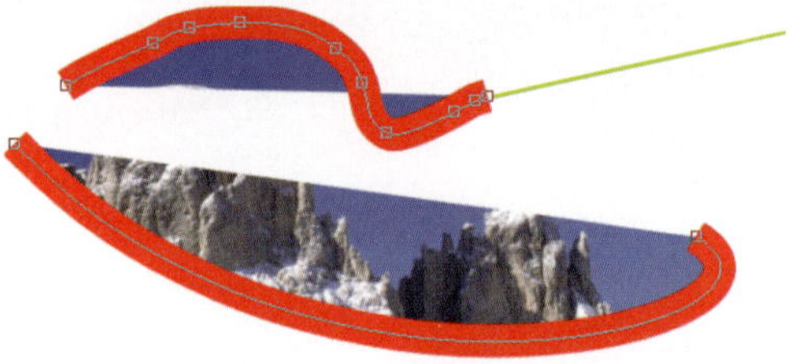

3. . . . In the Tool Options palette, select the Drawing Mode icon then a segment type. Drag out a new contour

To join contours, drag one node over another. When "JOIN" appears below the pointer, release the button.

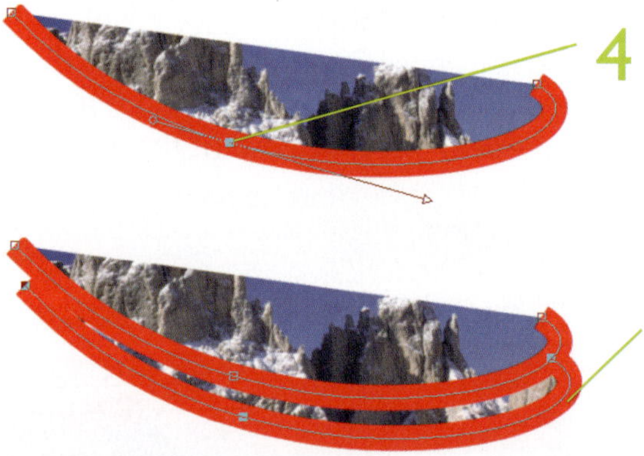

4. To duplicate a contour, click one of its nodes. Hit Ctrl+D to paste in the copy at the same location or Ctrl+Shift+D for an offset copy

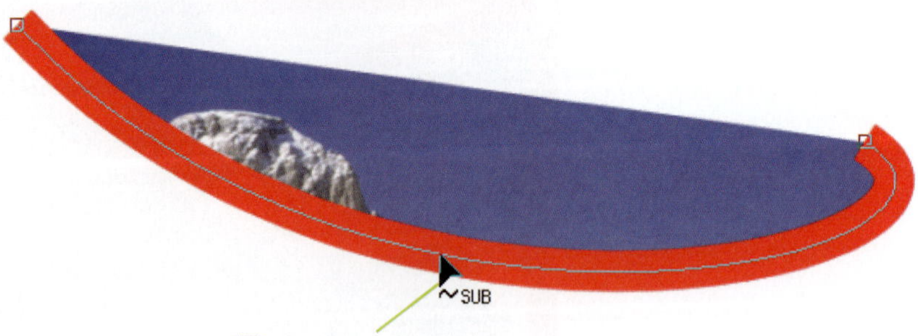

5. To move a contour, hold down Shift and drag

Using filters

In this chapter, you'll learn how to add a variety of creative effects to images or image selections. You'll do this by applying any of Paint Shop Pro's numerous filters.

Finally, you'll create your own filters and save these as presets.

Covers

Chapter Four

Using filters

In Paint Shop Pro, the distinction between filters, deformations and effects is sometimes less than precise.

Paint Shop Pro provides numerous effects that you can use to enhance your photographs etc. Effects are organized under various categories. Filters are specialized effects that enhance images or image selections by varying the color of every pixel ("picture element") in line with its current color and the colors of any neighboring pixels.

You can also create and apply your own filters, for some really distinctive and original effects.

Applying a filter

Filters only work with images with 16-million colors or more (if they have fewer colors, hit Ctrl+Shift+0) and 256-color grayscales.

1 Optionally, pre-select part of the relevant image or select a layer in the Layer palette

2 Pull down the Effects menu and click Effect Browser

3 Select Edge Effects in the tree

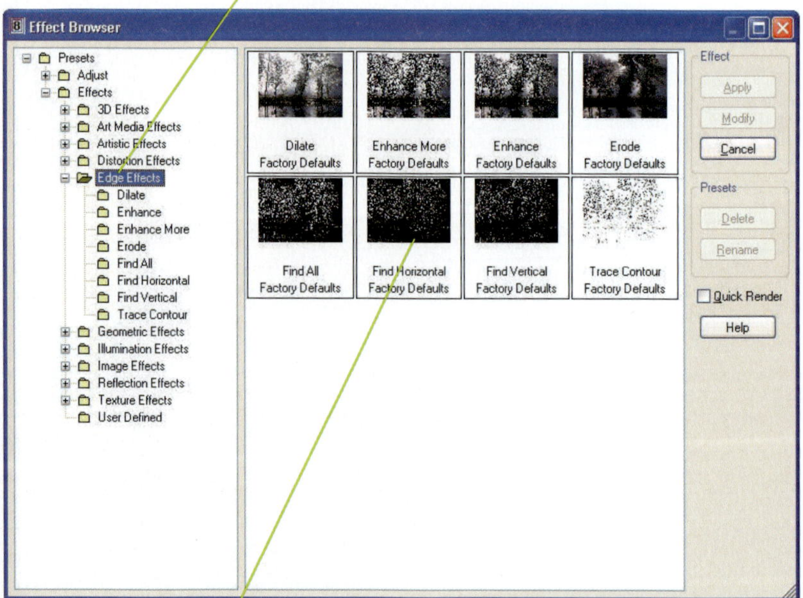

You can customize some filters before applying them. Just click the preview then hit Modify. Complete the dialog.

4 Double-click a filter preview to apply it

You can also use a menu route to apply edge filters. Pull down the Effects menu, click Edge Effects and then make a choice.

Filter Gallery

Because many filters can't be customized (you can only apply them out-of-the-box) applying the same filter twice can often give superior results.

Paint Shop Pro ships with numerous filters. Some of the most useful are detailed in this chapter.

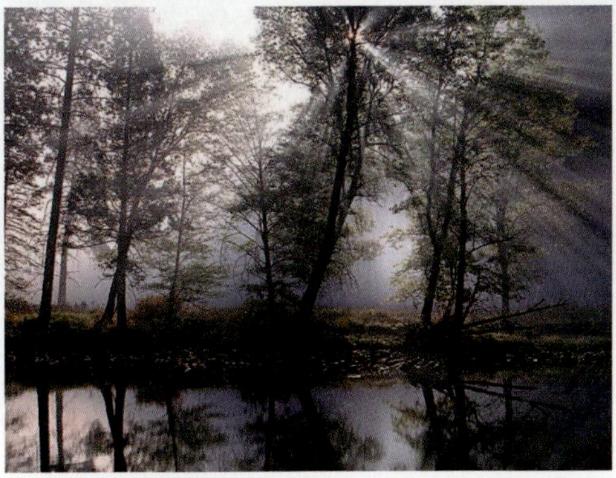

Compare this image (unchanged) with examples of filters below and later in this chapter

Example filters

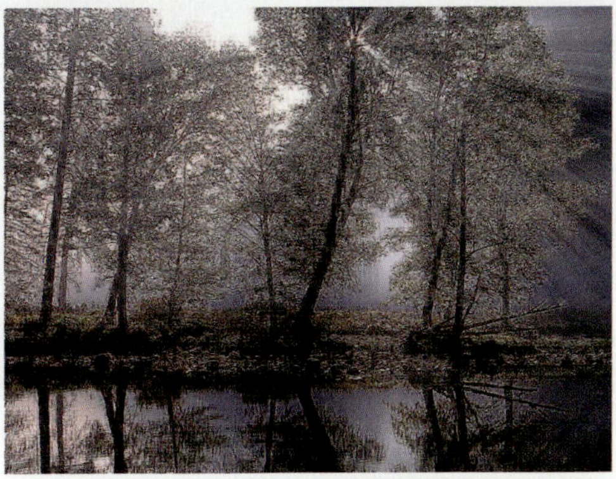

Enhance

Use the Enhance More filter (it works by amplifying edge contrast) to increase image clarity. (For a similar but reduced effect, use the Enhance filter.)

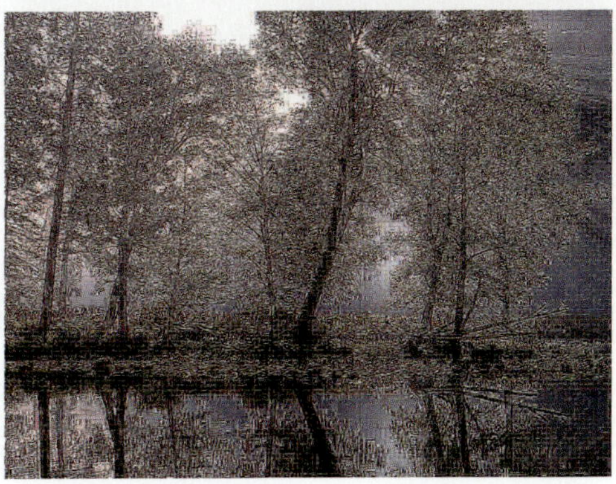

Enhance More

The Dilate filter enhances light areas in an image.

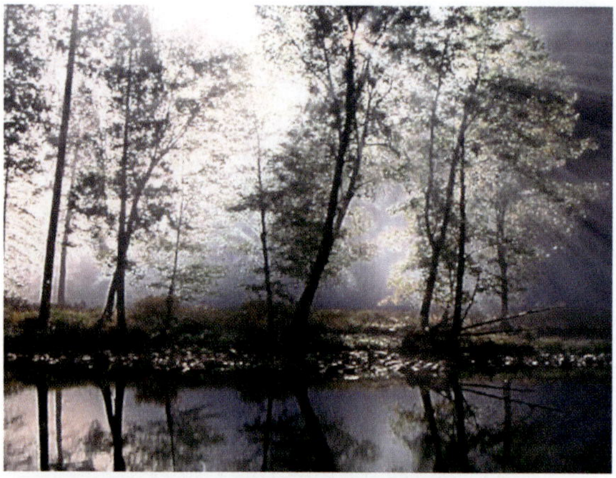

Dilate

Erode emphasizes edges by applying a stronger contrast to them.

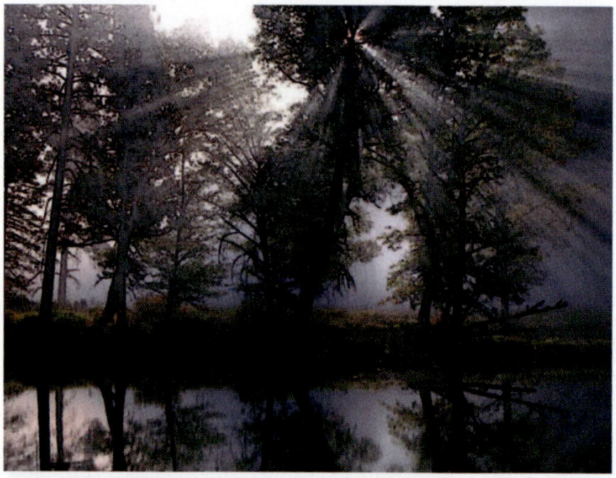

Erode

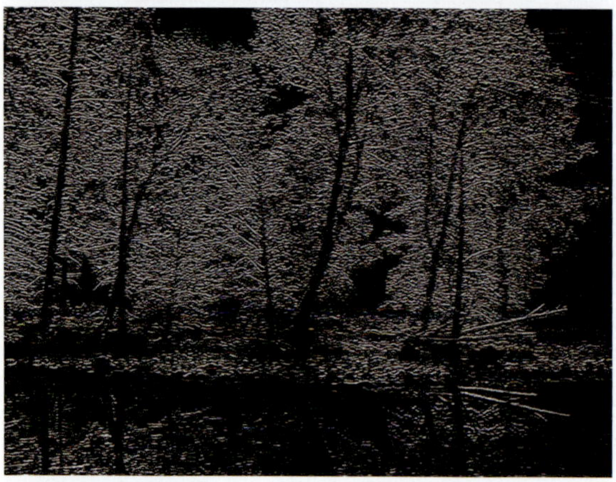

Find Horizontal

Use the Find Horizontal and Find Vertical filters when you need to identify – and emphasize – those parts of an image which have significant horizontal or vertical color transitions. (They work by darkening an image and then stressing the edges.)

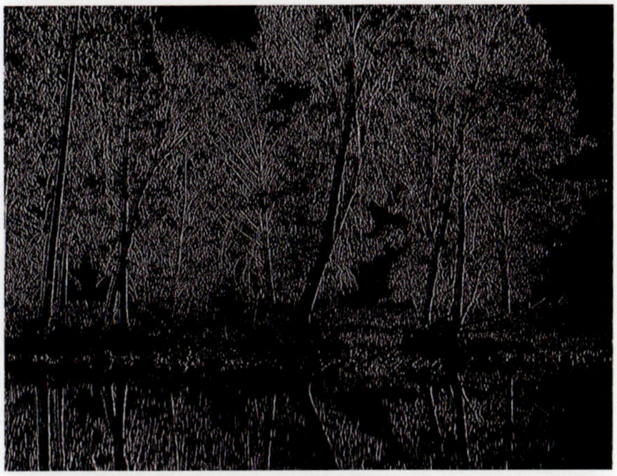

Find Vertical

Use the Find All filter (it works by darkening an image and emphasizing its edges) to increase image clarity.

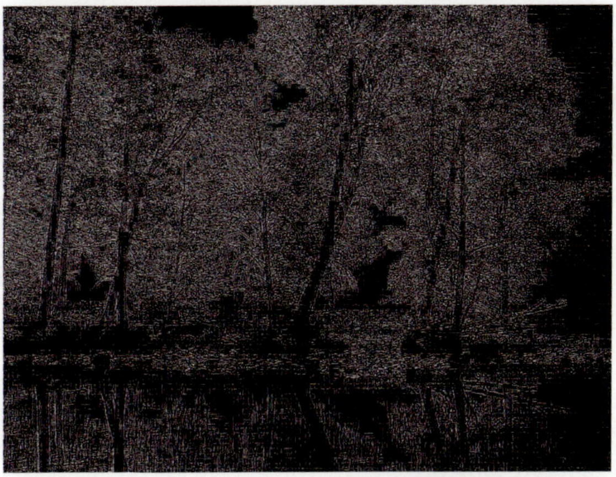

Find All

The Trace Contour filter is a specialist edge filter which, effectively, outlines images by defining a border around them.

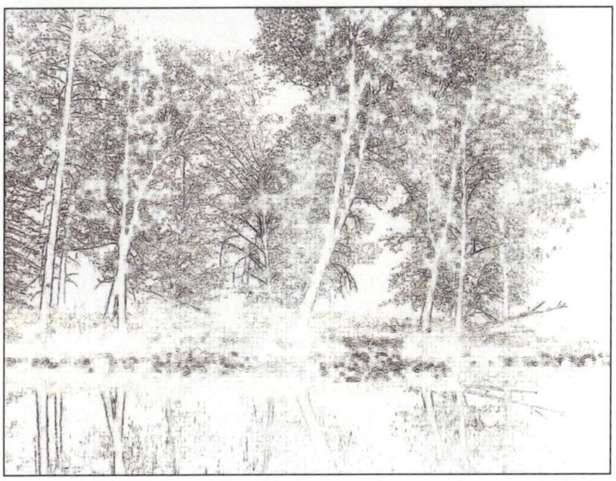

Trace Contour

Paint Shop Pro offers more specialized filters. For example, use the Deinterlace filter to correct video images.

Additional filters

You'll also find filters in the Adjust part of the Effect Browser hierarchy (and in the Adjust menu).

1 Select Adjust in the tree

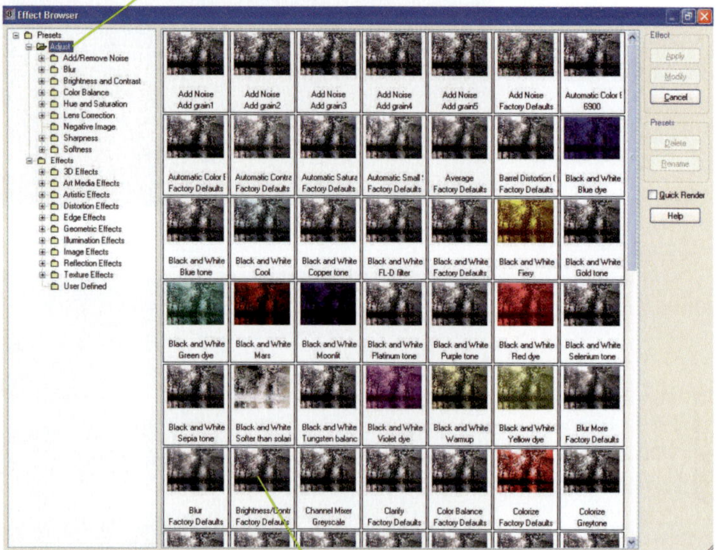

2 Double-click a filter preview (arranged alphabetically) to apply it

Scanned in JPEG images? You'll likely find they have "artifacts", unwanted color leakage or blocky-looking colors. Use the JPEG Artifact Removal filter to correct this problem.

If this doesn't work, try the Moiré Pattern Removal filter.

Use the Despeckle filter to blur all of an image except those locations (edges) where meaningful color changes take place.

Examples

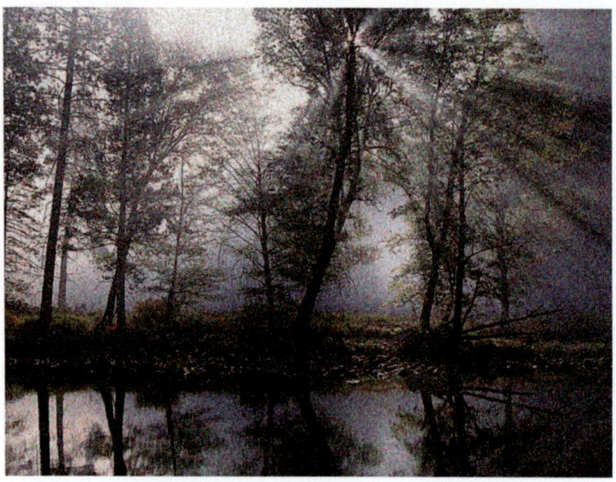

Add Noise

Use Add Noise (in moderation) to remove imperfections from images.

...cont'd

The Blur and Blur More filters reduce contrast and facilitate color transitions.

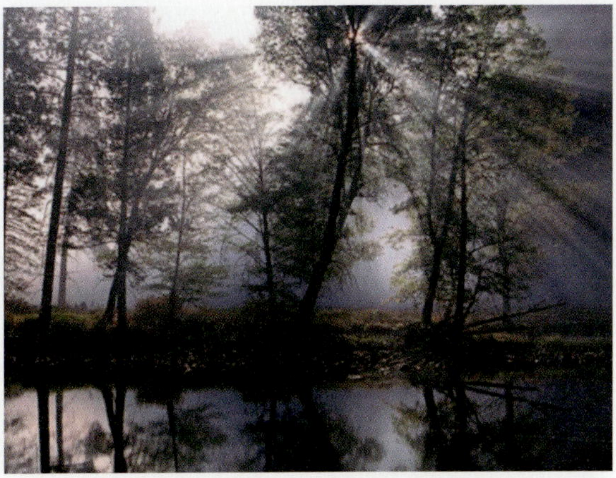

Blur

Use the Average filter to remove noise which is spread over the whole of an image. (This filter is also useful with pictures whose color depth you've increased.)

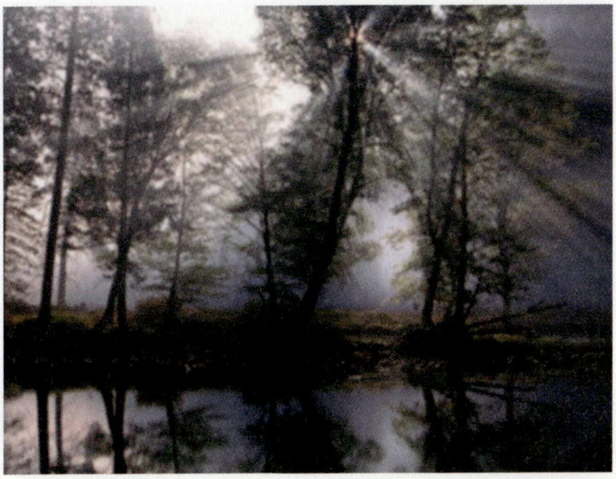

Blur More

Use the Edge Preserving filters to get rid of noise without losing edge definition.

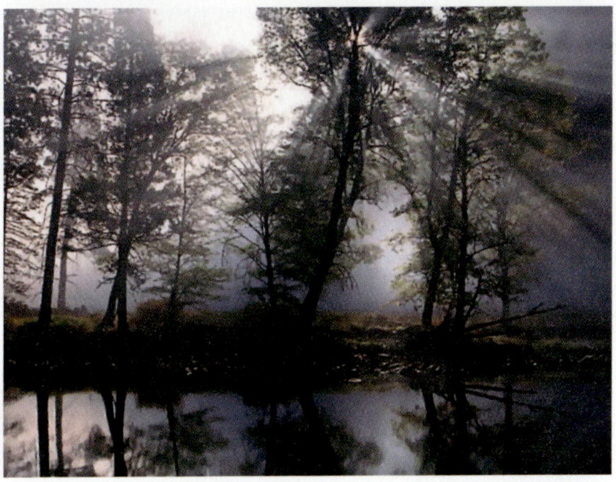

Edge Preserving – Watercolor

Motion Blur makes an image look as though it was moving when the photograph was taken. Use the Motion Blur dialog to specify a strength and angular direction.

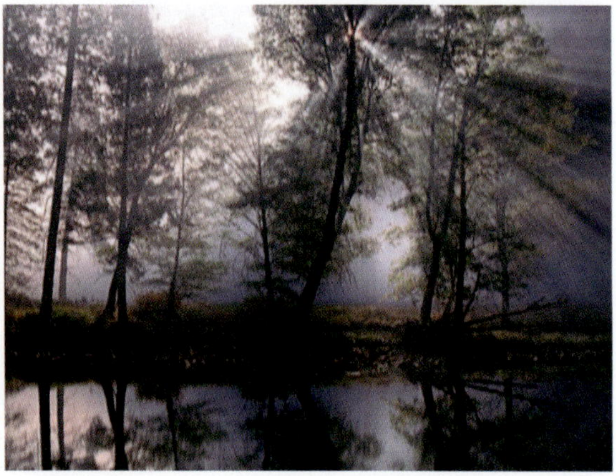

Motion Blur

Sharpen and Sharpen More intensify contrast between contiguous pixels and thus improve image focus.

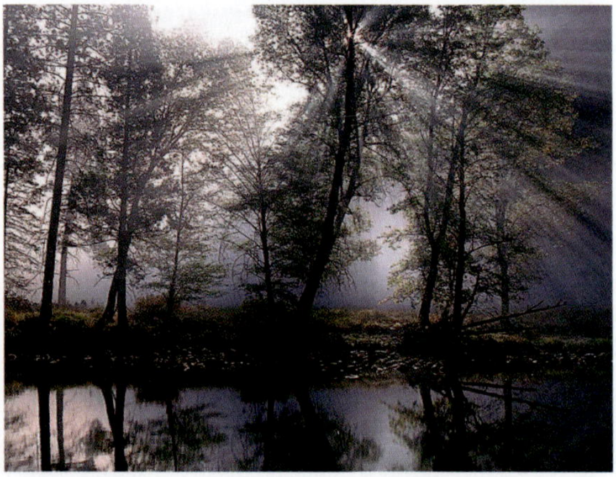

Sharpen

Use the Salt and Pepper filter to remove noise/specks (e.g. dust) from photographs. It works best when you apply it to a predefined selection.

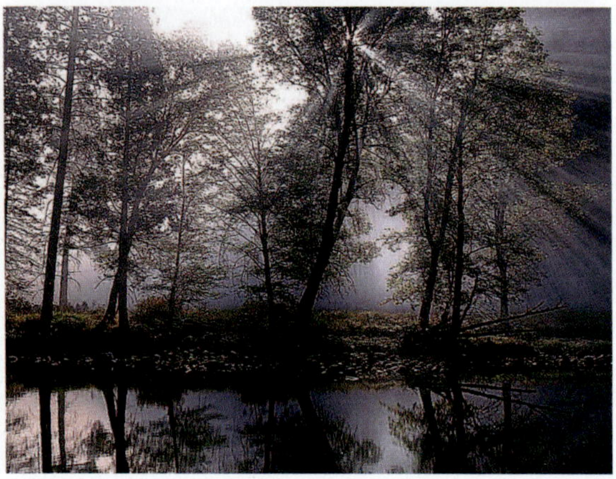

Sharpen More

The Soft Focus filters produce results that are close to a specific camera filter.

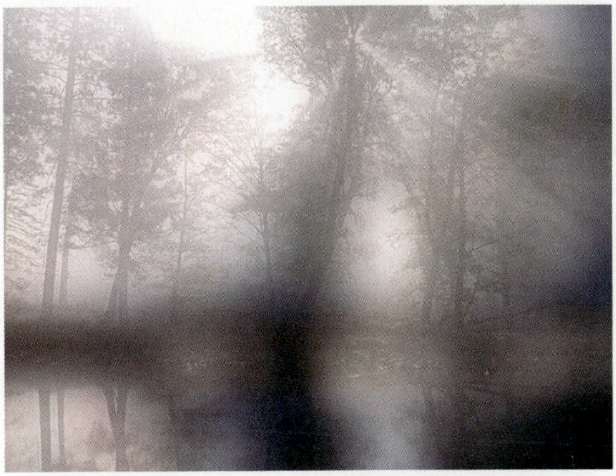

Soft Focus – Fog

Use the Soften (not shown) or Soften More filters to diminish image graininess.

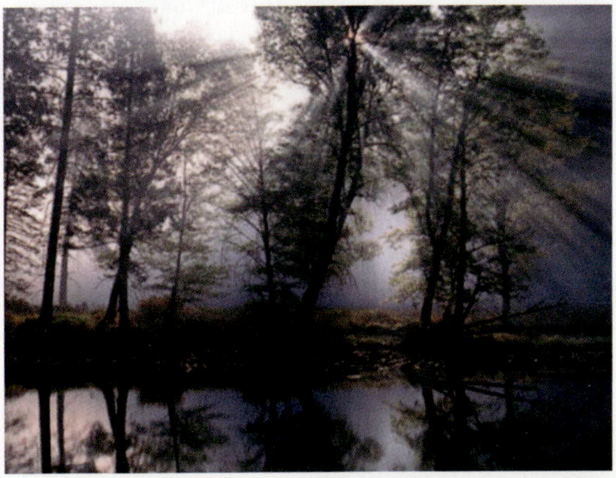

Soften More

Unsharp Mask is the sharpening filter preferred by professionals. It can produce some pretty dramatic effects.

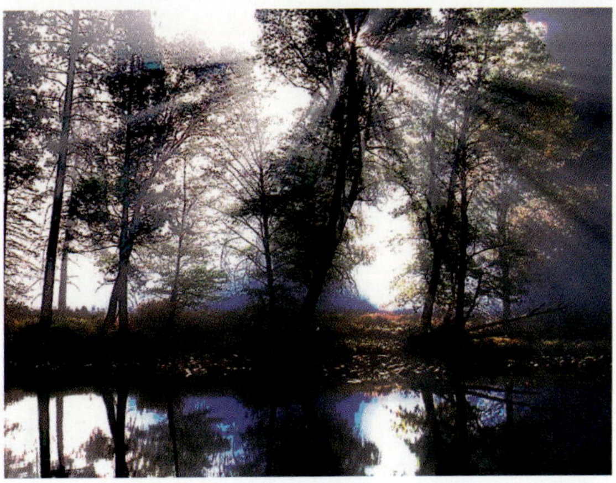

Unsharp Mask

Creating your own filters

You can define your own filters, easily and conveniently. Once created, new filters can be saved as presets.

1. Pull down the Effects menu and click User Defined

2. Select a preset

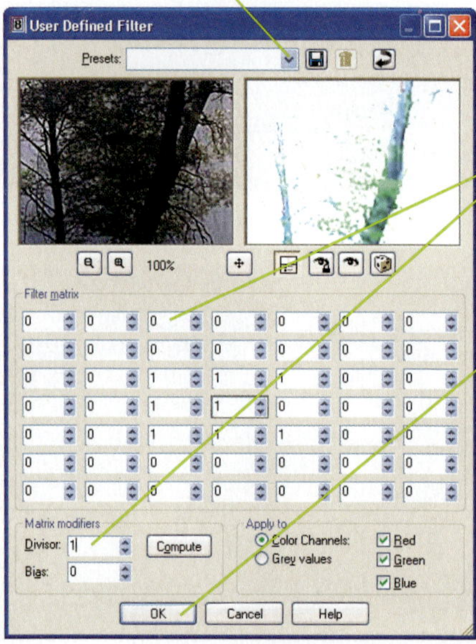

3. Or enter your own filter parameters

4. Click OK

5. The original image on page 103 after applying a user-defined filter

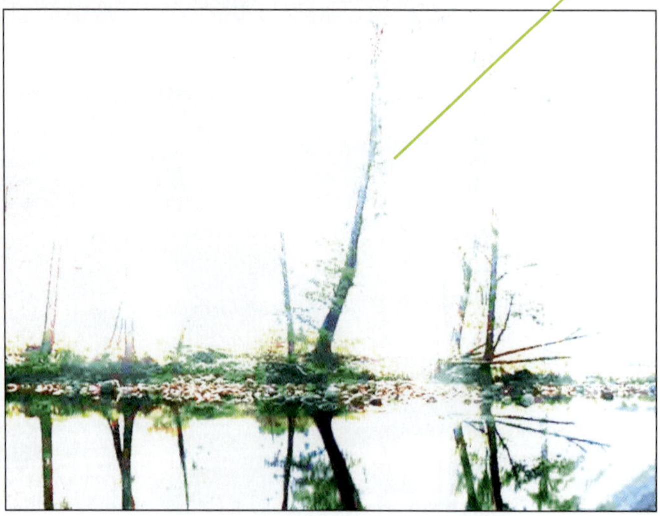

Stuck for somewhere to start? Try hitting the Randomize button (you can also do this in any other modifiable filter):

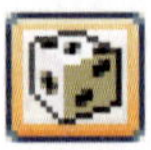

When you get an effect which is something like what you want, amend the settings manually.

Using deformations

Chapter Five

In this chapter, you'll distort images or selections with specialized effects called deformations. Then you'll learn how to utilize additional manual techniques which are not only handy (you can use them to correct photographic misalignments), they're also fun (you can create some seriously warped effects with them).

Covers

Using deformations

Deformations enhance images (or image selections, if you've pre-selected part of a picture) by transferring data from one image area to another. This makes them more spectacular than filters.

Deformations only work with colored images with more than 256 colors (hit Ctrl+Shift+0 to increase their color depth if they don't match up) and 256-color grayscales.

Applying a deformation

1. Optionally, pre-select part of the relevant image or select a layer in the Layer palette (F8)

2. Pull down the Effects menu and click Effect Browser

3. Under Effects, select Distortion Effects or Geometric Effects

In Paint Shop Pro, the distinction between filters, deformations and effects is sometimes less than precise.

You can also use a menu to apply deformations. Pull down the Effects menu and make the appropriate choices.

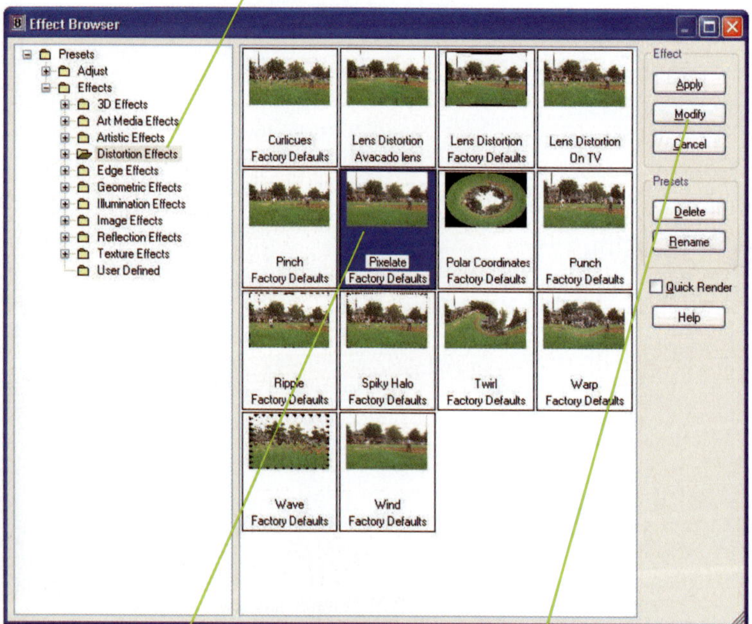

4. Double-click a deformation preview to apply it

5. Alternatively, you can customize a deformation before applying it. Just click the preview then hit Modify. Complete the dialog

Stuck for somewhere to start? Try hitting the Randomize button when you modify a deformation:

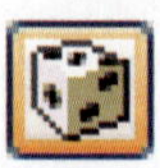

Deformation Gallery

Paint Shop Pro ships with numerous deformations.

Experiment with applying more than one deformation to images (or the same deformation more than once) – the effects can be dramatic.

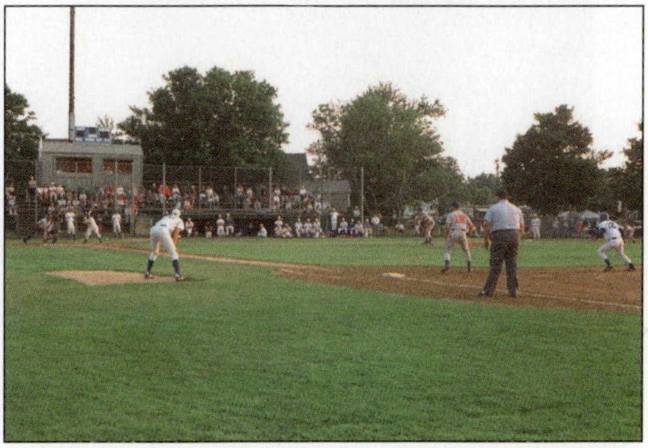

Compare this image (unchanged) with examples of deformations below and later in this chapter

Example deformations

The Circle deformation produces a "fish-eye" effect.

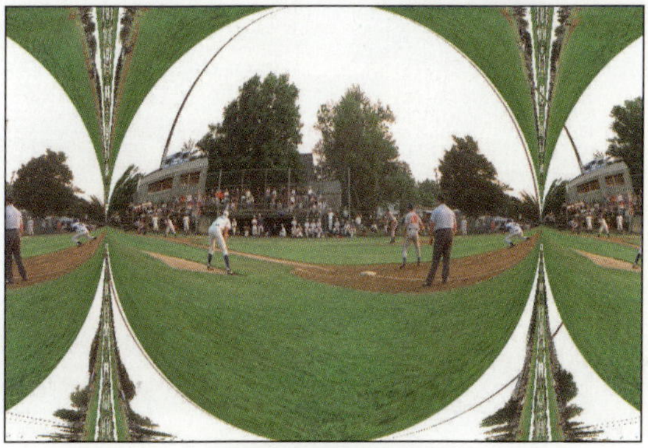

Circle

The Curlicues deformation splits images into curled columns.

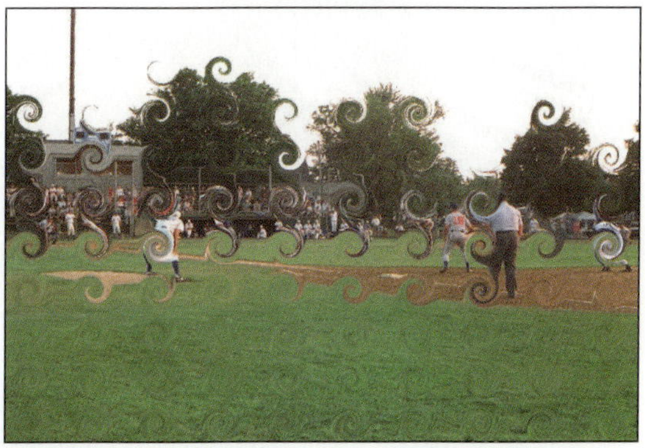

Curlicues

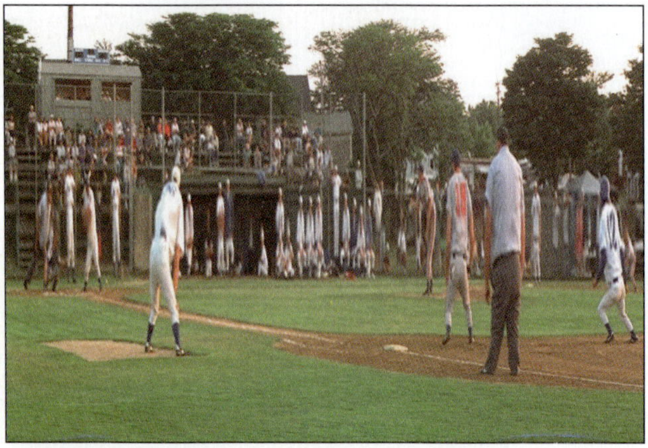

Cylinder Horizontal

This isn't an illusion: the Cylinder Vertical has a horizontal effect and vice versa. Go figure!

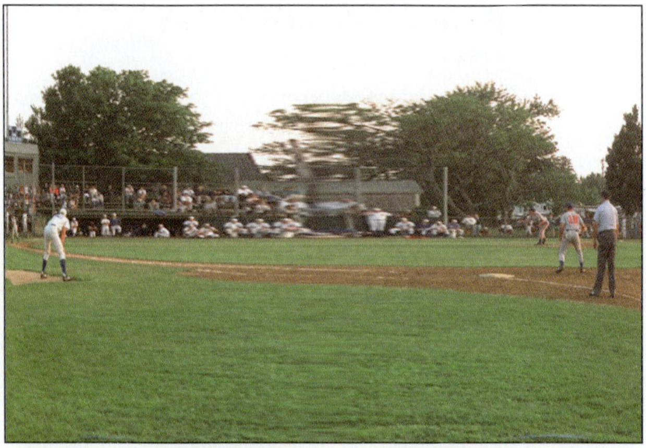

Cylinder Vertical

Self-explanatory, but you can achieve results which aren't just "straight" pentagons by varying the Edge mode setting when you customize the Pentagon deformation.

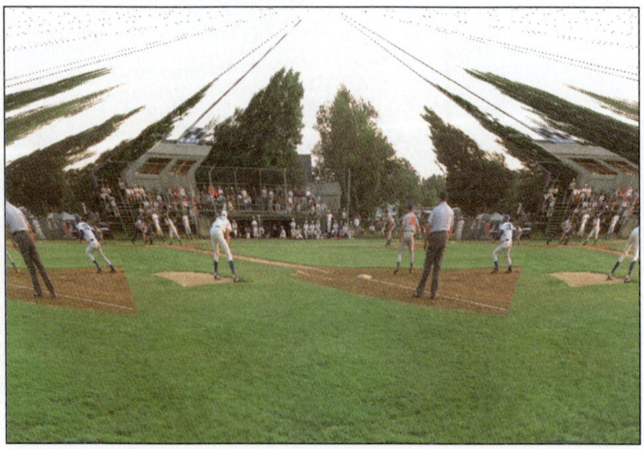

Pentagon

The Perspective Horizontal deformation slants an image horizontally. (The Perspective Vertical deformation does the same, only vertically.)

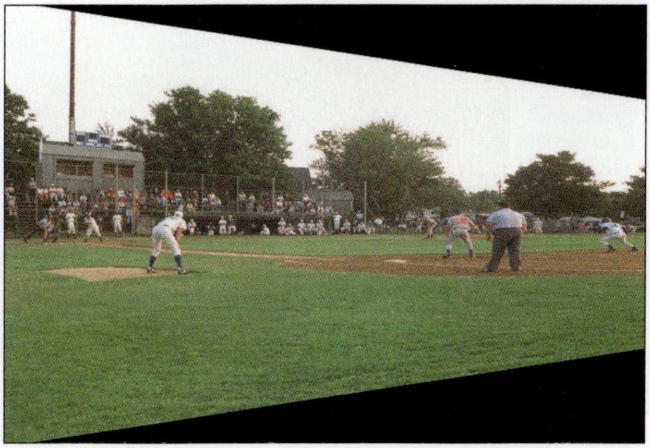

Perspective Horizontal

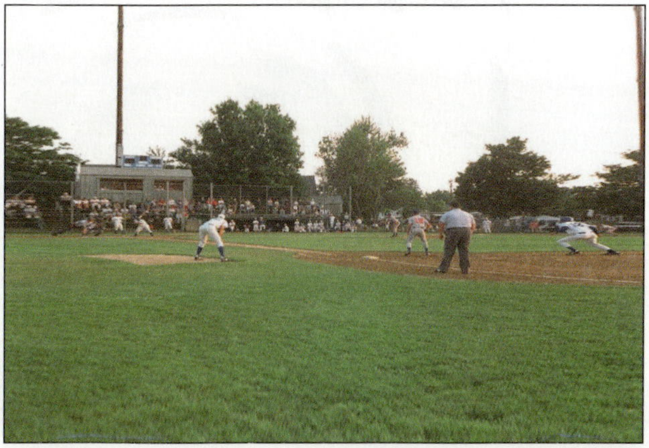

Pinch

When you customize this deformation, try varying the Edge mode setting.

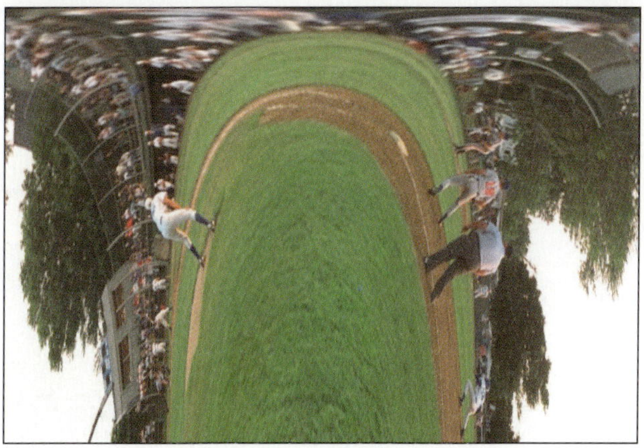

Polar Coordinates

Punch imposes the opposite effect to Pinch.

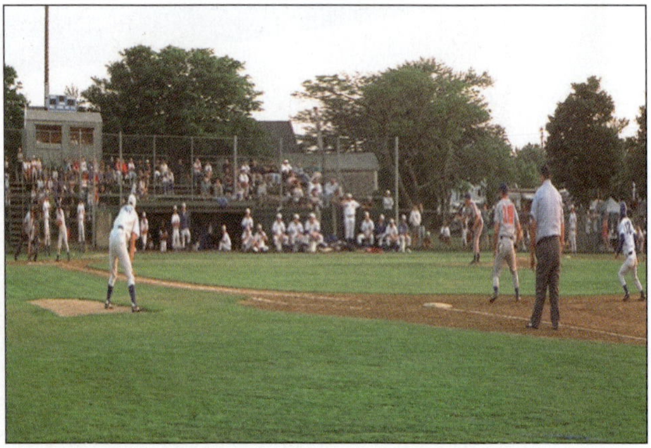

Punch

Ripple defines concentric rings around an image's midpoint.

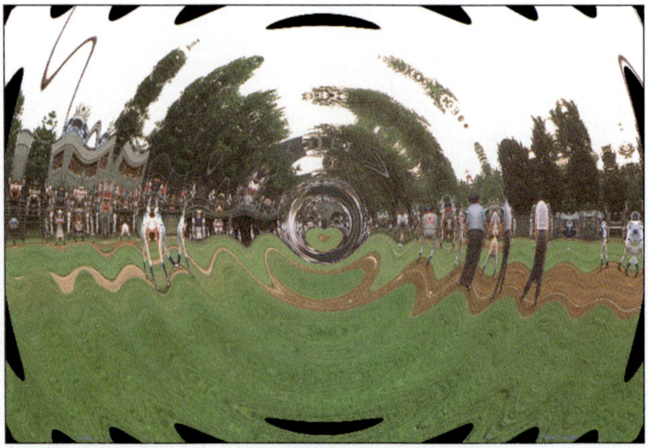

Ripple

For some reason, you'll find this deformation under Effects/ Reflection Effects in the Effect Browser.

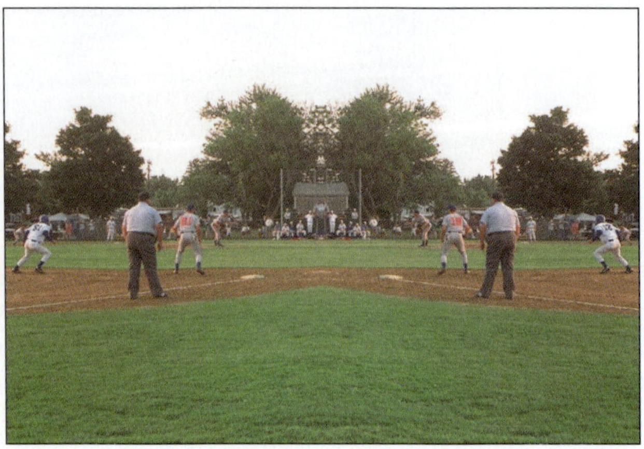

Rotating Mirror

The Skew deformation slants images. *(See page 119.)*

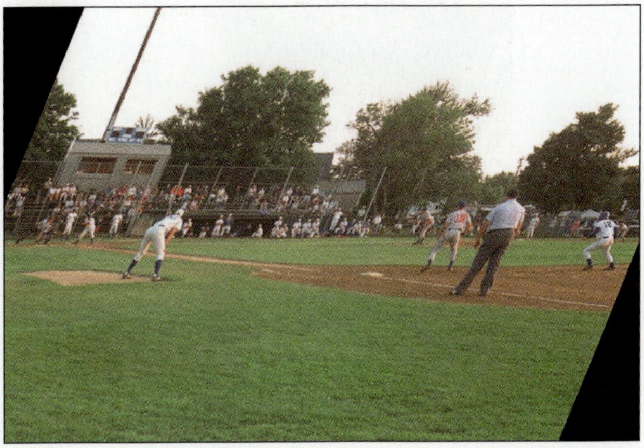

Skew

Spiky Halo applies a crown of waves arranged radially.

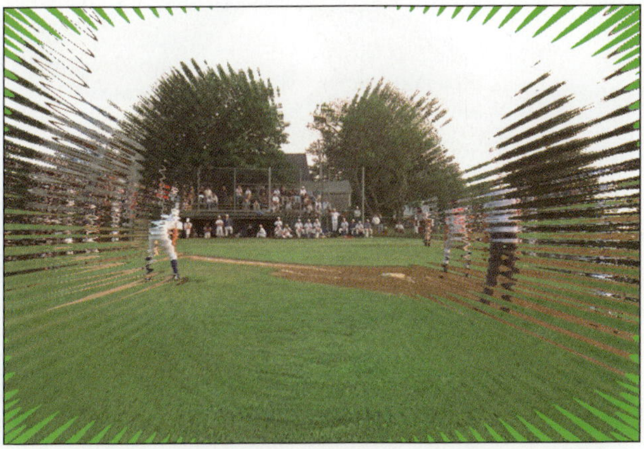

Spiky Halo

The Twirl deformation rotates an image around its center.

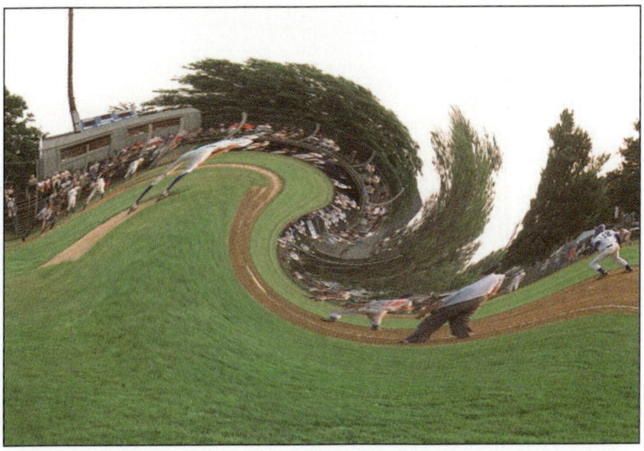

Twirl

The Warp deformation magnifies an image's center in relation to the remainder.

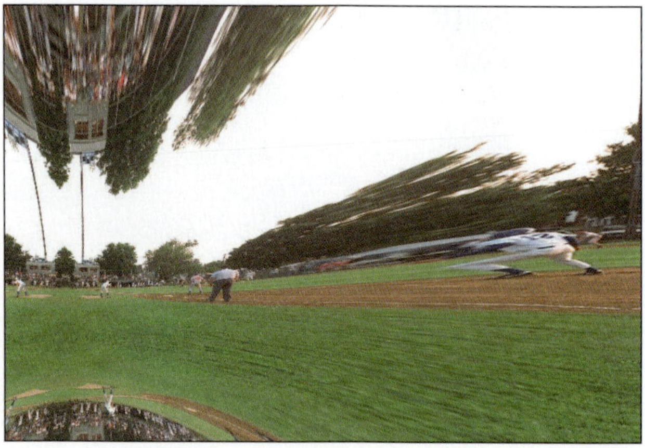

Warp

The Wave deformation imposes undulating vertical and horizontal lines – customizing this deformation can get pretty psychedelic.

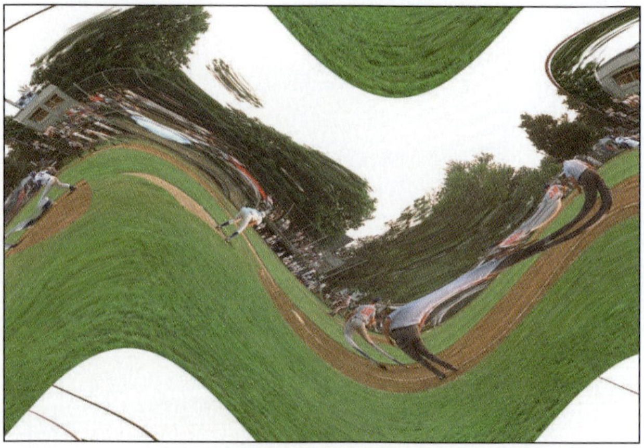

Wave

Wind applies the effect of wind coming from the left or right.

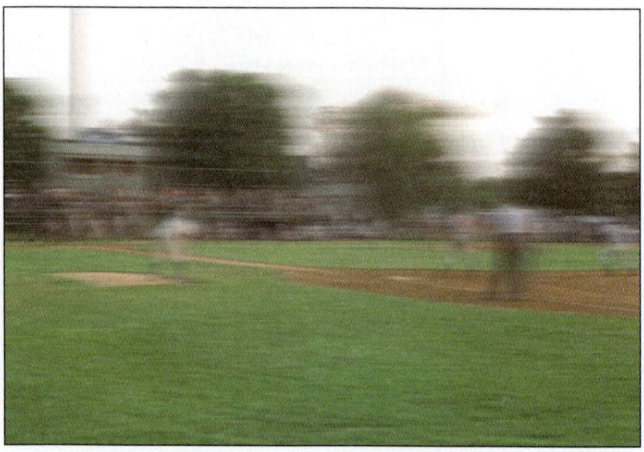

Wind

Using the Deform tool

Paint Shop Pro 8 has various deformation techniques that you can use to correct digital photographs (or just to produce interesting and fun effects).

If you define a selection, Paint Shop Pro will prompt you to promote it to a full layer. Hit OK in the dialog.

Deforming manually

1 Select the layer you want to deform (if you're working on the Background layer, promote it first – Layers, Promote Background Layer) or define a selection area, if appropriate

2 Click here in the Tool palette then click Deform. Or just press D

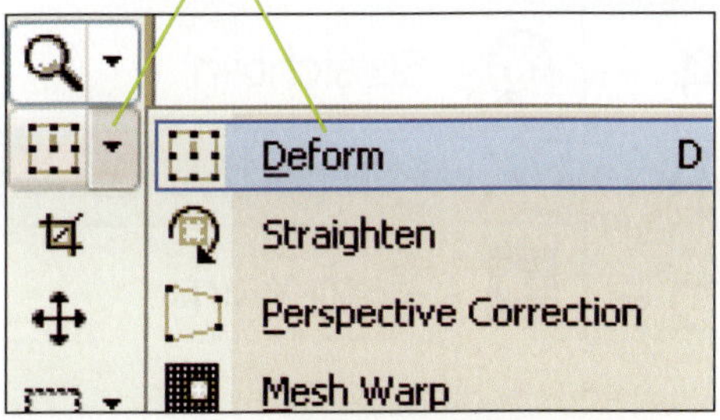

3 Optionally, turn on the Grid to aid realignment (Ctrl+Alt+G)

Hold down Shift as you drag a central handle to skew the image.

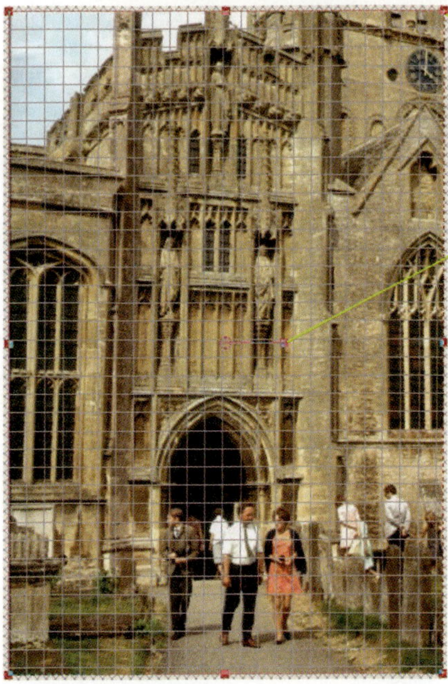

4 Hold down Ctrl and drag a corner handle to edit the perspective

5 Or place the mouse pointer over this – when the pointer changes to two circular arrows, drag to rotate

Hold down Ctrl and Shift to distort the image. This is more for fun than image correction.

Increase the Canvas size (Image, Canvas Size) if, as a result of using the Deform tool, any parts of the image are no longer visible.

Using the Perspective Correction tool

You can also adjust image perspective more directly.

If you define a selection, Paint Shop Pro will prompt you to promote it to a full layer. Hit OK in the dialog.

1 Select the layer you want to deform or define a selection area, if appropriate

2 Click here in the Tool palette then click Perspective Correction

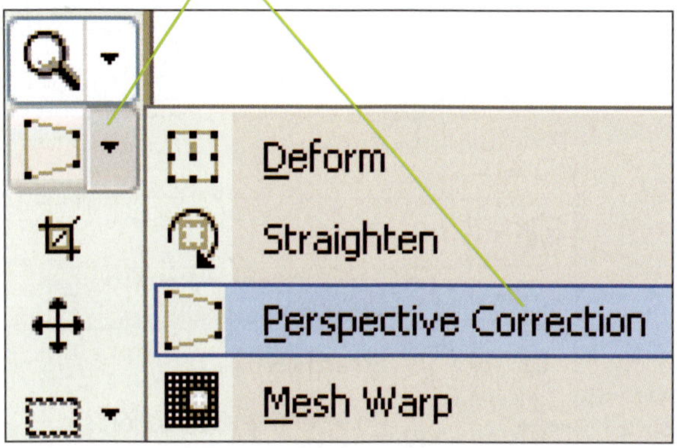

3 If the Tool Options palette isn't onscreen, hit F4

4 Check Crop image to revert the image to its original size after the perspective has been changed

5 Optionally, enter a value here to display grid lines

You can save Perspective Correction presets for reuse later – click here to access the Presets dialog:

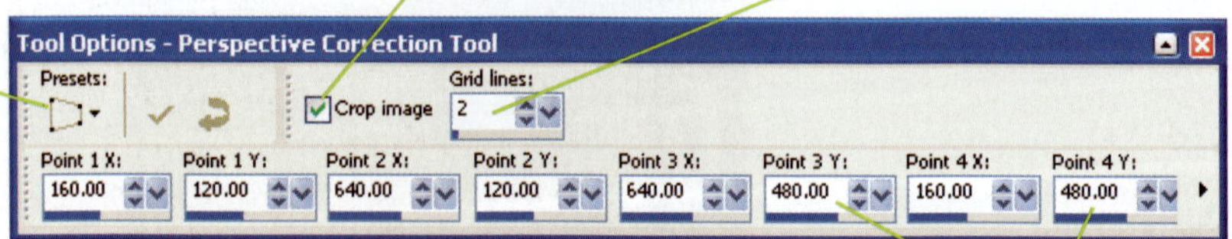

7 Optionally, fine-tune the bounding box position by entering precise values in the various X and Y fields

6 A bounding box appears – drag the corners till the box defines an area which ought to be 100% straight

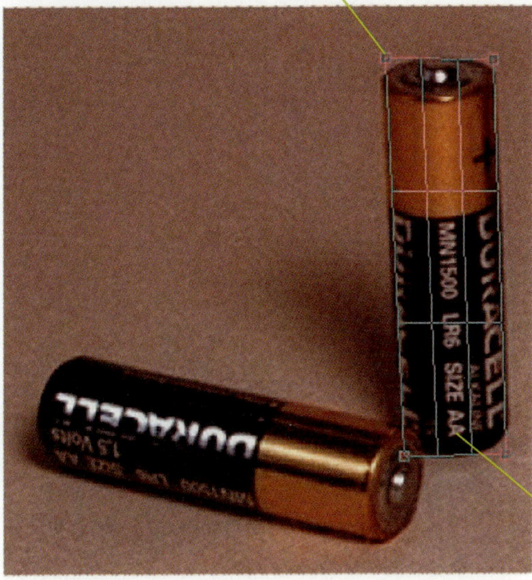

8 Double-click inside the box

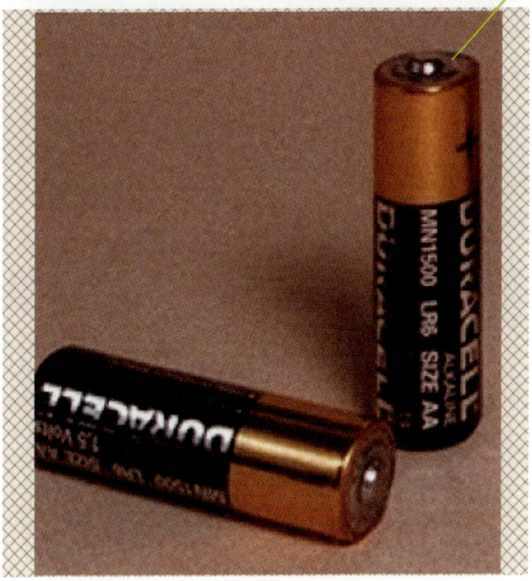

HOT TIP

Sometimes, only subtle changes are required with this tool.

9 If the effect isn't quite what you want, hit Ctrl+Z. Vary the box position slightly then repeat Step 7

Using the Straighten tool

You can straighten images by rotating them on-the-fly around a user-defined line.

If you define a selection, Paint Shop Pro will prompt you to promote it to a full layer. Hit OK in the dialog.

1 Select the raster layer you want to deform or define a selection area, if appropriate

2 Click here in the Tool palette then click Straighten

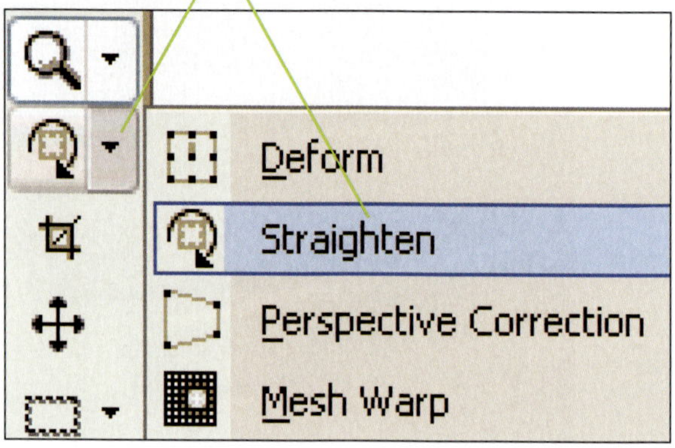

3 If the Tool Options palette isn't onscreen, hit F4

You can save Straighten presets for reuse later – click here to access the Presets dialog:

5 Select a straightening type – Auto suits most purposes

4 Check Crop image to revert the image to its original size after it's been straightened

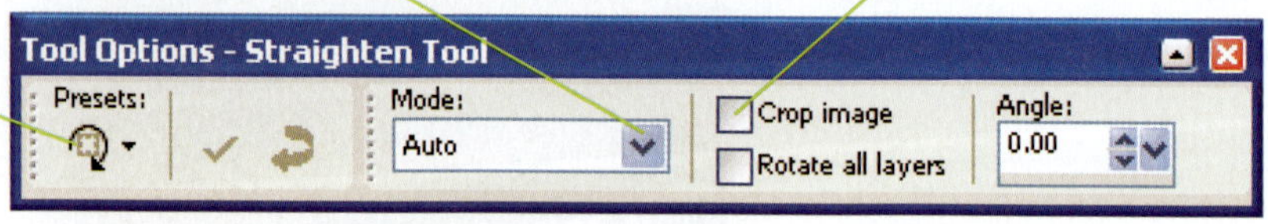

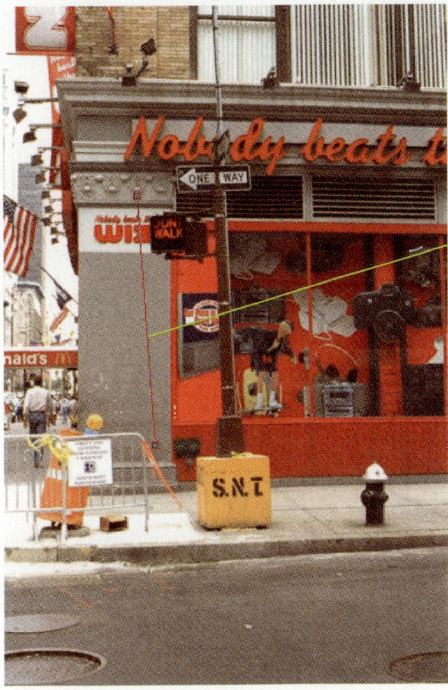

6 A straightening bar appears – drag the ends till the bar aligns with the image part you want to straighten

DON'T FORGET

This tool works best with images with strong vertical/horizontal components.

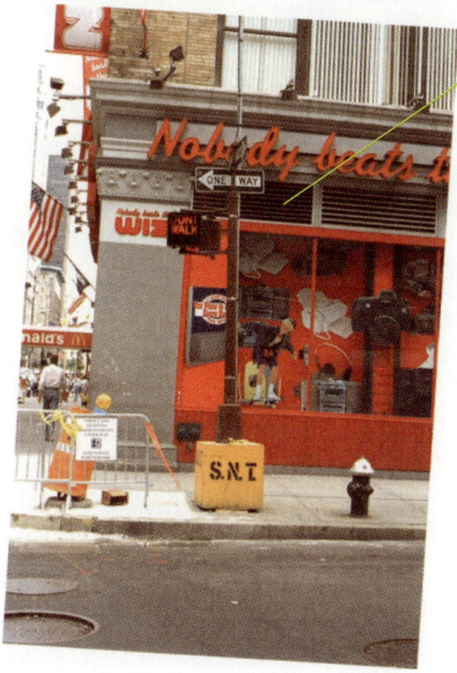

7 Double-click the image

8 If the effect isn't quite what you want, hit Ctrl+Z. Vary the bar position slightly then repeat Step 7

HOT TIP

Increase the Canvas size (Image, Canvas Size) if this operation results in any parts of the image no longer being visible.

Using the Mesh Warp tool

You can warp images on-the-fly.

If you define a selection, Paint Shop Pro will prompt you to promote it to a full layer. Hit OK in the dialog.

1 Select the layer you want to deform or define a selection area, if appropriate

2 Click here in the Tool palette then click Mesh Warp

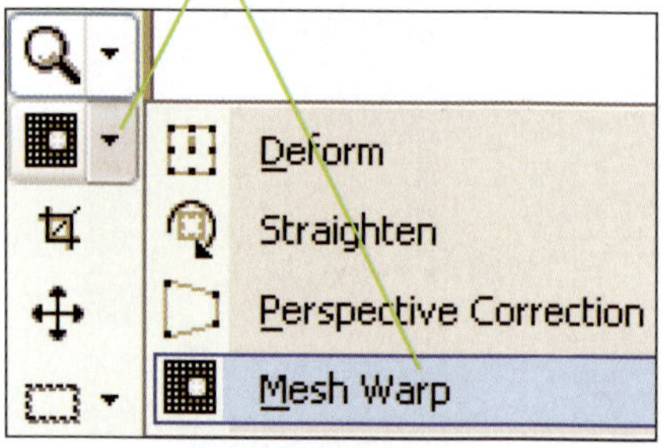

3 If the Tool Options palette isn't onscreen, hit F4

Use the Warp brush instead when you want to blend the area being warped with the rest of the image.

4 Check this for a high-quality warp

5 Customize the mesh grid

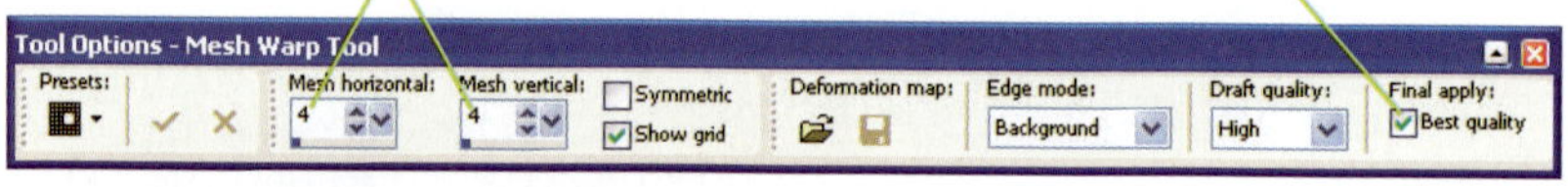

Hold down Ctrl (as here) to deform with a smooth curve or Shift to deform the entire row or column.

6 Drag a node to warp it

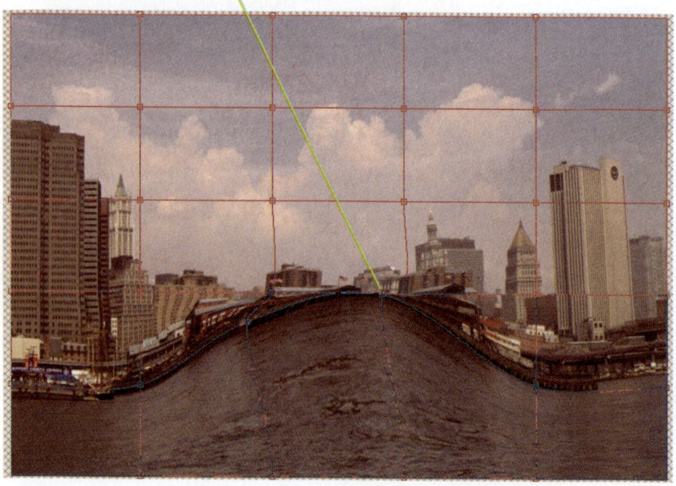

Using deformation maps

This is a really neat feature: you can save details of the nodes and lines you've created with the Mesh Warp tool as special "deformation maps" and then apply these to other images.

Saving deformation maps

1 After you've applied a mesh warp deformation, hit this button in the Tool Options palette:

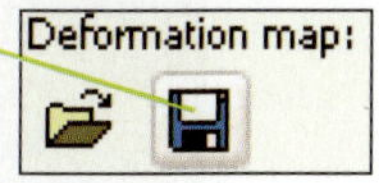

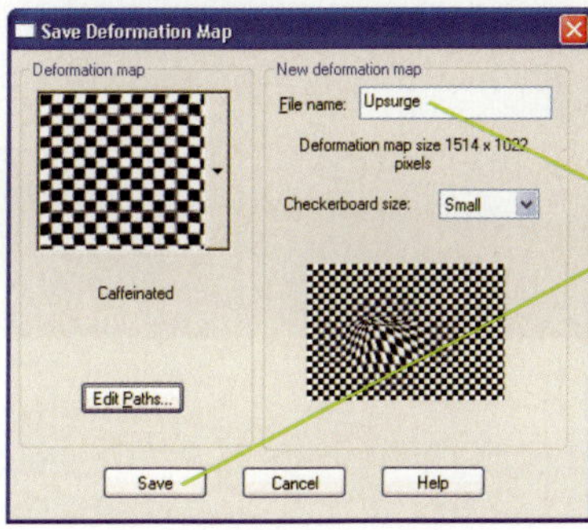

2 Name the map then hit Save

Loading deformation maps

1 Hit this button in the Tool Options palette:

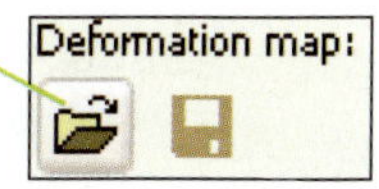

2 Select a map

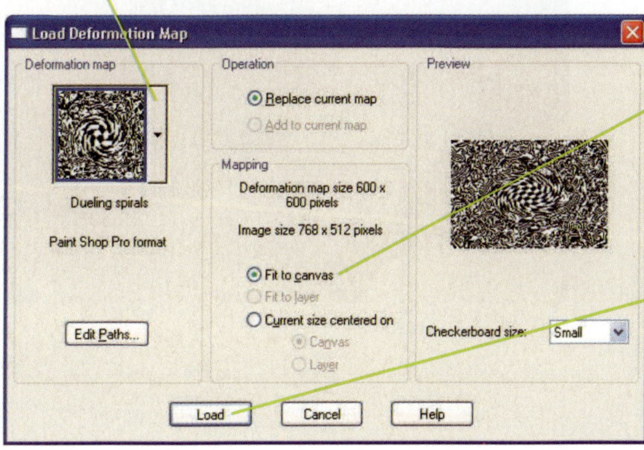

3 Select a placement

4 Click Load

5 An image before a deformation map has been applied:

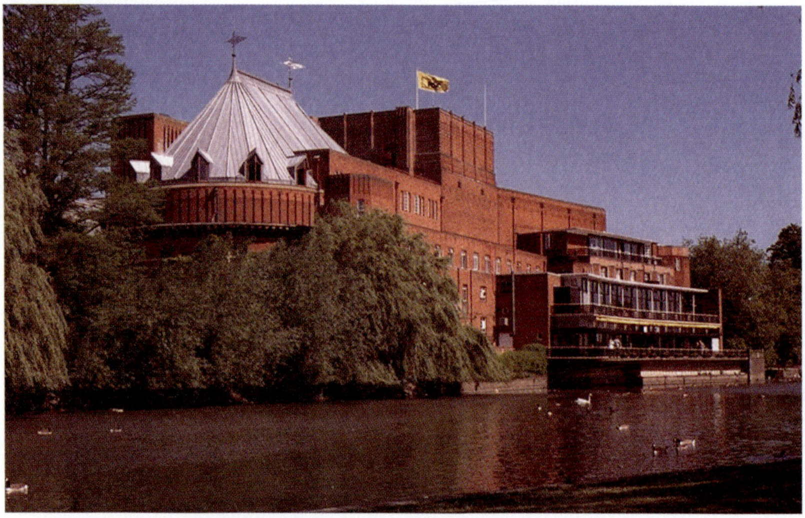

6 After applying the predefined "Dueling spirals" deformation map:

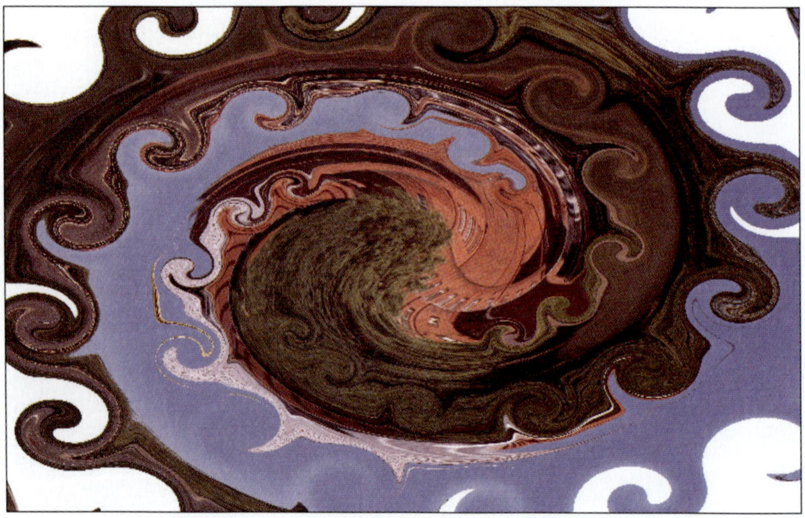

Using the Warp brush

You can also deform images with the use of a special Paint Shop Pro brush.

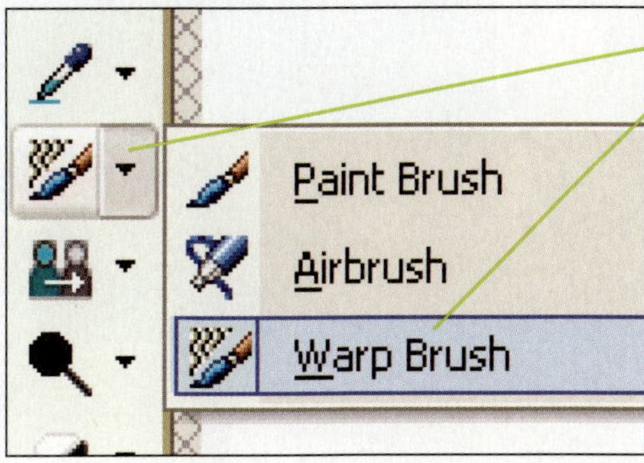

1 Click here in the Tool palette then click Warp Brush

2 If the Tool Options palette isn't onscreen, right-click the Tool Palette and select Palettes, Tool Options (or just hit F4)

Remember you can save Warp Brush presets for reuse later – click here to access the Presets dialog:

4 Select a warp mode (check them out to see what they can do)

3 Customize these fields, especially Strength (range: 1–100)

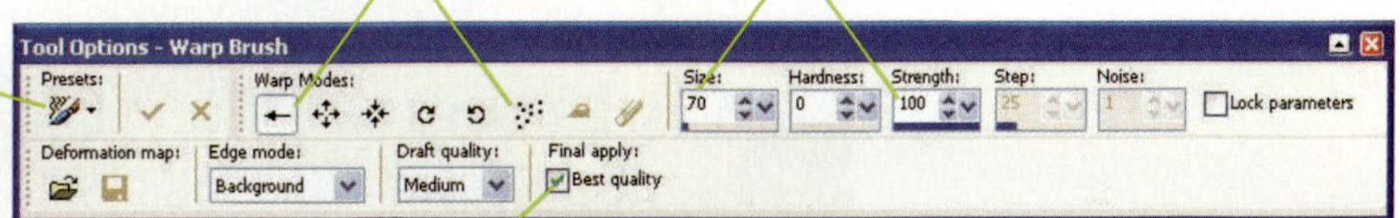

5 Check Best quality for optimal results

You can save Warp brush effects as deformation maps. See page 125 for how to do this.

6 Make sure your Brush Variance settings are optimized (see page 61 for how to do this)

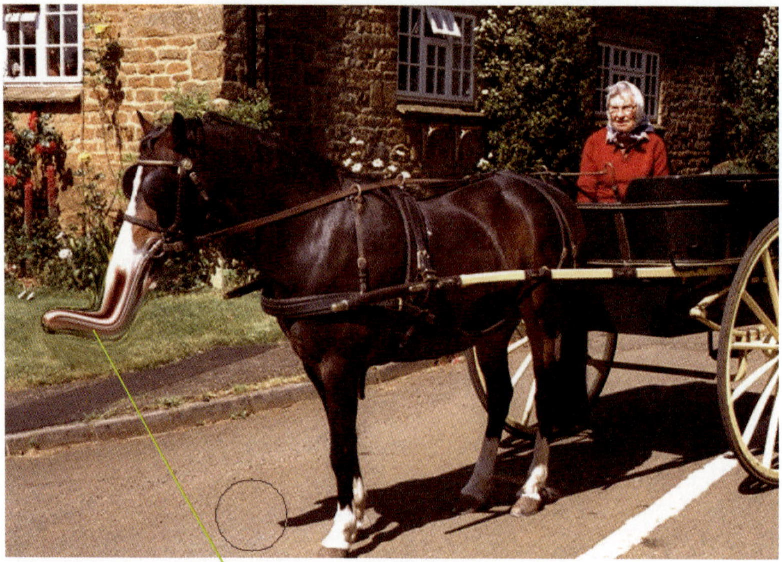

Push performs a smearing action in the direction of the brush stroke. Expand pushes pixels out from the center. Other warp modes are:

- *Right Twirl and Left Twirl – rotate pixels around the brush's center*
- *Noise – move pixels randomly under the brush*
- *Iron Out and Unwarp – use these to undo warps*

7 Drag over the image to deform it (this is Push: )

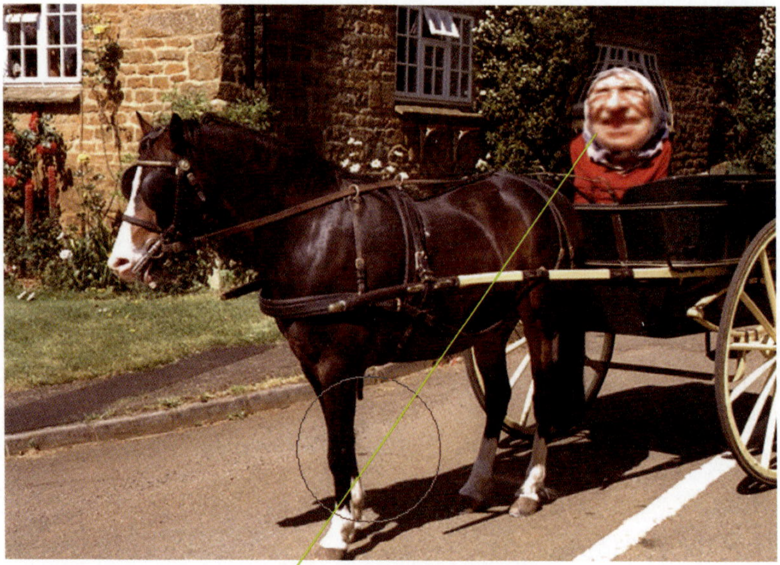

8 Drag over the image to deform it (this is Expand: )

Using effects and plug-ins

In this chapter, you'll enhance images or image selections by applying any of Paint Shop Pro's numerous special effects and third-party plug-ins. You'll also apply 3D effects to image selections; magnify sections with the Magnifying Lens effect; turn images into seamless patterns for use as Web backgrounds; and use specialized effects to enhance/correct photographs.

Covers

Chapter Six

Using effects

Paint Shop Pro also provides numerous special effects. These include artistic effects, texture effects, effects which apply or reflect light and additional effects that you can use to correct photographs.

Why not customize Paint Shop Pro so you can launch the Effect Browser with a keyboard shortcut? See page 14.

Applying an effect

1 Optionally, pre-select part of the relevant image or select a layer in the Layer palette (F8)

2 Pull down the Effects menu and click Effect Browser

3 Under Effects, select an appropriate category (Art Media Effects, Artistic Effects, Image Effects, Illumination Effects, Reflection Effects or Texture Effects)

Effects only work on colored images with more than 256 colors, 256-color grayscales and (with certain effects) grayscales converted to 16 million colors.

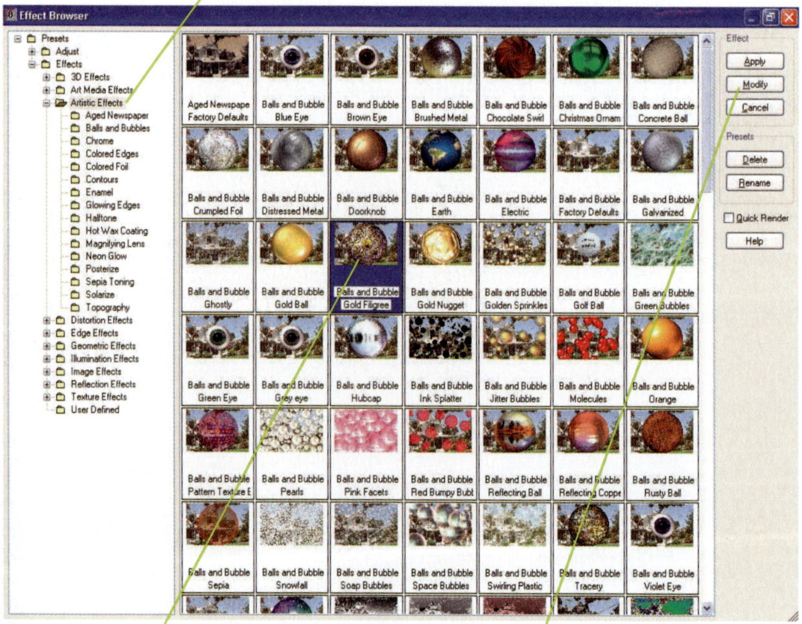

4 Double-click a preview to apply it

Stuck for somewhere to start? Try hitting the Randomize button when you modify an effect:

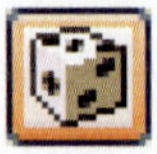

5 Alternatively, you can customize an effect before applying it. Just click the preview then hit Modify. Complete the dialog

Effect Gallery

Experiment with applying more than one effect to images or the same effect more than once.

Paint Shop Pro ships with numerous effects. Some of the most useful are detailed in this chapter.

With some effects (e.g. Solarize), selection areas are ineffective unless the image is 16 million colors.

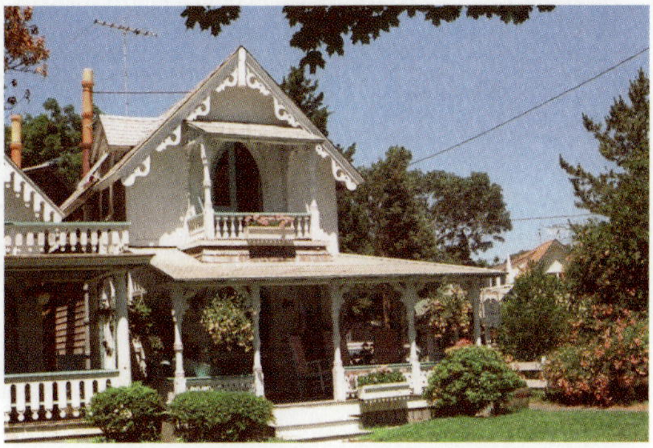

Compare this image (unchanged) with examples of effects below and later in this chapter

Example effects

Aged Newspaper mimics the effect of an ageing newspaper and resembles Sepia Toning's 19th century mode. Apply Aged Newspaper to a grayscale image then convert it to 16 million colors.

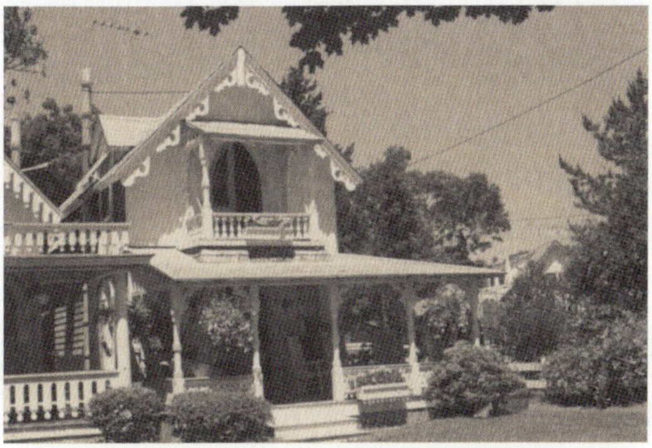

Aged Newspaper

Paint Shop Pro comes with 43 varieties of the Balls and Bubbles effect. However, there are loads of settings you can configure so you can easily make thousands of your own and save them as presets.

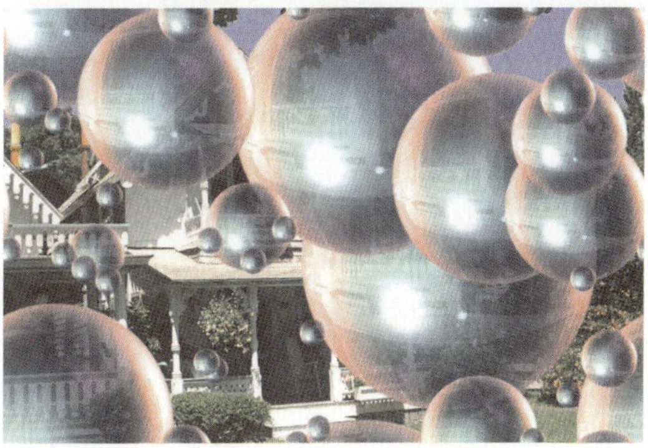

Balls and Bubbles (Space Bubbles)

You can specify whether the blinds are horizontal or vertical.

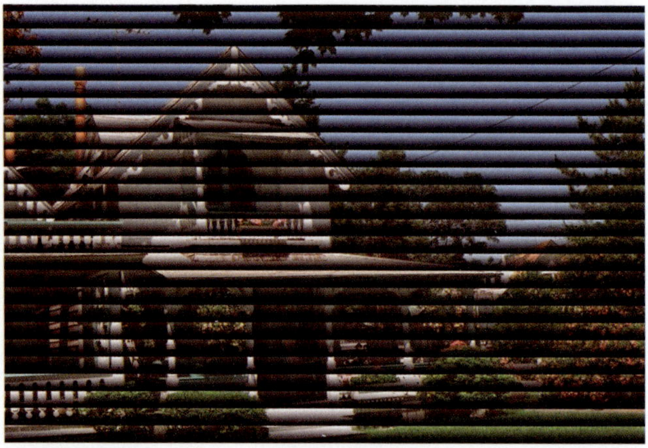

Blinds

Brush Strokes makes images look like watercolors. There are 38 presets – this is "Impressionist".

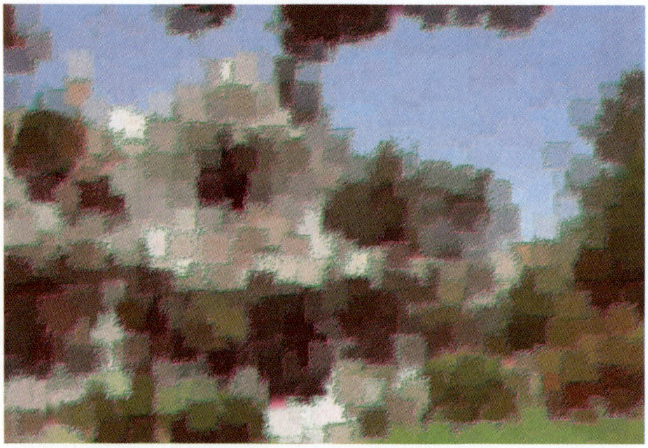

Brush Strokes

Charcoal converts to black and white and then mimics the effect of being drawn with charcoal. If the Opacity setting is set to less than 100, some colors show thru.

(The Black Pencil effect is similar but gives more detail.)

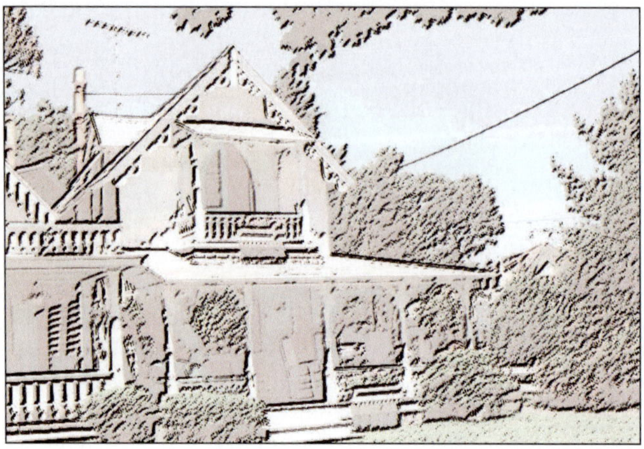

Charcoal

Chrome mimics applying a metallic patina to images. This example has the Use original color option checked. Uncheck it for a more metallic effect.

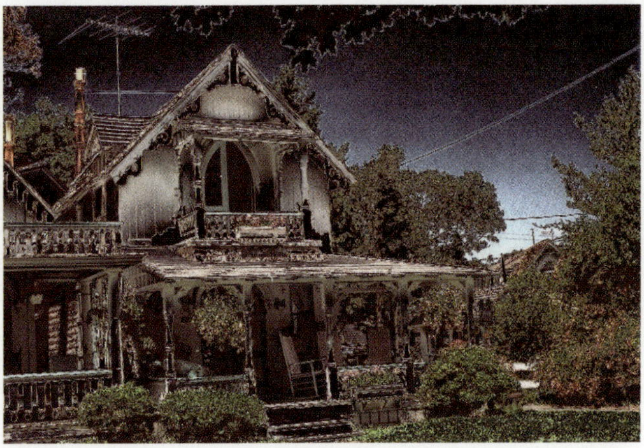

Chrome

Colored Foil combines a sculpted look with multiple colors.

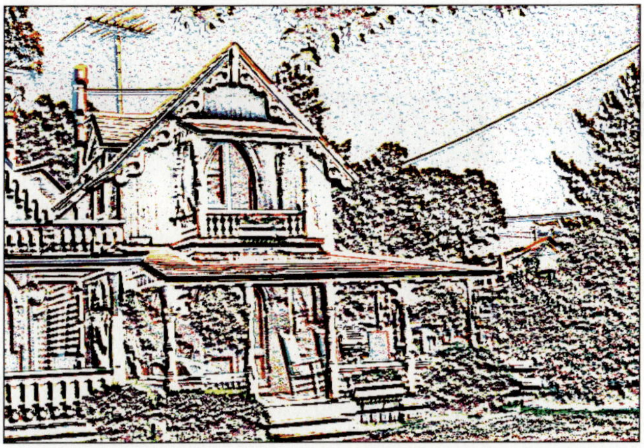

Colored Foil

Contours changes images into topographical maps (see also "Topography"). This is the Custom 1 preset.

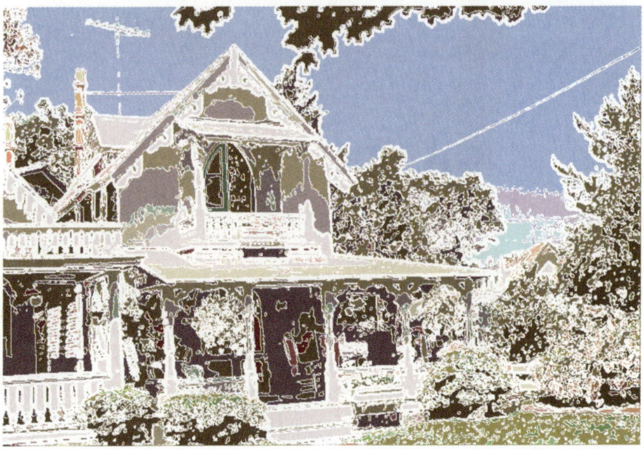

Contours

Emboss transforms the image into a bas-relief (shapes project from the background without becoming detached). Colors are also inserted when appropriate.

You can't customize the Emboss effect.

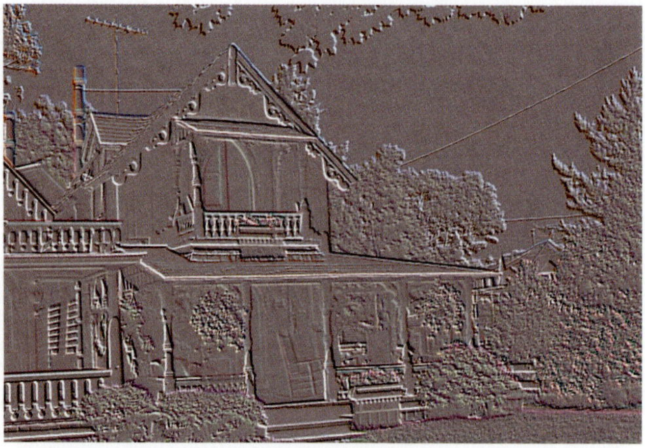

Emboss

Feedback makes an image appear to be reflected inwards in concentric mirrors.

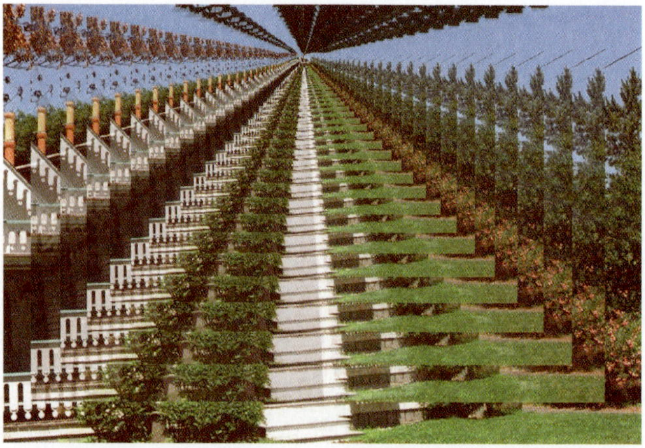

Feedback

Fine Leather incorporates embossing.

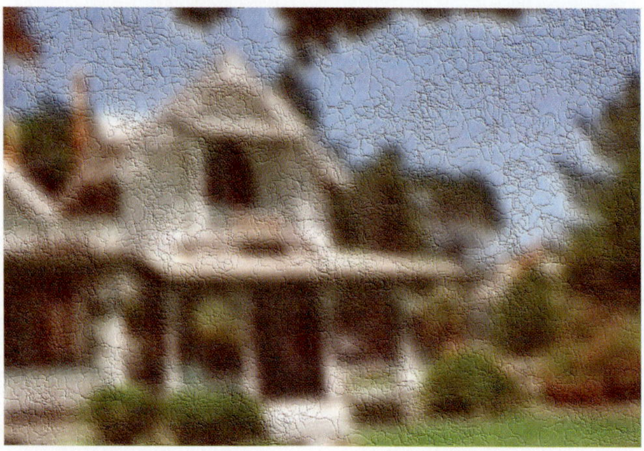

Fine Leather

Fur makes an image appear "bristly".

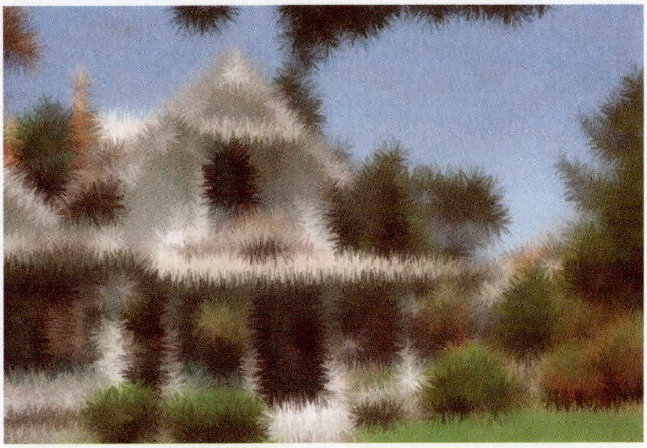

Fur

The 24 Halftone effects turn photographs into dot representations. Using Randomize with this version can get a little psychedelic.

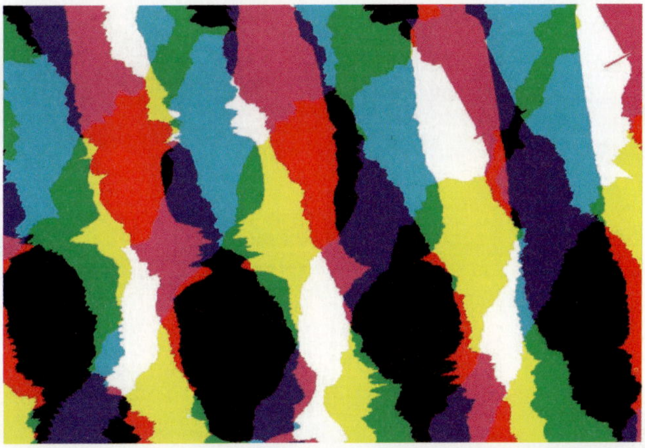

Halftone

Kaleidoscope isolates a pie-shaped section and converts this into a circular pattern.

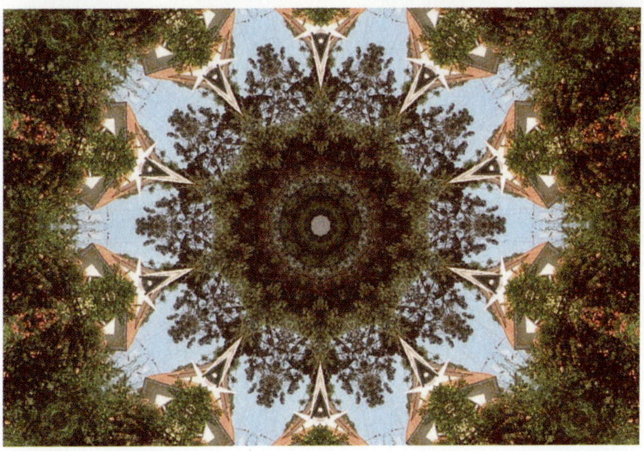

Kaleido-scope

Lights spotlights images – you can specify the number of spotlights. Here, a preset ("Sunset") has been applied.

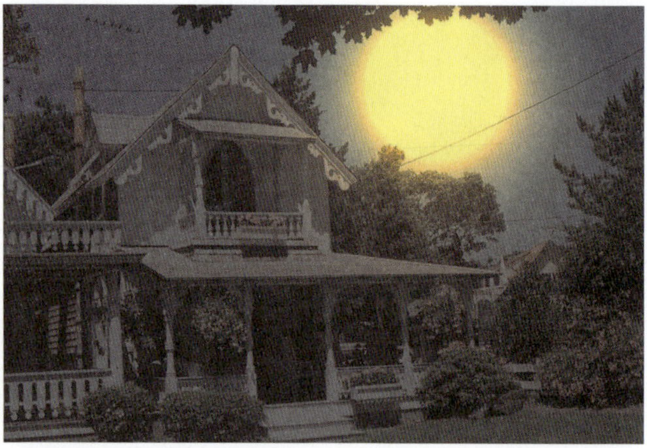

Light

Neon Glow makes images 3D and emphasizes edge contrast. Experiment with Randomize for wacky effects.

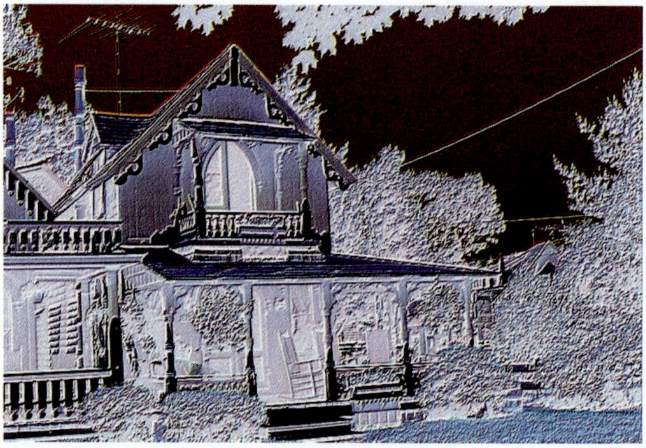

Neon Glow

This is the default Page Curl setting – try varying the curl and edge colors. You can also specify which corner curls.

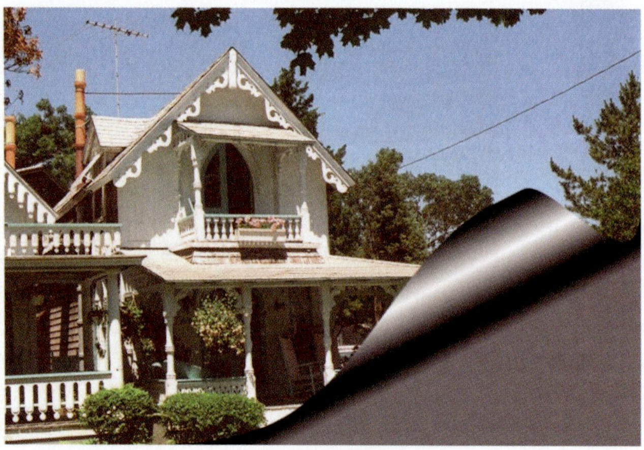

Page Curl

Pencil – as well as making an image look like a pencil drawing – also colors the edges. Varying the Color setting can have dramatic results, as can using Randomize.

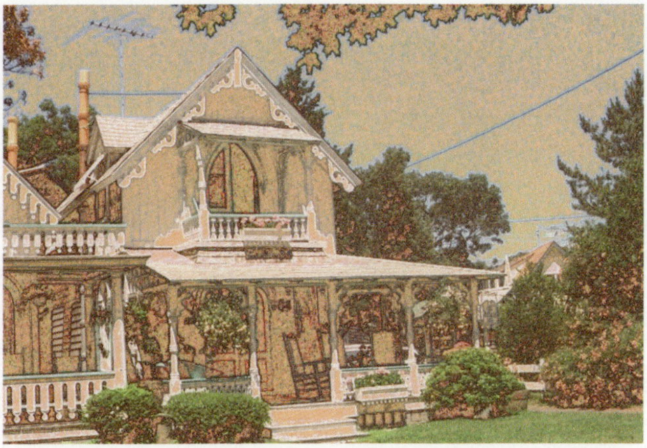

Pencil

Polished Stone makes an image look as if it's been carved out of a shiny surface.

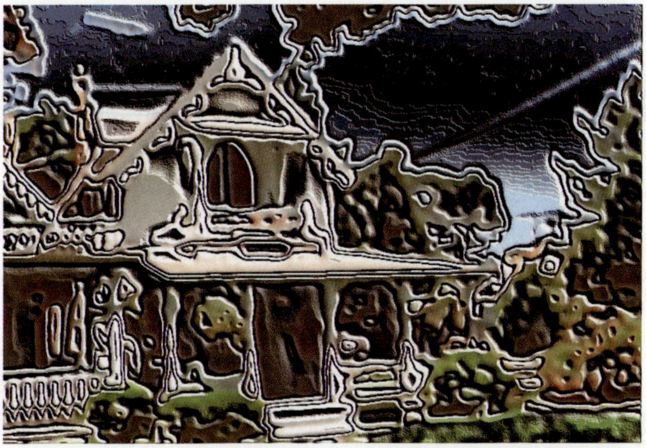

Polished Stone

Vary the Color and Luminance settings especially till you get the result you want.

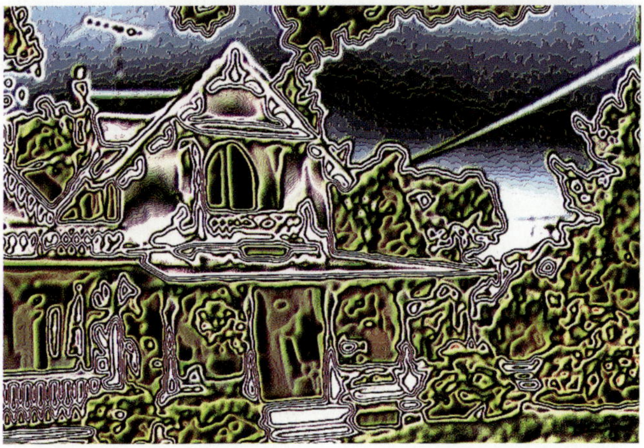

Sandstone

Sepia Toning makes an image look as if it was produced in the 19th century – to achieve this, grayscale it (Image, Greyscale) then convert it to 16 million colors (Ctrl+Shift+0) before applying the effect.

Alternatively, to give the image a more modern, 1940s feel, apply Sepia Toning to a 16-million-color image.

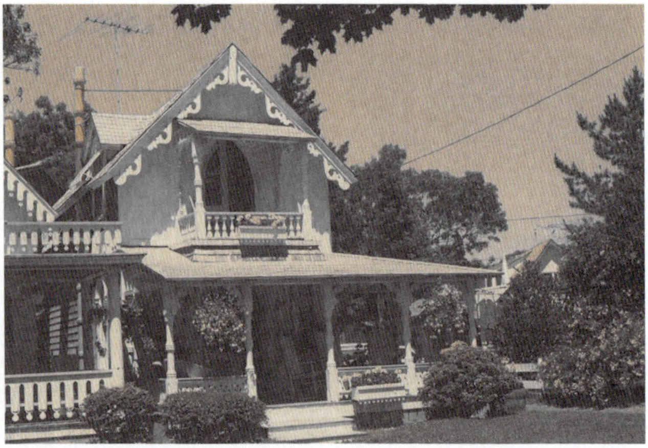

Sepia Toning

This is the "Psychadelic art" (sic) preset.

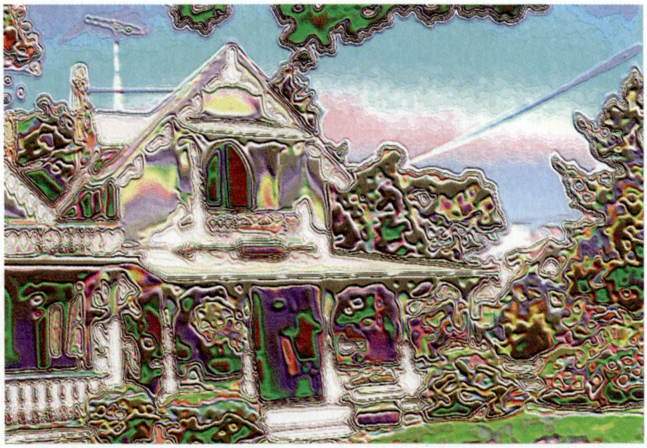

Soft Plastic

Straw-wall simulates applying straws to an image. For some reason, using Randomize really gives this effect way-out results.

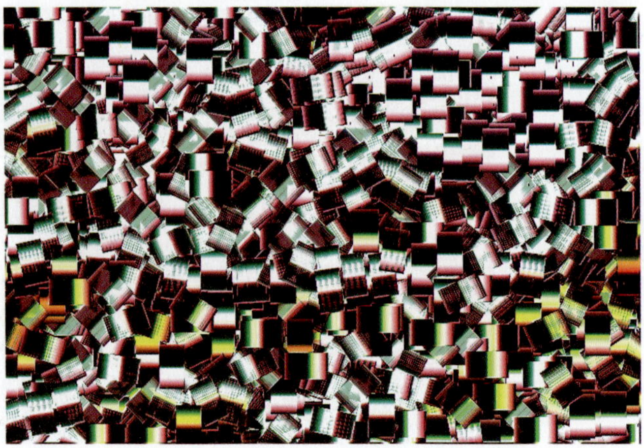

Straw-wall

Sunburst simulates viewing an image and its source of illumination through a lens. This is the "Center" preset.

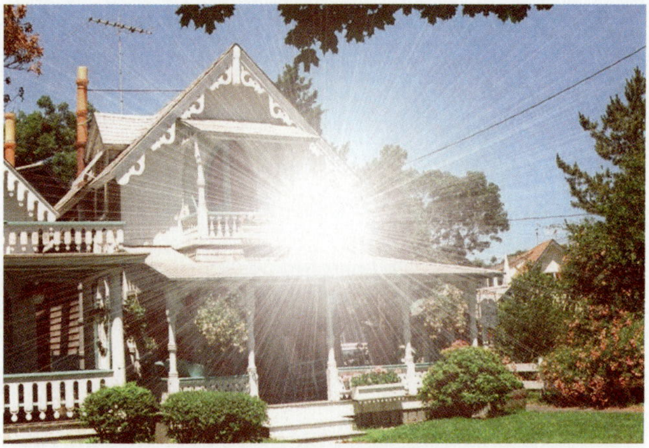

Sunburst

This is the "Stained Glass" preset.

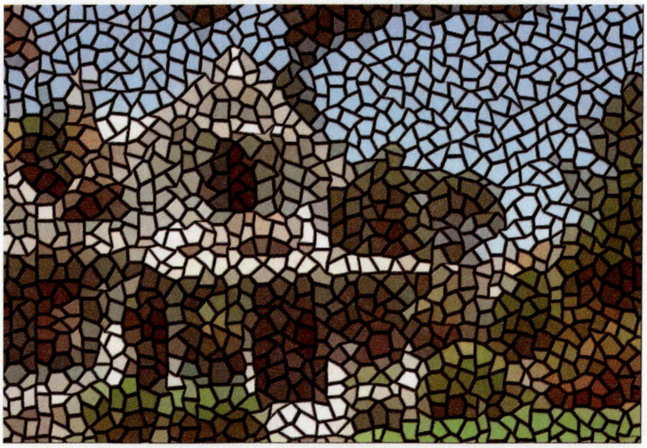

Tiles

Topography gives a 3D feel to an image. Again, Randomize can add a welcome flavor of exoticism.

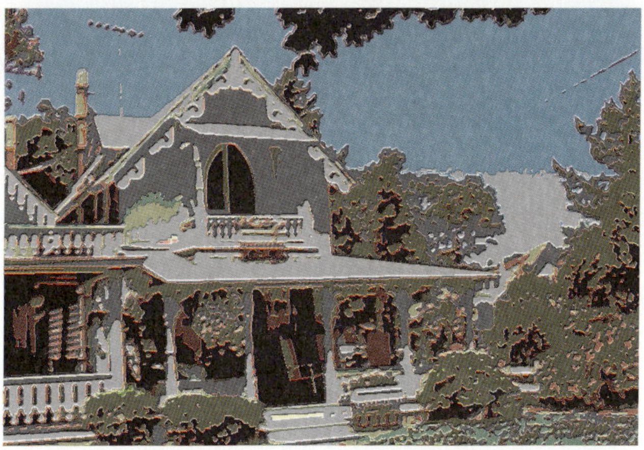

Topo-graphy

Applying the Magnifying Lens effect

With Paint Shop Pro 8, you can now apply a lens to an image and magnify the area inside it. There are 47 lenses to choose from and, of course, you can easily create your own and save them as presets.

Paint Shop Pro's magnifying lenses are a really cool feature – so cool, in fact, that we've used a customized one in this book (e.g. page 145).

1 In the Effect Browser select Effects/Artistic Effects/Magnifying Lens

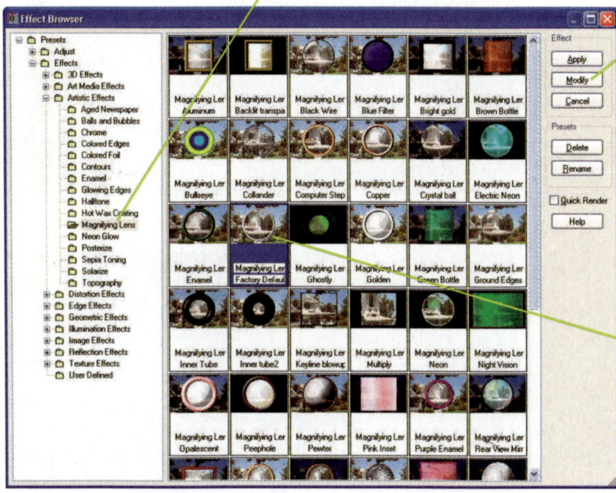

2 Select a preset or the Factory Default

3 Hit Modify

Hit the Diskette icon next to the Presets field to save your lenses for later use.

4 Use your mouse to resize and reposition the bounding box

Drag in the right-hand Preview box to view the relevant image area. Click the Zoom In or Zoom Out icons to adjust the magnification.

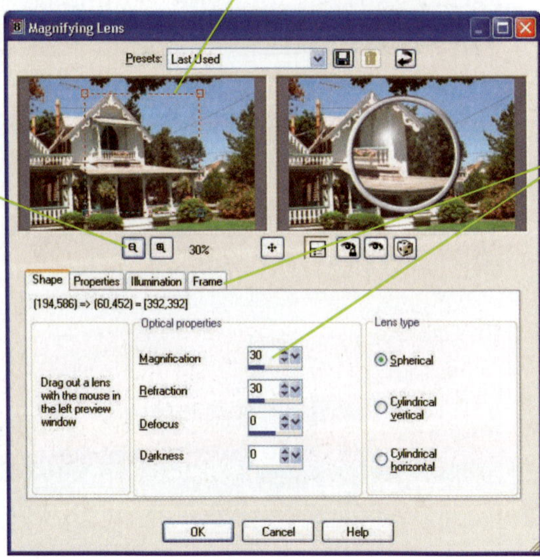

5 Work your way thru the tabs, adjusting the various settings, then hit OK

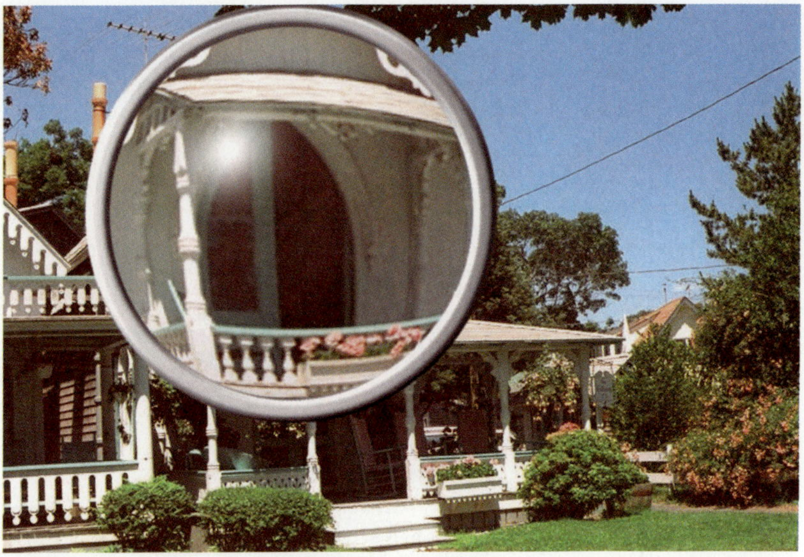

There are also some 50 "user-defined" effects (under Effects/User Defined) – these are actually supplied with Paint Shop Pro. Have fun trying them out.

6 Paint Shop Pro applies the lens – this is the "Factory Default" preset. Hitting the Randomize button, however, can produce slightly different results:

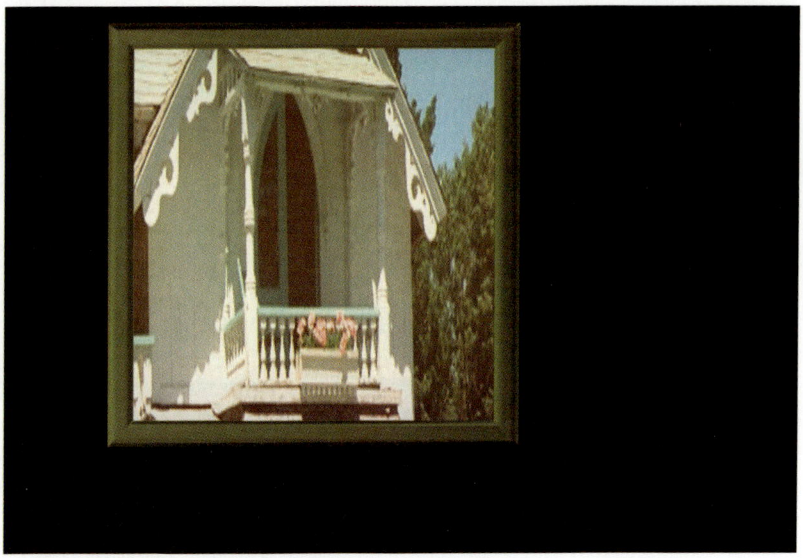

Tiling effects

You can tile images seamlessly.

1. In the Effect Browser, select Effects, Image Effects, Seamless Tiling. Click an effect then hit Modify

2. Drag the "bullseye" to set the offset (point of origin) of the tiling

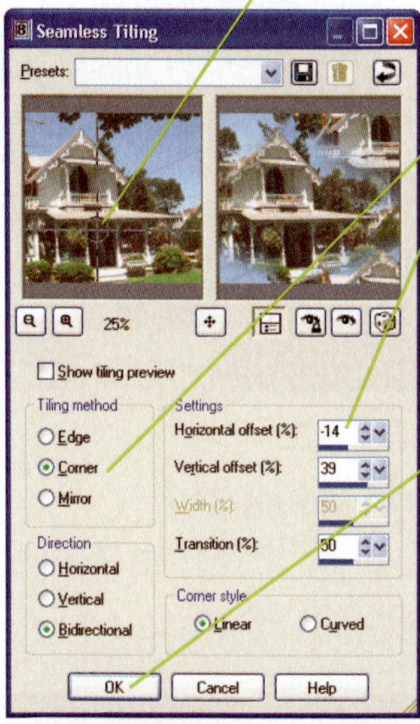

3. Choose a tiling direction, method and corner style

4. Hit OK

5. This is the Seamless Tiling – "Factory Default" preset

Seamless tiles are especially effective as backgrounds in Web pages. Alternatively, apply them with the Flood Fill tool.

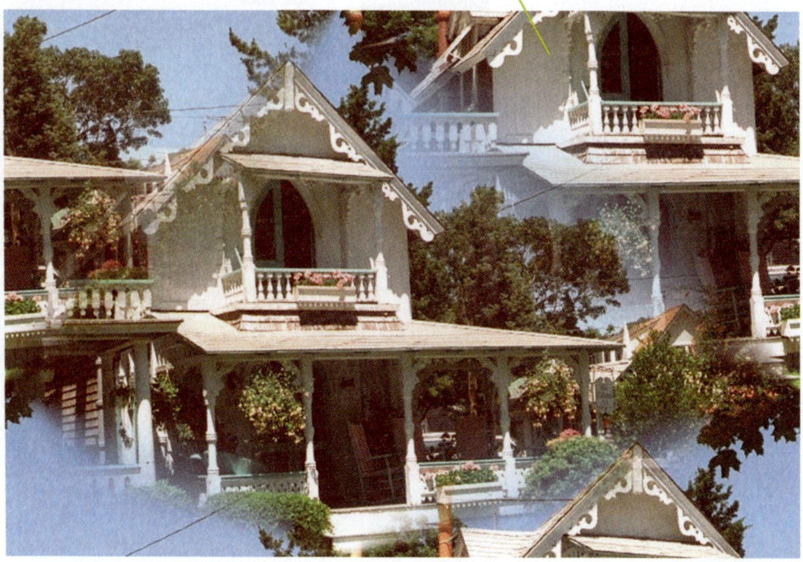

3D effects

Paint Shop Pro also ships with several neat 3D effects. These include Buttonize (very useful for websites), Chisel, Cutout and Drop Shadow.

Some 3D effects only function if you've pre-defined a selection area. With these, hit Ctrl+A if you want to work on the whole of an image.

Applying a 3D effect

1. If applicable, pre-select part of an image
2. In the Effect Browser, select Effects/3D Effects. Select a submenu e.g. Buttonize or Drop Shadow
3. Double-click an effect to apply it. Or select an effect, click Modify then complete the dialog

A Web button

If you want to drop-shadow the whole of an image, you'll have to increase the canvas first.

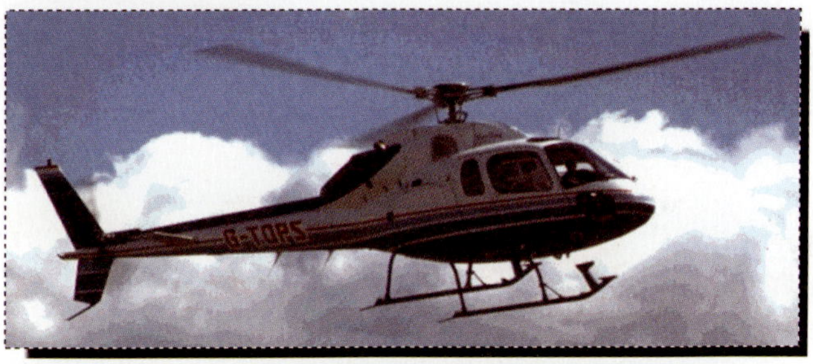

An image with drop shadow

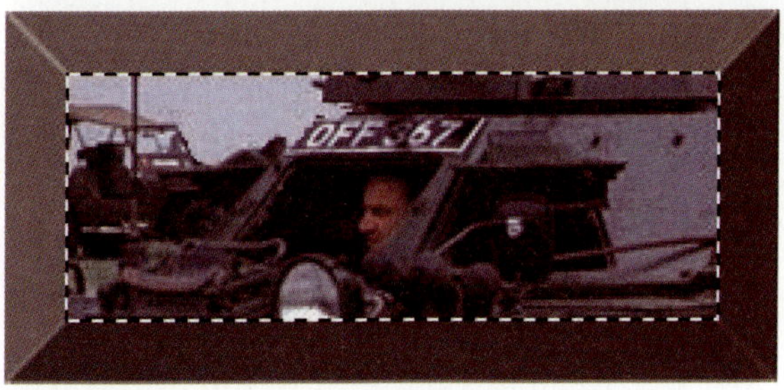

Chisel makes an image appear to have been cut out of stone

Photographic effects

You can use a variety of specialist effects to enhance photos – many of them are automatic. For example, you can:

- remove red-eye (flash light reflected from the subject's retina onto the film)
- remove moiré – see also page 106
- automatically erase scratches
- compensate for fade

If the overall condition of your photograph is poor, using the One Step Photo Fix option is a great choice: it adjusts a whole raft of attributes, including color balance, contrast, clarity and saturation. It also smooths edges and sharpens the picture. The best part is, it requires no user intervention.

(It isn't a cure-all, however: you may still have to remove scratches – see Step 3 and the facing page.)

Applying a photographic effect

1 Click Enhance Photo in the Photo toolbar

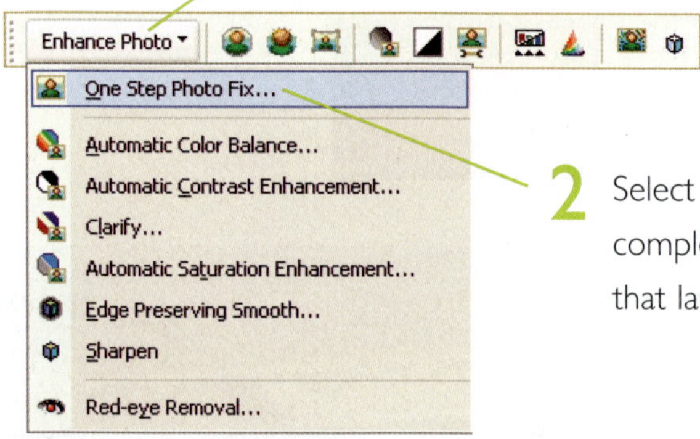

2 Select an option (also complete any dialog that launches)

3 Alternatively, some photographic effects are located on the Adjust menu. Click the appropriate submenu selection

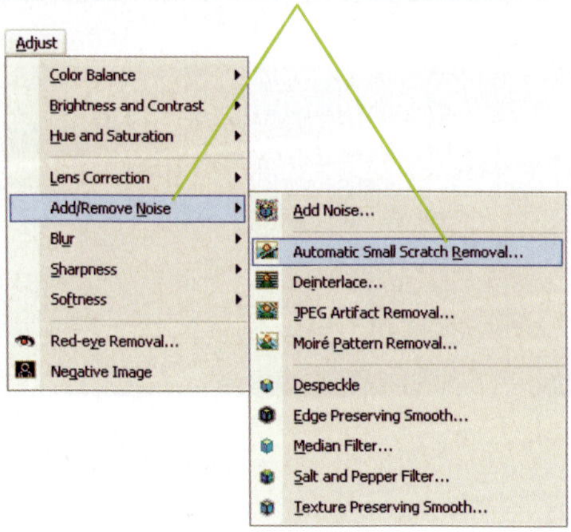

4 Complete any dialog that appears

To correct fade (the process whereby light distorts image colors) choose Color Balance, Fade Correction in Step 3.

Scratch removal in action

Use Automatic Scratch Removal on images with reasonably smooth backgrounds.

Want to turn photographs into negatives (this is fun but it's also useful – for example, you can scan in a photographic negative and turn it into a photograph)? Choose Effects, Artistic Effects, Solarize. Complete the dialog.

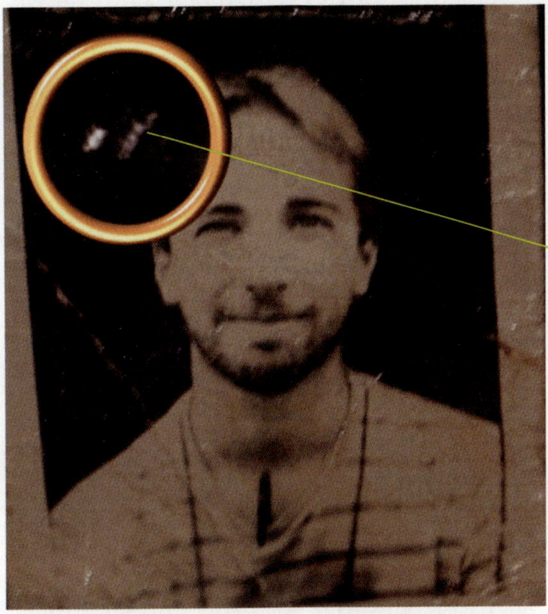

Scratches – this is an old photograph, so its quality isn't outstanding

Apply photographic effects several times, watching carefully to make sure the remainder of the image doesn't suffer and fine-tuning the settings as required.

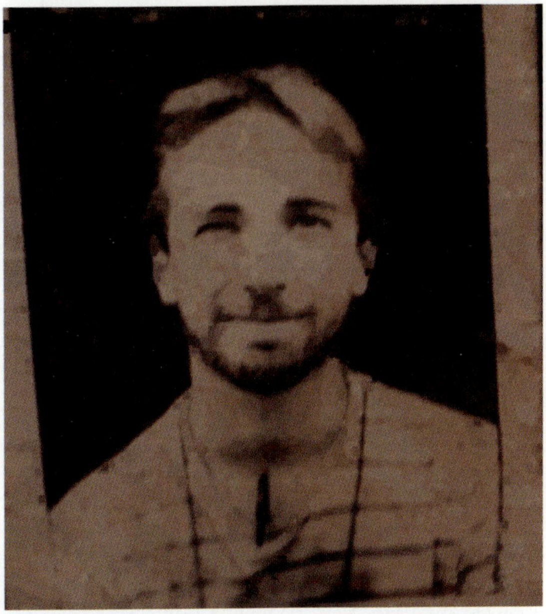

After several passes, the scratches are diminished

Using plug-ins

Paint Shop Pro 8 ships with a some third-party plug-ins which apply effects. Many of these are demonstration versions – this means that they're stamped with "DEMO" and so are basically unusable. However, there are two which are fully functional.

Plug-ins only work with colored images with more than 256 colors.

Applying a plug-in

1. If applicable, pre-select part of the relevant image

2. Pull down the Effects menu and click Plugins, Virtual Painter. Select Collage or Pastel

You can get lots of freeware plug-ins from ***www.cybia.com****. Since these are Photoshop-compatible, they should work with Paint Shop Pro 8. Just download them to* ***\Jasc Software Inc\Paint Shop Pro 8\PlugIns\Cybia****. Once they've been installed, Paint Shop Pro should recognize them automatically.*

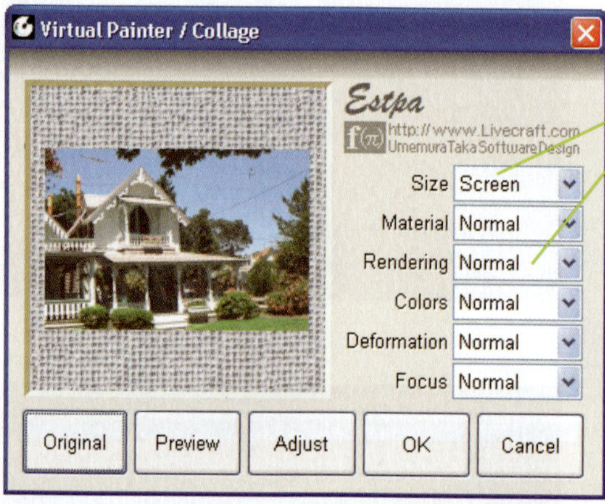

3. Customize the effect then hit OK

This is an example of the Collage plug-in. Most of the settings have three options: Subtle, Normal and Intense. Try adjusting these singly or together.

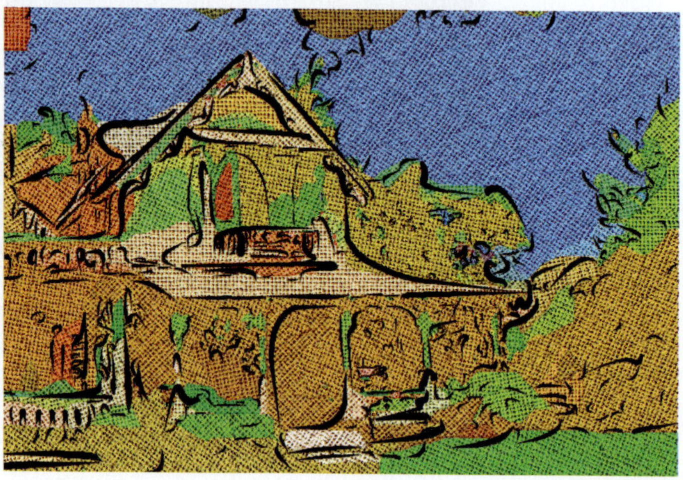

Paint Shop Pro and the Web

Chapter Seven

In this chapter, you'll learn how to customize and export images for use on the Web. Techniques you'll use include rollovers, slicing and mapping. You'll also send pictures by email directly from within Paint Shop Pro and upload them to Shutterfly, so other people can view them.

Covers

Image formats

Paint Shop Pro supports bitmaps (rasters), vectors and metas. Bitmaps consist of colored dots while vectors are defined by equations and give better results when rescaled. Metas are blanket formats which explicitly allow the inclusion of raster and vector data, as well as text annotations.

Paint Shop Pro recognizes a wide selection of bitmap, vector and meta graphic formats. These are some of the main ones:

Bitmap formats

PCX	Originated with PC Paintbrush. Used for years to transfer graphics data between Windows applications. Supports compression
TIFF	Tagged Image File Format. Suffix: .TIF. If anything, even more widely used than PCX, across a whole range of platforms and applications
BMP	Not as common as PCX and TIFF, but still popular. Tends to produce large files
TGA	Targa. A high-end format, and also a bridge with so-called low-end computers (e.g. Amiga and Atari). Often used in PC and Mac paint and ray-tracing programs because of its high-resolution color fidelity. Supports compression
PCD	(Kodak) PhotoCD. Used primarily to store photographs on CD. Paint Shop Pro will not export to PCD
GIF	Graphics Interchange Format. Just about any Windows program – and a lot more besides – will read GIF. Frequently used on the Internet. Disadvantage: it can't handle more than 256 colors. Compression is supported
JPEG	Joint Photographic Experts Group. Used for photograph storage, especially on the Internet. It supports a very high-level of compression, usually without appreciable distortion
PNG	Interlaced Portable Network Graphics. Now used increasingly on the Internet

The last three formats in the "Bitmap formats" table are most often used on the Internet:

- *GIF is suitable for line art and images of 256 colors or fewer*
- *JPEG is especially effective for photographs*
- *PNG is suitable for most images but not all browsers support it*

Vector formats

CGM	Computer Graphics Metafile. Frequently used in the past, especially as a medium for clip-art transmission. Less frequently used nowadays
EPS	The most widely used PostScript format. Combines vector and raster data with a low-resolution informational bitmap header. The preferred vector format

An example of a meta format is Windows Metafile (suffix: .WMF). This can be used for data exchange between just about all Windows programs.

Exporting files for the Internet

You can use steps 1–4 on page 21 to produce files suitable for Internet use. However, Paint Shop Pro makes it even easier to produce transparent GIF, JPEG and PNG files by providing specialized export dialogs.

This is the route for Internet gurus – if you want a simpler path to Web file creation, click the Use Wizard button in the dialog. Work thru the screens, answering the various questions, until your file is ready to be exported.

Exporting GIF/JPEG/PNG files

1 Pull down the File menu and click Export

2 In the sub-menu, click JPEG Optimizer, GIF Optimizer or PNG Optimizer

3 Complete the dialog that launches (the dialog varies according to which option is chosen in step 2)

Some PCs are limited to 256-color display. Images with more colors are "dithered" and are often distorted. As a result, it's a good idea to reduce images you create for the Web to 256 colors (Ctrl+Shift+3).

4 Optionally, select a preset

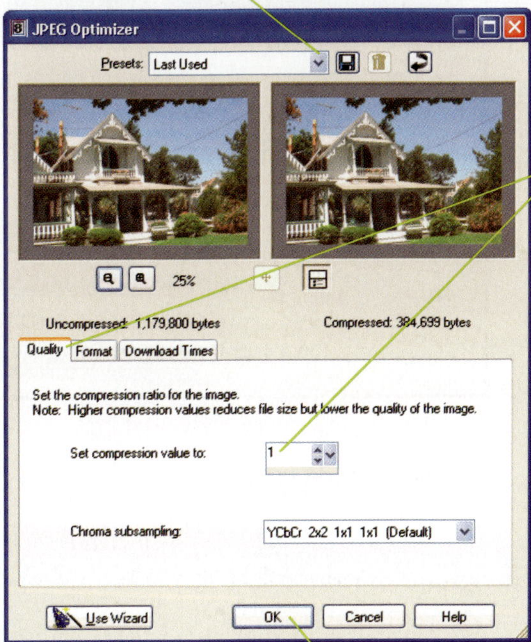

5 Activate each tab in turn, then complete the relevant options

6 Click OK

Before you export a layered picture for Web use, flatten it by pulling down the Layers menu and selecting Merge, Merge All (Flatten).

Image slicing

You can use a technique known as image slicing to save an image into smaller parts, in various formats and levels of optimization. This speeds up viewing of your site, not only because these optimized images take less time to download but also because those image parts used repeatedly (e.g. logos) are only saved once. Since many visitors will lose patience if a site takes too long to download, this is a vital consideration in website design.

To email the open image, choose File, Send. Paint Shop Pro opens your email client with the picture set up as an attachment.

Slicing consists of dividing an image into "cells" and editing them.

Creating cells

1 Choose File, Export, Image Slicer

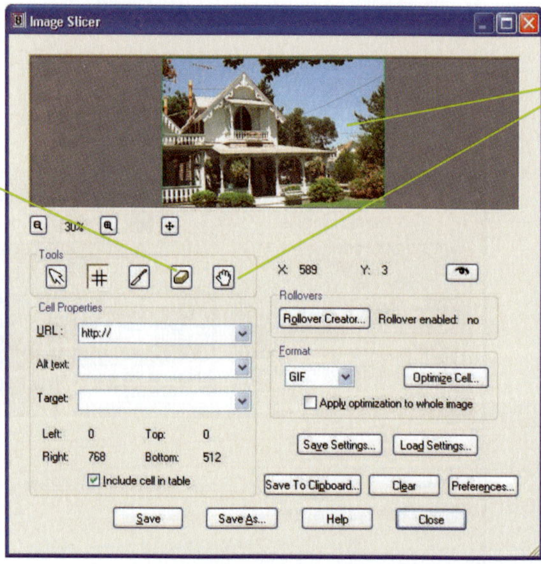

2 Click a tool (see Steps 3–4) then the preview

To delete a cell, click the Eraser button then click the cell border.

3 If you selected 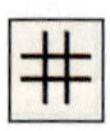 in Step 2, specify the number of rows and columns in the Grid Size dialog then hit OK

4 If you selected 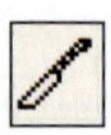 in Step 2, click and drag vertically over the image preview to create a vertical line then horizontally to create a horizontal line

You can create cells within cells, if you want. Just select a tool, click within one cell then define some more.

Editing/formatting cells

1 Click here then click a cell to select it

5 Click Save Settings to save cell details for reuse in this or other images

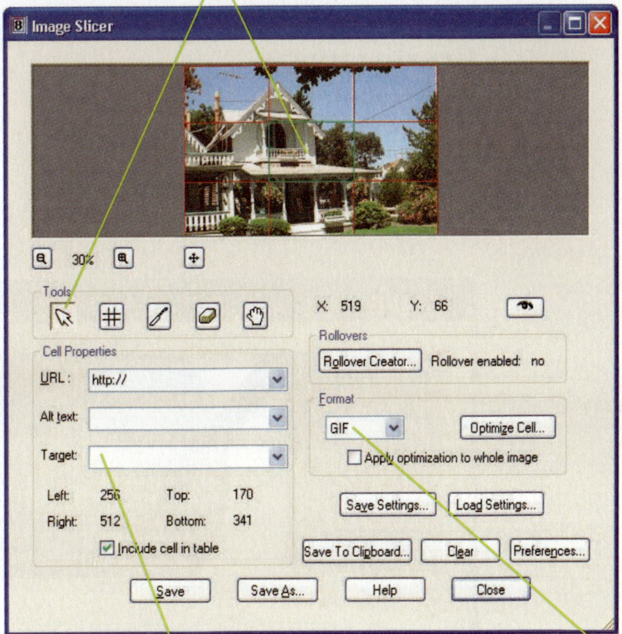

2 Complete the Properties section

3 Click in the Format box and select a format (e.g. GIF)

4 Click the Optimize Cell button and complete the dialog by activating each tab and selecting the relevant options in each

6 You'll need to insert the slice settings into the image's HTML code. Click the Save to Clipboard button then complete the dialog. Finally, open the HTML file and paste in the code at the right location

7 Click Close

HOT TIP

To preview your image in your Internet browser, click this button:

HOT TIP

Repeat 1–5 for each cell.

HOT TIP

Re step 2 – in the Target field you can choose from the following options:

- *_blank – the linked page opens in a new window*
- *_parent – the linked page opens in the parent window*
- *_self – the linked page opens in the same window*
- *_top – the linked page opens in the full browser window*

Image mapping

You can use a technique known as image mapping to create image areas (hot spots) which are linked to Internet addresses (URLs). The hot spots are actually cells and can be circles, rectangles or irregular. When the site visitor moves his/her mouse pointer over a cell, it changes to a hand – this indicates that clicking it will jump to another Web page.

Creating maps

To create a polygon, click to create a start point. Click elsewhere to create a line. Continue like this till you're thru – when the polygon is complete, right-click the image.

To delete a map area, click the Eraser button then click the area border.

1 Pull down the File menu and click Export, Image Mapper

3 Drag out a map shape – here, a circle

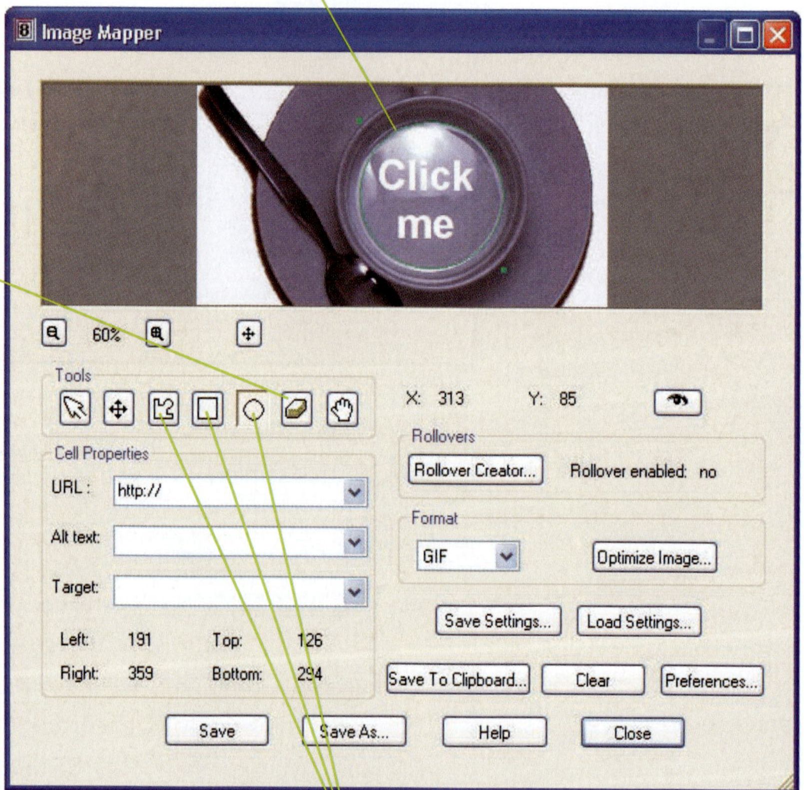

2 Click the Polygon, Rectangle or Circle tool, then click in the image preview

To preview your image in your Internet browser, click this button:

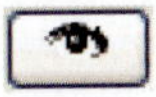

Hit Save Settings to save your area details for reuse in this or other images.

Re step 2 – in the Target field you can choose from the following options:

- *_blank – the linked page opens in a new window*
- *_parent – the linked page opens in the parent window*
- *_self – the linked page opens in the same window*
- *_top – the linked page opens in the full browser window*

Editing/formatting maps

1 Click the Pan tool then click in a map area to select it

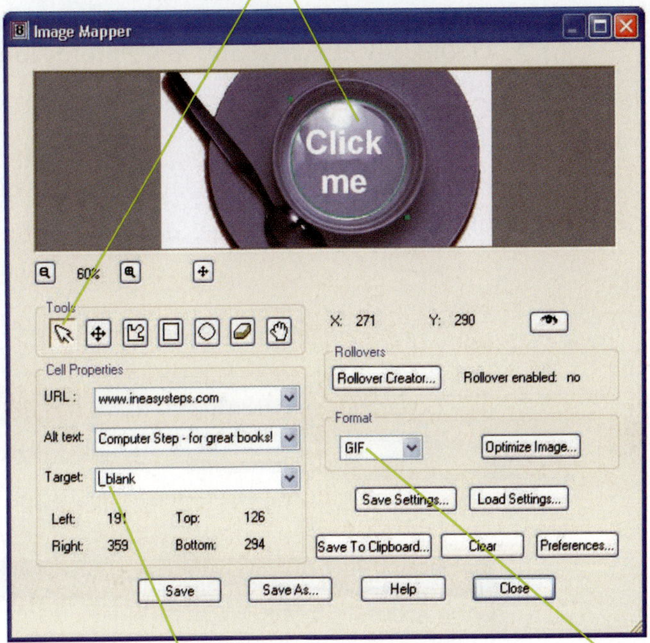

2 Complete the Properties section

3 Click in the Format box and select a format (e.g. GIF)

4 Click the Optimize Image button and complete the dialog that launches by activating each tab and selecting the relevant options in each

5 You'll need to insert the map settings into the image's HTML code. Click the Save to Clipboard button then complete the two dialogs that launch. Finally, open the HTML file and paste in the code at the right location

6 Click Close

Using rollovers

You can also use Paint Shop Pro to export "rollovers". Rollovers are images or image sections that change into something else when activated by passing the mouse over them, and are often used on the Internet, particularly in website navigation bars.

The use of rollovers can make websites look much more graphically effective, and more professional.

Creating rollovers

1 In the Image Slicer or Image Mapper dialogs, click the Pan tool 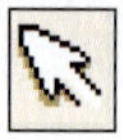 then select the cell you want to convert to a rollover

2 Hit the Rollover Creator button

3 Select an initiating mouse action

4 Click the mouse action's Open button then, in the Select Rollover dialog, select the image you want to use for the rollover

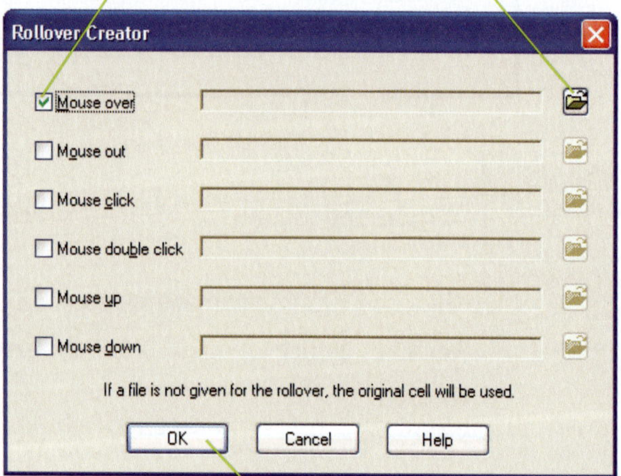

5 Repeat 3–4 for each action you want to associate with the rollover

6 Click here

Using Photo Sharing

To find out if Jasc has allocated new photo sharing services, choose Help, Jasc Software Online, Check for Updates.

Paint Shop Pro supports photo sharing. This means you can upload your images to online services and store them there. In this way, other folks can view them. At the time of writing, the only supported service is Shutterfly – check Jasc's website for details of any that may be added in future.

Enrolling with Shutterfly

1. Go to **http://jasc.shutterfly.com/home/signin_newuser.jsp**

Want to use a new photo sharing service (assuming Jasc has added one)? Choose File, Preferences, General Program Preferences. In the dialog, select the PhotoSharing tab. Select the service in the list.

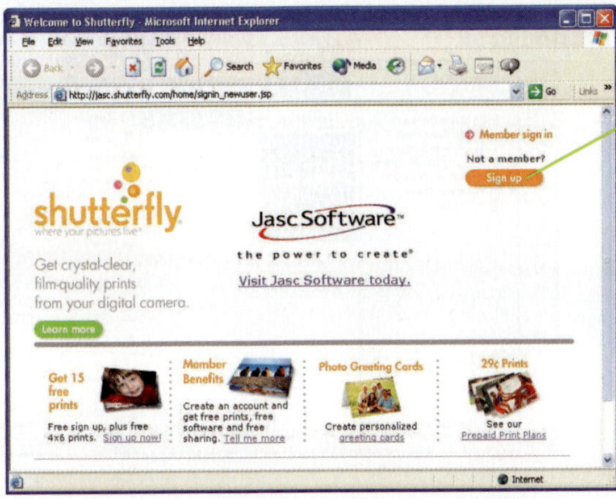

2. Click Sign up

Check out any special offers.

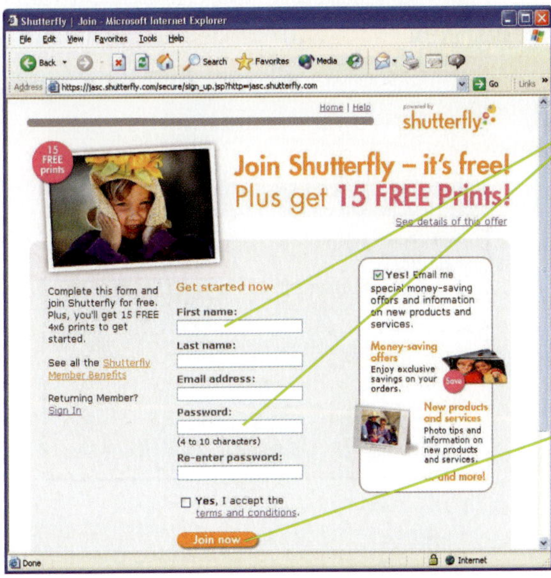

3. Enter your name, email address and a password

4. Click Join now

Uploading to Shutterfly

1 With your Web connection live, hit Ctrl+B

2 Locate and select the images you want to upload

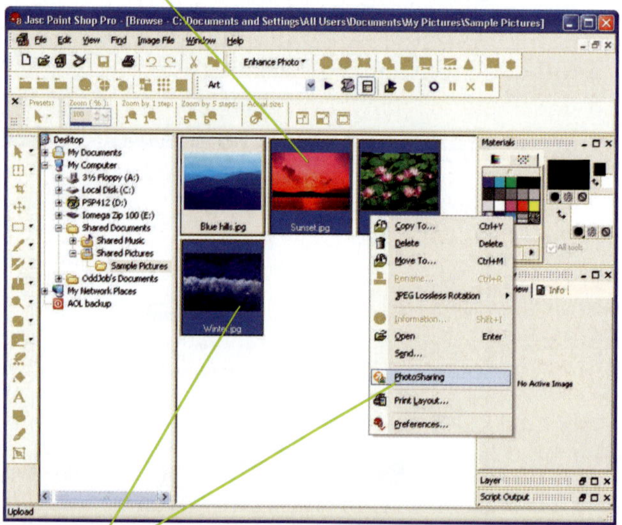

3 Right-click one image and select PhotoSharing

4 Optionally, rename the Shutterfly album where your images will be stored

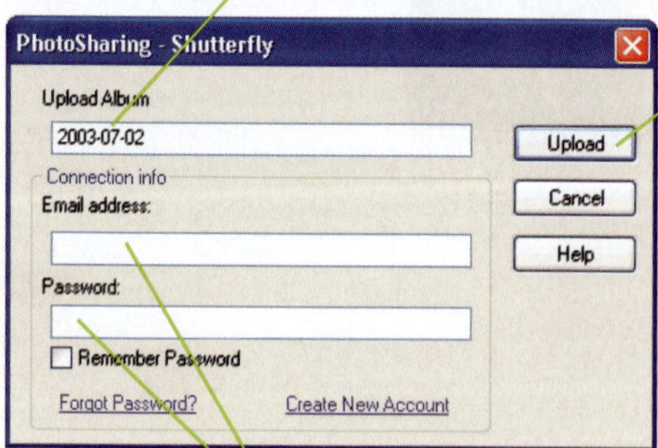

6 Hit Upload

7 Click Yes in the prompt to view Shutterfly's site

5 Enter your email address and password

Additional techniques

Chapter Eight

In this chapter, you'll enhance your use of images by working with layers and masks, advanced techniques that let you achieve unique effects. You'll also create workspaces (so you can have different configurations of Paint Shop Pro for each job you do) and use Autosave so you don't lose any work if Windows crashes. Then you'll learn how to apply borders/frames to images; crop images; work with histograms to readjust color values; and carry out other color corrections.

Finally, you'll print out your work, singly and with multiple images on the page.

Covers

Layers – an overview

You can paint (or apply effects to) specific layers. When you do this, unaffected areas in underlying layers remain visible until such time as you merge the layers.

You can add layers to Paint Shop Pro images. Layers are separate, transparent levels which add a new dimension to image editing, though they're not necessary for simple editing tasks. Memory permitting, you can have as many as 500 layers.

Types of layer include:

- raster (hosts pixel-related data)
- vector (holds vector objects e.g. shapes and text)
- adjustment (contains color correction data)
- mask (shows/hides underlying layers – see pages 164–168)

Vector layers can be added to any image, but raster and adjustment layers can only be created in grayscale images or images with at least 16 million colors. Layer editing and manipulation are undertaken via the Layer palette. This shows each layer and its sequence in the overall stack of layers. It also, in the case of a vector layer, displays icons representing each vector object:

For obvious reasons, mask and adjustment layers can't be the bottom layer.

Expand vector layers by clicking the +

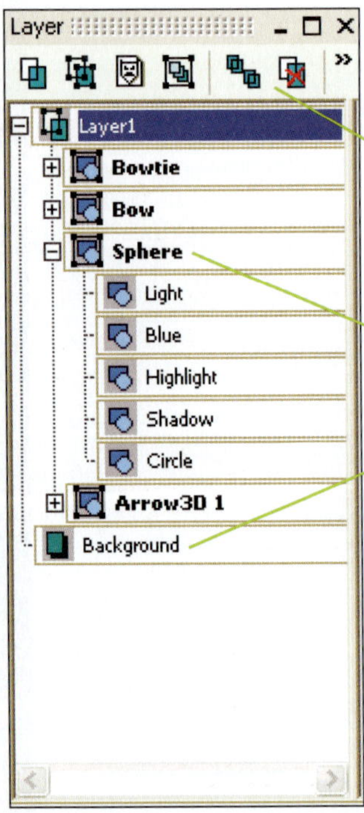

Toolbar

Vector object

Background layer – each new image has one. To promote it into a normal layer, right-click it in the palette. In the menu, select Promote To Layer

To launch the Layer palette, press L

Adding new layers

To create a new layer with default properties, hold down Shift as you click either of the layer creation buttons in the Layer palette toolbar.

Adjustment layers perform commands that are available on the Adjust menu; however, they don't change any pixels.

Use vector layers to create easily editable objects. They're really great for text.

1 In the Layer palette toolbar hit [raster layer button] to create a raster layer, or [vector layer button] to create a vector layer

2 Or pull down the Layer menu and do the following:

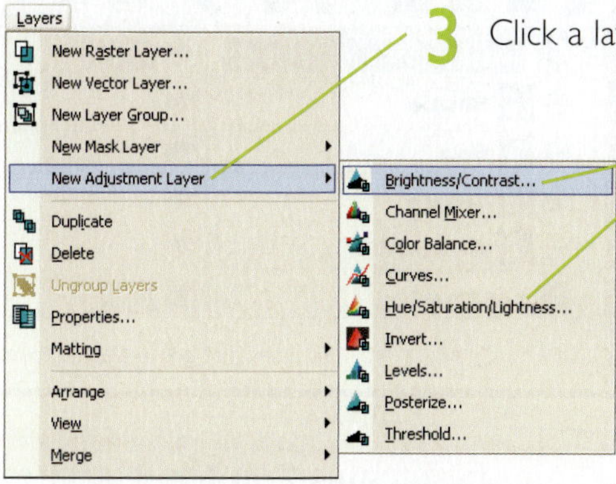

3 Click a layer type

4 If you chose New Adjustment Layer in Step 3, select a layer sub-type

5 Either way, carry out the following steps:

6 Name the layer

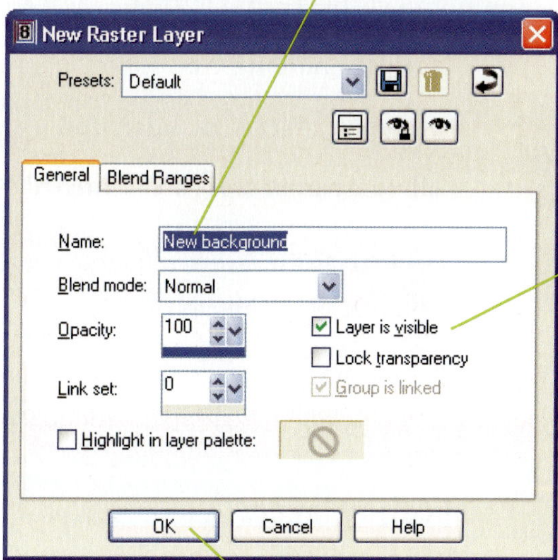

7 Work thru the tabs and their fields

8 Click OK

Using layers

As here, the Layer palette can also be dragged onto the screen – it then functions like a large toolbar.

Rearranging layers

1 If the Layer palette isn't onscreen, press L

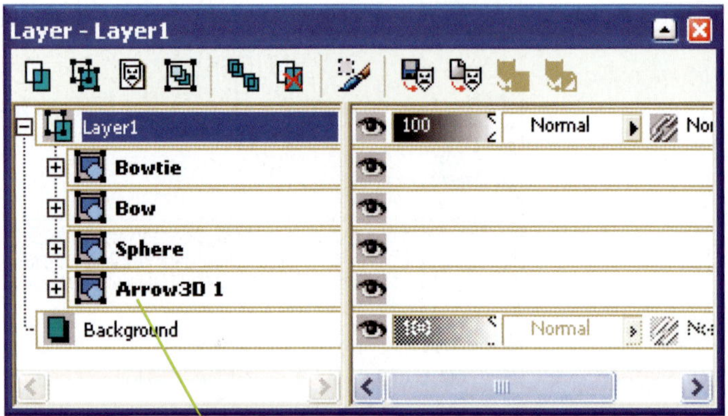

2 Click a layer, then drag it up or down to a new location in the palette – this is called "promoting" it

To delete a layer, right-click it in the Layer palette. Click Delete in the menu.

Layer information is retained when you save your images to Paint Shop Pro's native format and to Adobe Photoshop format.

Merging layers

When you merge layers, you join all the component layers (or simply all visible layers) into one. As a result:

- they can no longer be edited independently
- all vector objects are rasterized
- all transparent areas are whitened

1 To merge all the layers within an image, pull down the Layers menu and select Merge All (Flatten)

2 Or, to merge only those layers currently visible within an image, pull down the Layers menu and select Merge Visible

Use duplicated layers to try out changes.

Duplicating layers

1 Hit this button in the Layer palette toolbar: 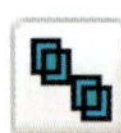

Other actions on layers

Hiding/showing layers or layer objects

1. In the Layer palette, click a layer's (or a vector object's) Visibility button to hide it – the button changes to: 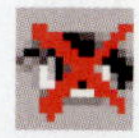

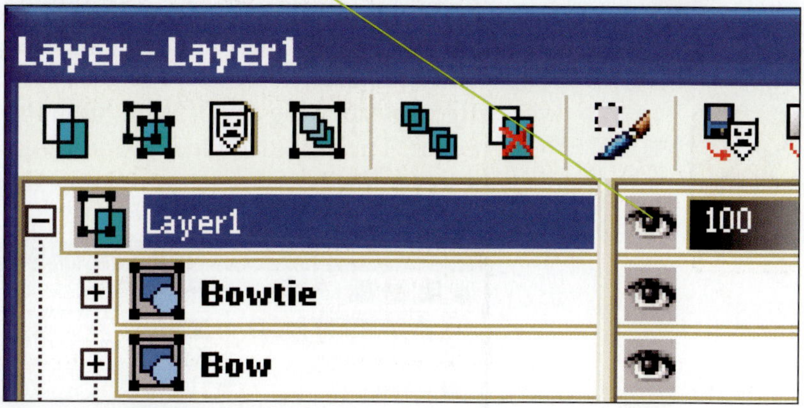

Current (visible) layers which hold no data are transparent.

Hold your mouse pointer over a layer's name to view a handy thumbnail.

Viewing/hiding all layers

1. To view or hide all layers, pull down the Layers menu and click View, All or View, None respectively

Inverting layers

1. To make all invisible layers visible (or vice versa), pull down the Layers menu and click View, Invert

Transporting selected layers to other images

1. In the Layer palette, drag the layer you want to copy onto the active image – the copied layer appears above the active one

Transporting all layers to other images

The destination image must be grayscale or 16-million-color.

1. Hit Ctrl+B to launch the Browser
2. Drag the thumbnail for the image whose layers you want to copy onto the destination image

Blending layers

Using blend modes

One great way to work with layers is to blend them. This simply involves controlling the way pixels on the layer to be blended interact with those on underlying layers.

By default, the blend mode of all layers is "Normal". This means that pixels are blended with all underlying layers, not merely the one immediately below it. You can create some really unique effects by applying any of Paint Shop Pro's 20 additional blend modes. The way each mode works can get quite technical – however, the best way to get to know them is to work thru them.

HOT TIP: You are likely to get some cool effects by dragging the Opacity slider.

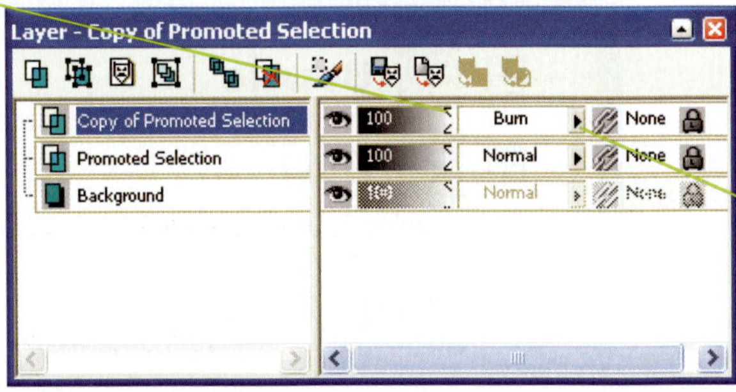

Select a blend mode

Using blend ranges

You can produce effects that are even more unique by limiting the pixels affected by blend modes.

1. Select a blend mode then double-click the layer

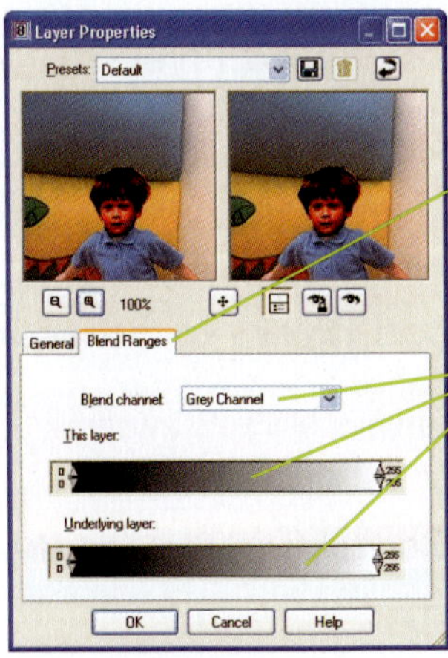

2. Select this tab

3. Select a channel then drag the upper and lower arrows to set opacity levels

HOT TIP: The choice of channel determines how opacity is set.

Tips for using layers

1. Want to work on a photograph? You mostly won't need to use layers. For example, if you just want to crop out unwanted areas, why use layers? They'd just make the job unnecessarily complex

2. So why use layers? Let's say you wanted to make major changes to a photograph. Create a duplicate of the background layer then turn off the background's visibility. Now work away on the copy: if you don't like what you come up with, just delete the copy layer and there's no harm done

HOT TIP

You can organize layers (it doesn't matter what type, except that adjustment and mask layers can't be at the bottom) into logical groups that you can manipulate like normal layers.

In the Layer palette, right-click the first layer and select New Layer Group. Complete the dialog. Now drag any further layers you want to include onto the new group.

3. Want to add text? Don't do this directly onto the background. Instead, create a new vector layer and create the text here. Why? The text is much more easily editable

4. Use blend modes and ranges to customize how layers interact

5. Want to create a new vector illustration? Create each object on its own layer to aid editing

6. If vector objects on separate layers are logically related (e.g. someone riding a cycle) link them so if you move one onscreen, you move them all (you can also link groups):

HOT TIP

To move layers onscreen, drag them with the Move tool.

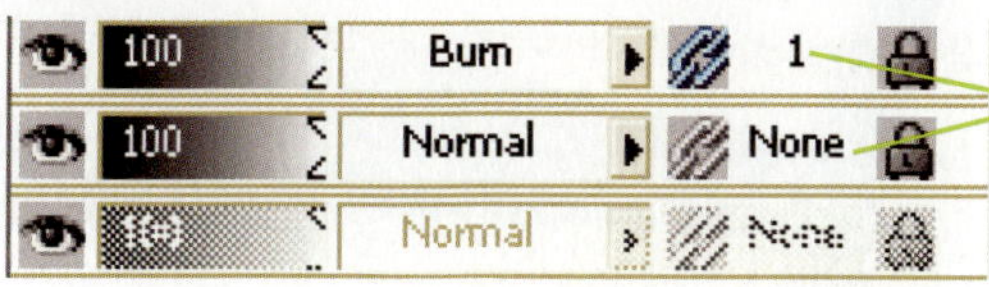

Click in this field repeatedly till all layers you want to link have the same number

Linking only relates to the Move tool: it has no effect on the Layer palette stacking order

7. If you're working with multiple layers, turn off layer visibility selectively till you get the best result

Masks – an overview

Because masks are bitmaps, all bitmap tools work with them. Also, in those tools which have bitmap and vector modes (e.g. the Preset Shapes tool), only the bitmap component is operative on masks.

Masks are 256-color grayscale bitmaps which are overlaid over image layers. They contain "holes"; you perform editing operations on the areas displayed through the gaps. The holes can be created via selection areas, other images or channels. Alternatively, the mask can be as large as the underlying layer.

To an extent, then, masks can be regarded as stencils. However, they also act as advanced selection areas. For example, you can control the extent to which a mask operates by defining the grayscale content:

- painting with black augments masking
- painting with white effaces masking
- any intervening shade of gray allows a portion of the effect you generate to take effect

You can apply any filter, deformation or effect which can be used with grayscale images.

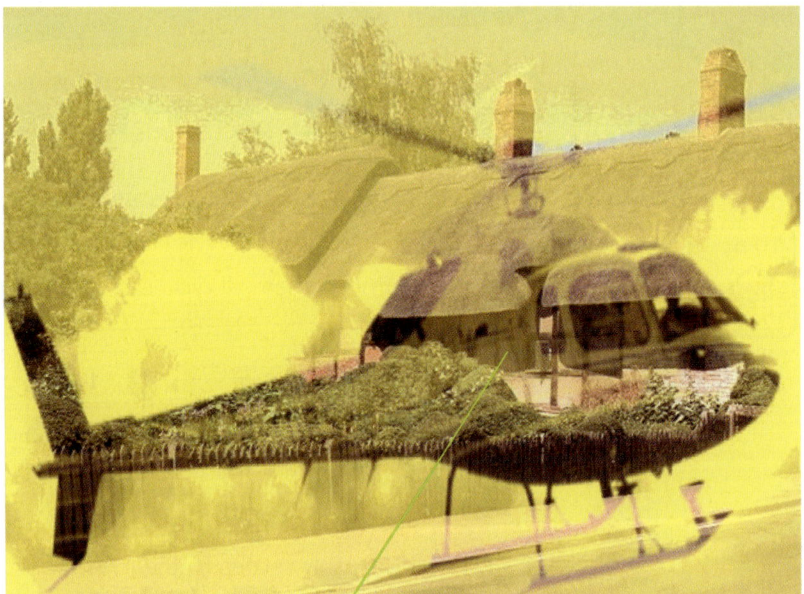

Here, a separate image has been applied as a mask and a fill has been applied to it

Layer masks

You can't apply masks to a background layer – instead, promote it first.

Masking an entire layer

1 Select the layer you want to mask

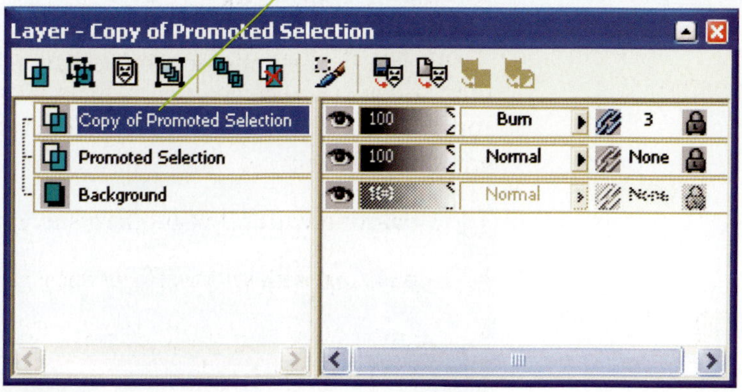

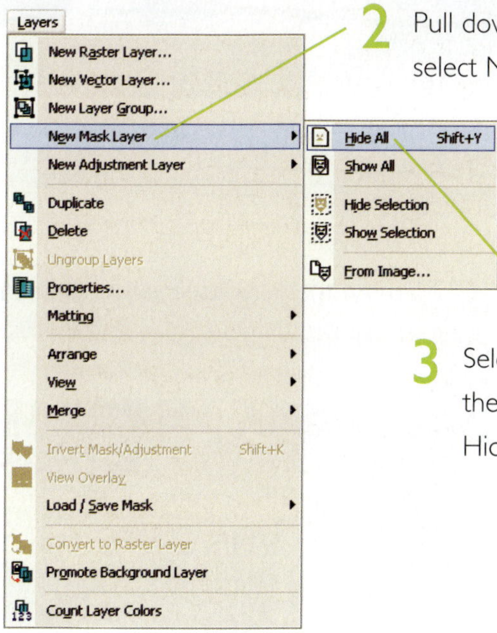

2 Pull down the Layer menu and select New Mask Layer

When you create any kind of mask, the mask layer and the active layer are automatically grouped. As a result, the mask only applies to this layer.

3 Select Show All to view all the underlying pixels or Hide All for the reverse

You can edit the mask later to mask selective areas.

4 To view the mask within the image itself, toggle this button next to it in the right-hand Layer palette pane:

Selection masks

Selection masks are masks which contain a hole (the hole being supplied by the selection area). By default, any changes you make apply to the hole, not the surrounding area.

Creating a selection mask

1 Define the appropriate selection area

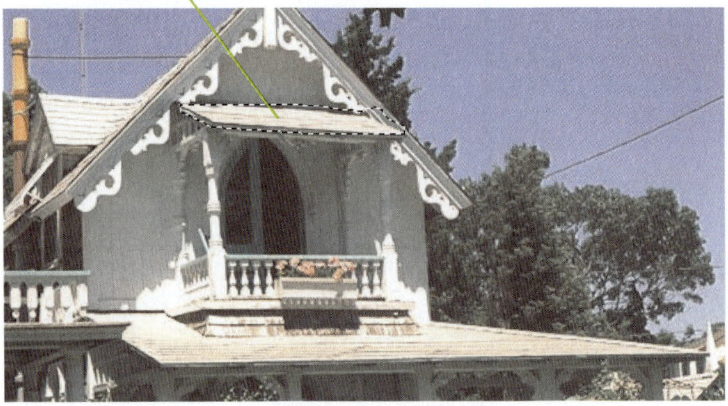

2 Pull down the Layer menu and select New Selection Layer. Then select Hide Selection or Show Selection

3 To make the mask itself visible (this applies to all mask types), hit Ctrl+Alt+V

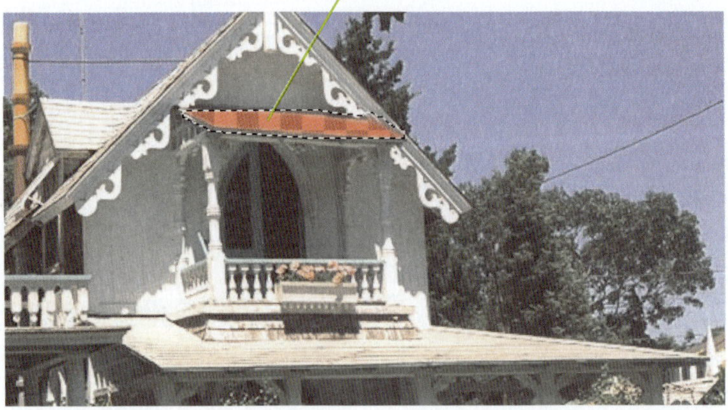

Press Ctrl+D to remove the original selection area.

Image masks

This technique can produce really remarkable effects.

Creating masks from images

If you've split an image into RGB, HSL (Hue, Saturation and Lightness) or CMYK channels (Image, Split Channels...), you can select one in Step 4 to apply it as a layer.

1 Open the image you want to use as a mask and then the image you want to insert it into

2 In the destination image, select the layer you want to mask

3 In the Layers menu, click New Mask Layer, From Image

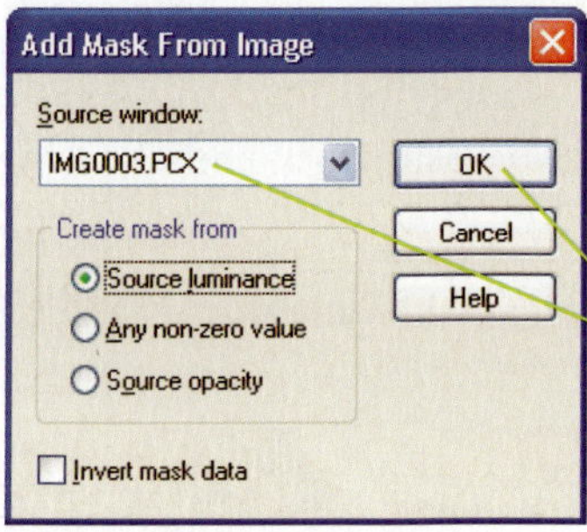

4 Select the mask image then hit OK

Created a cool mask? Save it to disk for reuse. Choose Layers, Load/Save Mask, Save Mask To Disk.

Loading masks from disk

1 You can also load masks from disk. This is especially useful as Paint Shop Pro comes with numerous masks ready for use

Select the orientation (how the mask fits the image). Entries under "Options" only apply if you chose the "As is" (the mask is applied without resizing) orientation.

2 In the Layers menu, choose Load/Save Mask, Load Mask From Disk then complete the dialog

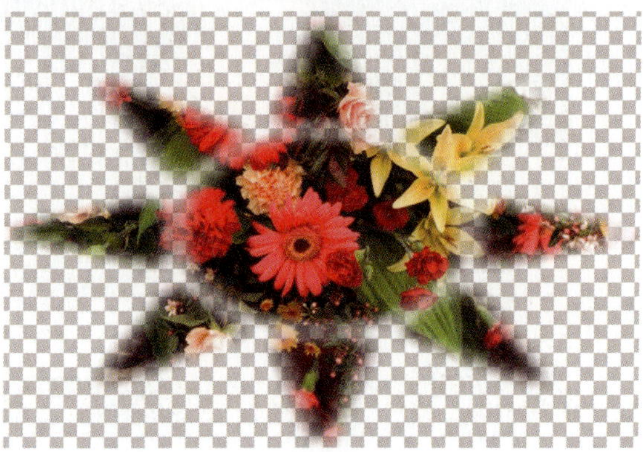

Mask 181 has been applied to an image

Editing masks

Paint Shop Pro has a special mode in which you can edit masks. This can involve varying the extent of the mask or controlling the degree (if any) of masking.

A quick way to dramatically change a mask is to invert its transparency by hitting Shift+K.

Amending a mask

1. Select the mask layer in the Layer palette then hit Ctrl+Alt+V to view the mask overlay – completely masked pixels are shown in red while those which are partially masked are in paler red

When you select a mask layer, the Materials palette shows grayscales.

2. Paint with any of the painting tools to amend the mask area (e.g. via the Brush tool) or its extent (e.g. gradient fills). Remember:

   - painting with black adds masking
   - painting with white removes the mask
   - painting with gray shades applies differing mask levels

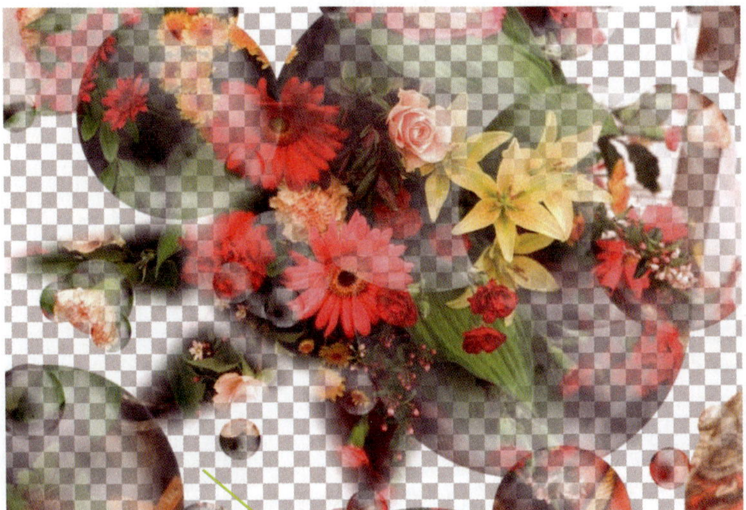

The Space Bubbles Balls and Bubbles effect has been applied to the mask layer on page 167

You can add any filter, deformation or effect to masks (but the process may take longer than usual).

3. Edit the mask layer's opacity or visibility in the same way you would any layer's

Color corrections – an overview

Paint Shop Pro lets you make various adjustments to image color distribution. To help you decide which amendments are necessary, you can call up a special window: the Histogram viewer. Look at the illustrations below:

Unless you're an image editing guru, you're not likely to need to use the Histogram window. If you do use it, bear these points in mind:

- *a wide horizontal spread means the image can be corrected*
- *if Greyscale is checked and the spread is largely at the left, the image is too dark (and vice versa)*
- *spikes contain a lot of pixels*

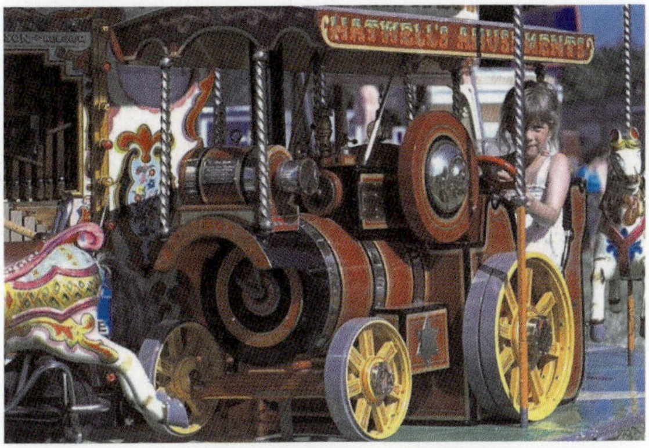

The original image

Spike

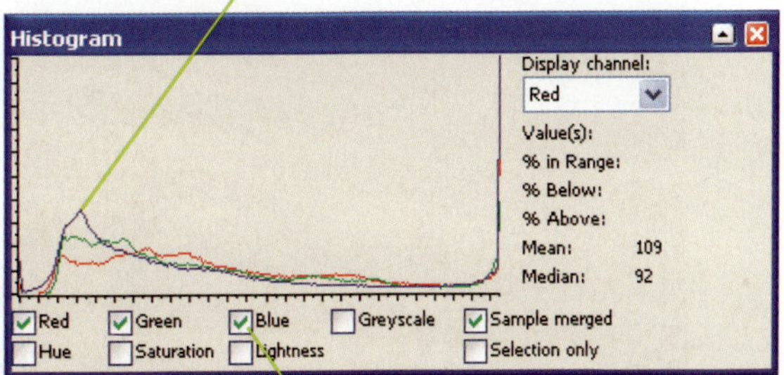

... and its histogram (to launch the Histogram window, press F7)

Here, the RGB (Red/Green/Blue) components have been checked – you can also select grayscale, hue, saturation and lightness values

If Sample merged is checked, the Histogram window graphs all layers.

Move your mouse pointer over any point in the Histogram window to display (on the right) the percentage of pixels that are below or above it or in the same range. (You can also drag out a selection in the window and get the same information.)

The Histogram window displays, along the horizontal axis, the three RGB components (Red, Green and Blue). The vertical axis against which these are plotted represents each component's share of colors in pixels.

The far left of the horizontal axis represents black, the far right white. Spikes indicate a concentration of a particular value (e.g. Red).

Histogram functions

You can carry out two principal histogram-based operations on images: Equalize and Stretch.

Equalize rearranges image pixels so that those around the midpoint of the relevant histogram are pushed nearer the high and low brightness levels (see page 169 for more information). The result is normally an averaging of image brightness.

Stretch has somewhat the opposite effect. In images where black and white are not included in the histogram, it ensures the colors do span the full spectrum.

Applying Equalize or Stretch

1. If appropriate, define a selection area
2. Hit Shift+E to apply Equalize or Shift+T to apply Stretch

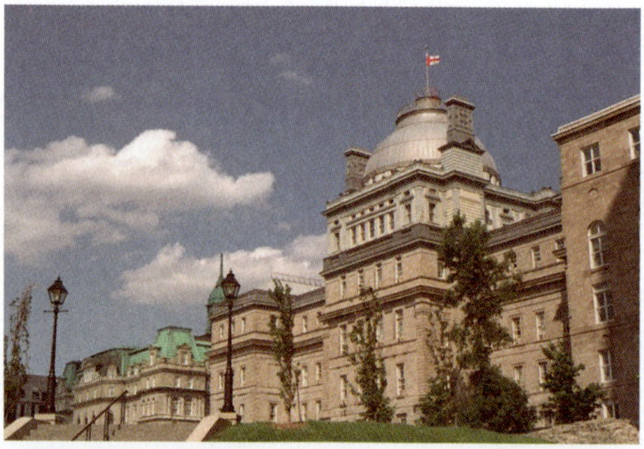

An unchanged image

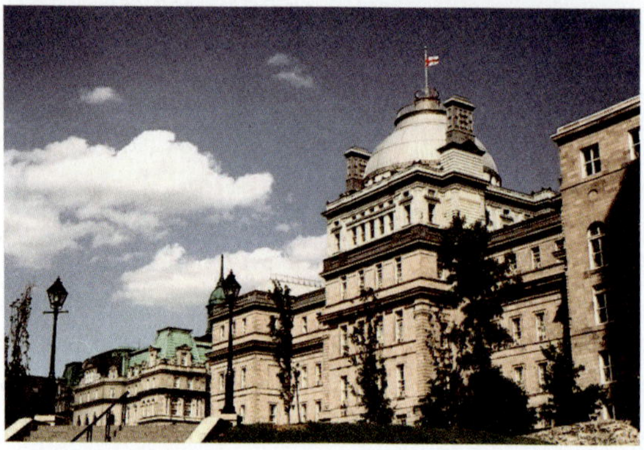

... and after applying Equalize

Framing images

When you've got your image looking really good, you can frame it. Well, not really, but you can apply a cool frame within Paint Shop Pro itself.

1 Choose Image, Picture Frame

2 Select a frame

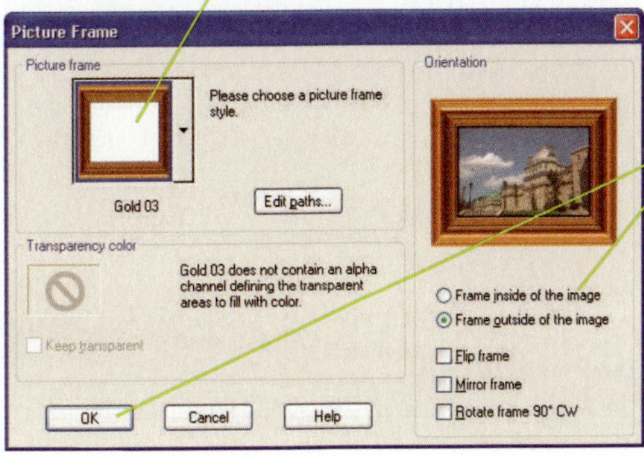

3 Choose a position then hit OK

To border an image, pull down the Image menu and select Add Borders. Specify a color and which sides you want bordered.

4 Why not frame images you've applied special effects to?

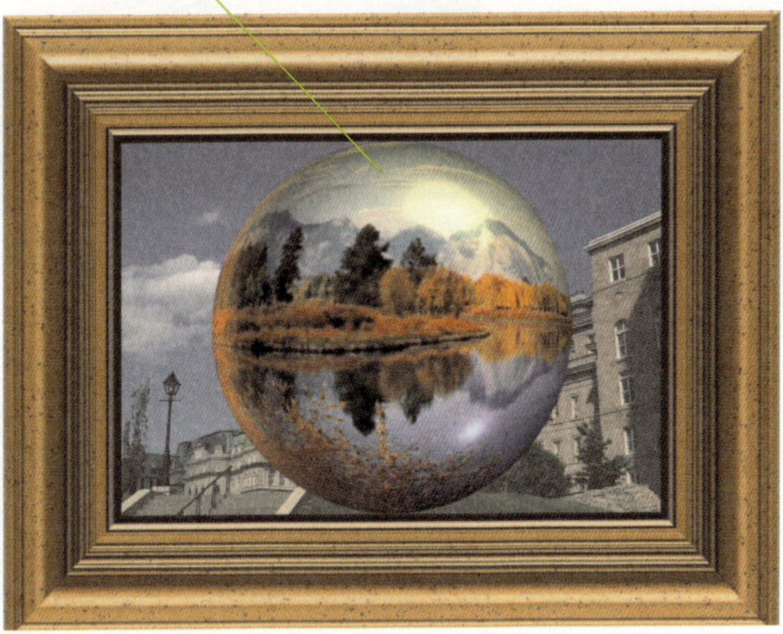

Cropping images

You frequently will need to crop images. This just means telling Paint Shop Pro what part of an image you want to keep and discarding the rest.

The Crop tool comes with lots of presets. Just click the Presets button on the Tool Options palette when the Crop tool is active.

Method 1

1 Define a selection area

2 Hit Shift+R to discard the image area outside the selection

Method 2

The advantage of using the Crop tool method is that you can also use the tool to adjust the crop area you've just defined:

- *to move (but not resize) the crop rectangle, click inside it and drag to a new location*
- *to resize the rectangle, drag one of the sides or corners in or out*

1 If you're working on a background layer, promote it

2 Hit R to launch the Crop tool

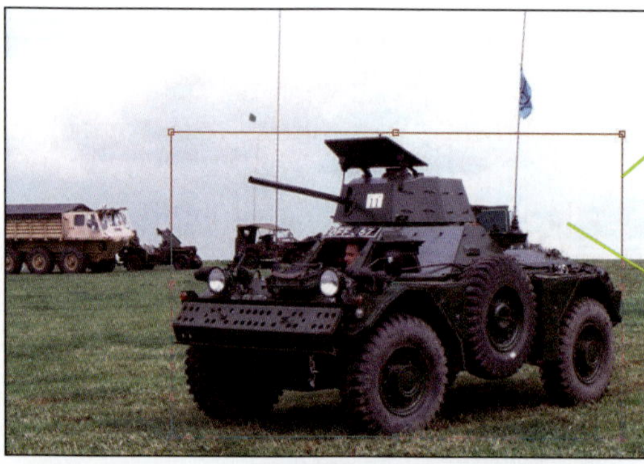

3 Drag out a selection area

4 Double-click inside it

You can also use the Tool Options palette to redefine the Crop tool area.

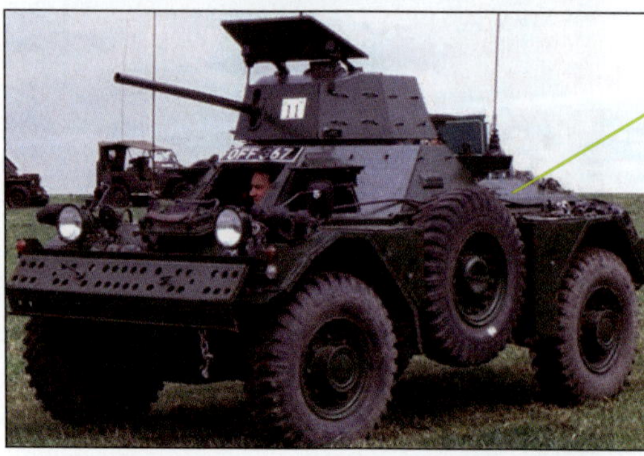

5 The image is cropped

Using workspaces

You can save details of your current "workspace" to disk. By this, Paint Shop Pro means all your palettes, toolbars, zoom settings, grid/ruler settings and open images. Why do this? So you can have different configurations for different editing purposes. It's a bit like having lots of different versions of Paint Shop Pro.

When you create a workspace, you're prompted to save any unnamed images, and any previously named but amended files are saved automatically.

The workspace only stores details of where the relevant files are located, not the files themselves.

Saving workspaces

1 Hit Shift+Alt+S

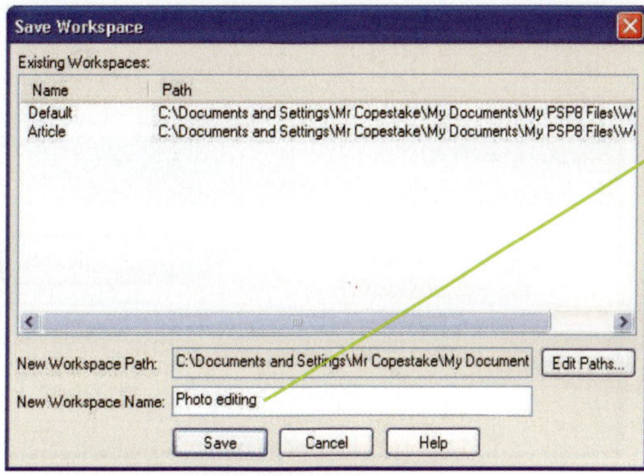

2 Name the workspace then hit Save

Want to delete an unwanted workspace? Hit Shift+Alt+D and complete the dialog that launches.

One pre-supplied workspace mimics the appearance of version 7 of Paint Shop Pro.

Loading workspaces

1 Hit Shift+Alt+L

2 Double-click a workspace

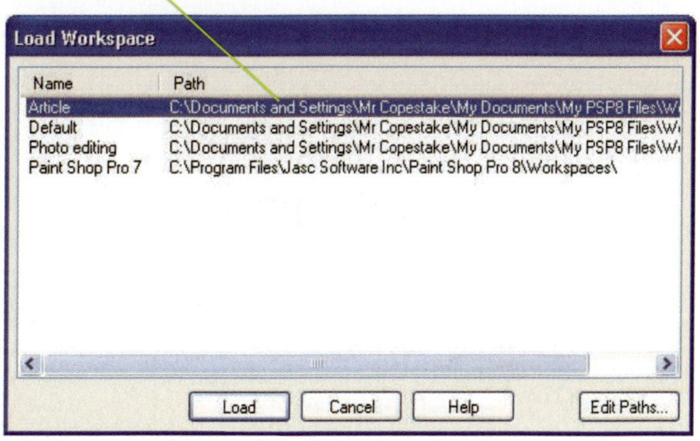

Using Autosave

If Windows or Paint Shop Pro crash suddenly, you run the risk of losing much or all of your ongoing work. However, you can prevent this by activating Paint Shop Pro's Autosave feature. When active, Autosave stores temporary details of active images. After any crash, Paint Shop Pro searches for these when you restart it. If it finds them, it reloads the temporary images.

Activating Autosave

1 Choose File, Preferences, Autosave Settings

2 Check Enable autosave

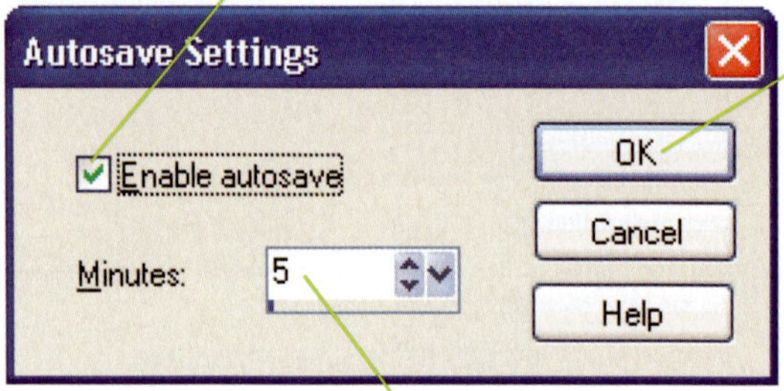

4 Click here

3 Enter the interval at which Paint Shop Pro saves its temporary files

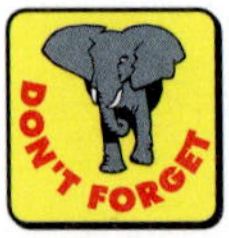

For "User", substitute the appropriate user name.

By default, Paint Shop Pro saves its temporary files in your C:\Documents and Settings*User*\Local Settings\Temp folder. However, you can change this if you want.

Specifying a new temporary file location

1 Pull down the File menu and click Preferences, File Locations

2 In the File Locations dialog, activate the Undo/Temporary Files file type on the left

3 On the right, type in the new folder address then click OK

Printing single images

You can print the active image or several on one page.

Printing the active image

1 Hit Ctrl+P

2 Select a printer

3 Adjust your printer's settings

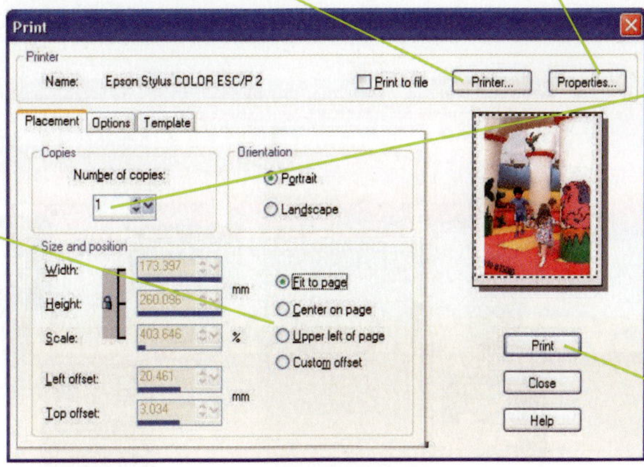

4 Type in the no. of copies

9 Start printing

Select a print orientation in the Orientation section then (if you haven't chosen a template) allocate a size/position option:

5 To print corner crop marks, center crop marks or registration marks, select the Options tab and check the relevant option(s). Crop and registration marks help commercial printers ensure print and color accuracy and mainly apply to PostScript output. If you're printing to a desktop printer, you won't require any of these features

To print to a file (e.g. for submission to a commercial printer), check Print to file and complete the dialog that launches.

6 To print the filename – or any title entered in the Current Image Information dialog (see page 16) – check Image Name under the Options tab

7 Under Options, check Greyscale to print out in gray shades

Want to print out your image in negative? Just select the Options tab and check Negative.

8 Select the Template tab to print a template (see also overleaf) with your image or to have your image fill a template. Check Print to template then choose one in the dialog

Printing multiple images

Paint Shop Pro has a neat way to print more than one image on the same page: the Print Layout Window.

1 Choose File, Print Layout

2 All currently open images are shown as thumbnails (to open more, in Print Layout choose File, Open Images and complete the dialog)

If the layout you're printing is one you use frequently, save it as a template so you can reuse it. Choose File, Save Template. Complete the dialog – check Save with images if you want the images currently displayed to open when you reopen the template.

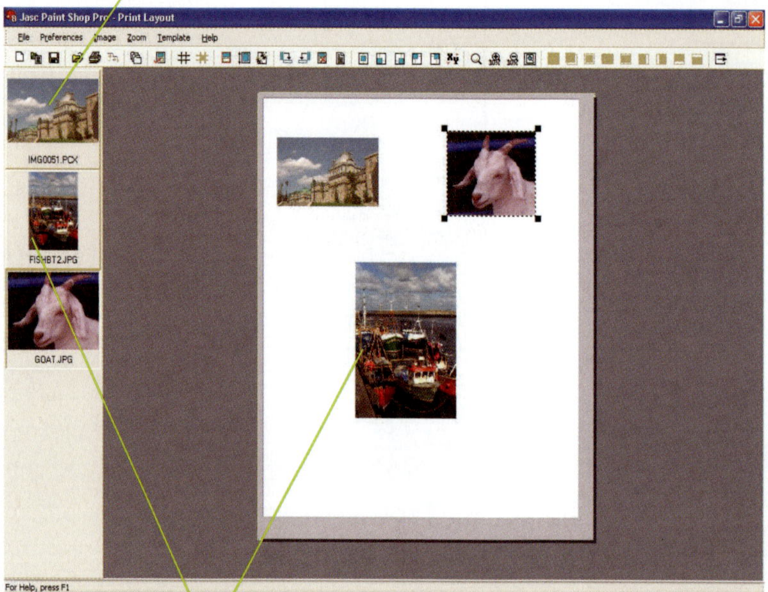

You need to ensure you print images with the correct resolution. Use the following guide:

- *300 dpi (dots per inch) printing – image resolution 72–120*
- *600 dpi printing – image resolution 125–170*

To set an image's resolution, use the Resize dialog (page 19)

3 Drag the thumbnails you want to print onto the page

4 Use the mouse to move and/or resize the images on the page. Or choose Preferences, Auto Arrange to have Paint Shop Pro do it for you

5 Optionally, click an image and apply any relevant menu commands (e.g. to view information about the image, select Image Information in the Image menu)

6 Ready to print? Choose File, Print

Using scripts

In this chapter, you'll learn about a great productivity tool. You'll record just about any Paint Shop Pro procedure and save it as a script. You can then apply this at any point, just by selecting and running the script. You can also edit scripts and even apply the same script to multiple images in one go.

Covers

Chapter Nine

Generating and playing scripts

Folks skilled at programming can find out more about Python (Paint Shop Pro's scripting engine) at ***http://www.python.org/****.*

Also, a useful guide to scripting called "Scripting How To.pdf" is automatically installed to ***\Paint Shop Pro 8\Learning Center\PDF Files****.*

A long-awaited feature in Paint Shop Pro 8 is the ability to automate lengthy tasks. We all have things we do fairly often, and these frequently are complex procedures. The good news is that you can now record these as "scripts". The bad news is that there are certain restrictions:

- customizations of the user interface can't be scripted
- operations involving the Materials or Tools palette can't be recorded on-the-fly (but they can be written with a text editor, which requires some programming expertise)
- some plug-ins may not be scriptable

Recording a script

1 Make a written note of the actions you want to record

2 Launch the Script toolbar (View, Toolbars, Script)

If in doubt, stick with the wizard defaults.

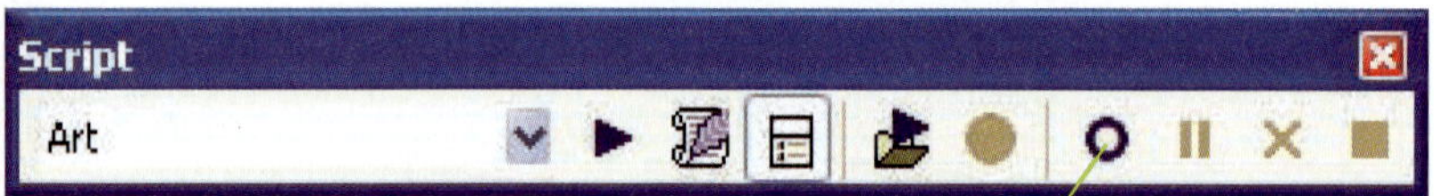

3 Click here

4 Carry out the actions you listed

Presets are scripts. So, basically, are print layouts.

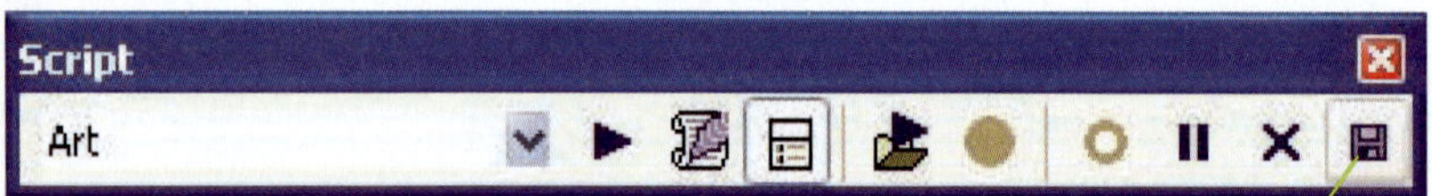

5 Click here

You can have up to 9 BoundScripts. These are special scripts which can be dragged onto toolbars and menus and can be assigned keyboard shortcuts.

Because of the connection with Python, scripts can be "restricted" or "trusted". Most of the difference has to do with security; in practical terms, the main point is that some commands (like File, Save As) can't be run from protected scripts.

Want to perform script housekeeping? You can do this by running the ScriptManager script.

6 Go to the right folder then name the script

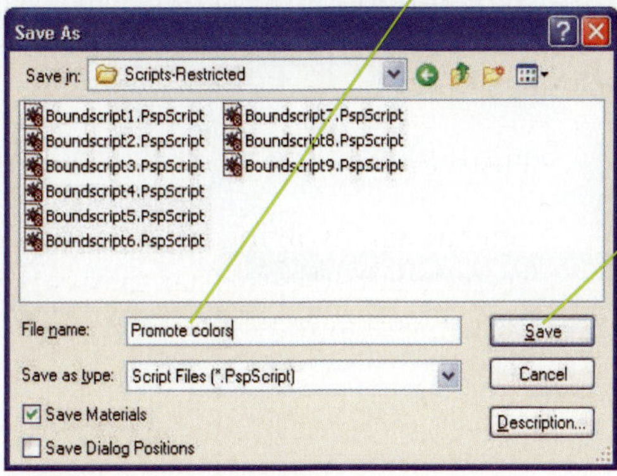

7 Click Save

Running a script

1 Select a script

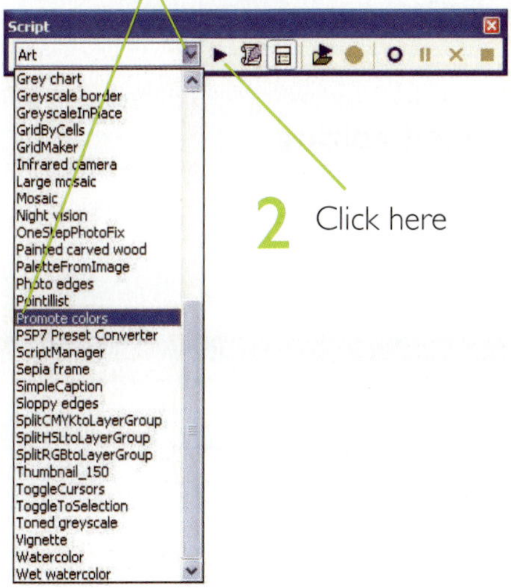

2 Click here

3 Alternatively, if the script isn't visible in the list, hit this button:

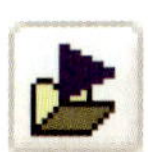

4 In the dialog, find the script, select it then hit Open to run it

Editing scripts

Paint Shop Pro has a built-in script editor which should enable just about anyone to edit some aspects of scripts. Programming gurus can also edit scripts in text editors like Notepad.

Can't find the script? Choose File, Script, Edit and locate then open it with the dialog that launches.

If the script was created with a text editor, this dialog doesn't appear. Instead, the script opens in your default text editor.

Using the built-in editor

1 Select a script in the Script toolbar then click this button: 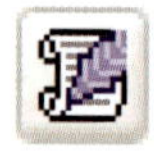

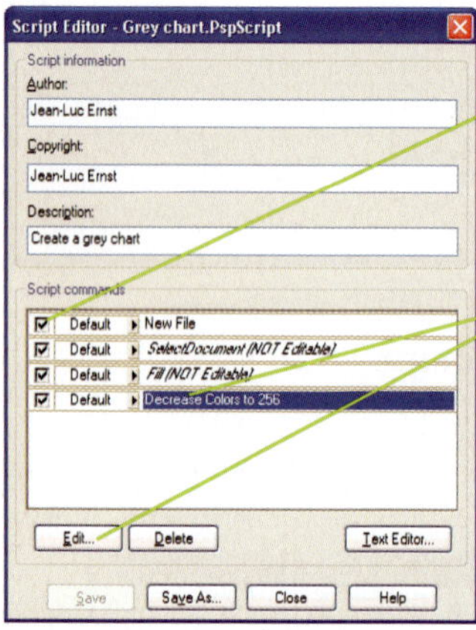

2 Uncheck a script component to disable it

3 Select a component (some can't be edited) then hit Edit. Modify the command's settings in the originating dialog etc.

Advanced editing

You can apply scripts to multiple files at once. Hit File, Batch, Process. Go to the folder which hosts the files you want to process then flag them. Select a Save Mode, choose a script then customize the output format/folder. Hit Start to begin the batch process.

1 Want to edit a script at source? Hit Text Editor in the Script Editor dialog

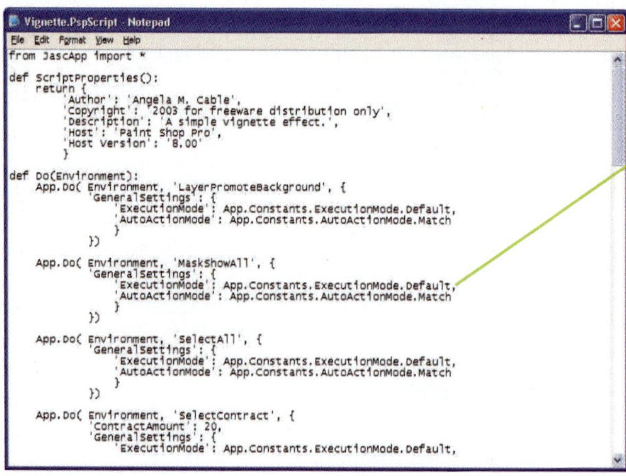

2 Edit it in the usual way

Animation Shop

In this chapter, you'll learn how to create animated images and banners for use on websites. You'll also customize completed animations by adding transitions, effects and text effects to individual frames; inserting new frames; resizing animations; and optimizing them for Web/presentation use.

Finally, you'll export frames directly to Paint Shop Pro (so you can make use of its more advanced editing capabilities) and preview your animations in your Web browser prior to uploading.

Covers

Chapter Ten

Creating animations

You can use a companion program called Animation Shop to animate images. This is fun and useful, particularly as you can create animations for websites.

Animations consist of frames (images) viewed successively. Be prepared to create quite a few – broadly, the more frames, the better the result likely to be.

Creating an animation

The easiest way to create animations is to use a special wizard.

1. Hit Shift+A

2. There are several stages in the wizard. Work thru each one:

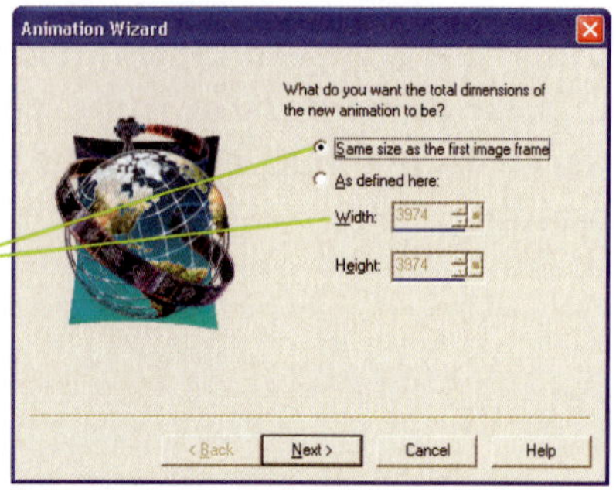

- specifying the frame size
- specifying the canvas color
- specifying the frame position
- specifying animation properties
- adding new frames

Animation properties include having animations play continuously, or "loop".

If in doubt, stick with the wizard defaults.

3. To run your animation, select Animation in the View menu

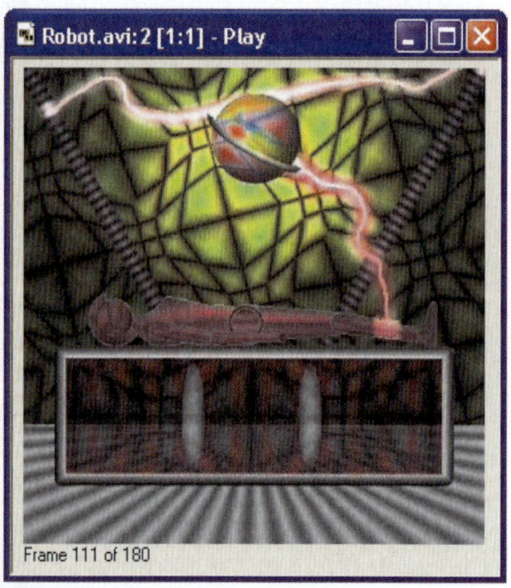

An animation in the course of being run

Animation Shop will open (Ctrl+O) and convert animations in third-party formats like .avi.

Creating an animated banner

You can create banners with animated text – great on the Web.

To insert a new blank frame, click the frame you want the new one to precede or follow then press Ctrl+T or Ctrl+Shift+T respectively.

To insert a frame with content, choose Animation, Insert Frames, From File. In the dialog, click Add File and select one or more animation files. Click Open. Complete the remainder of the dialog then hit OK.

1. Hit Shift+B
2. There are several stages in the wizard:
   - specifying the background

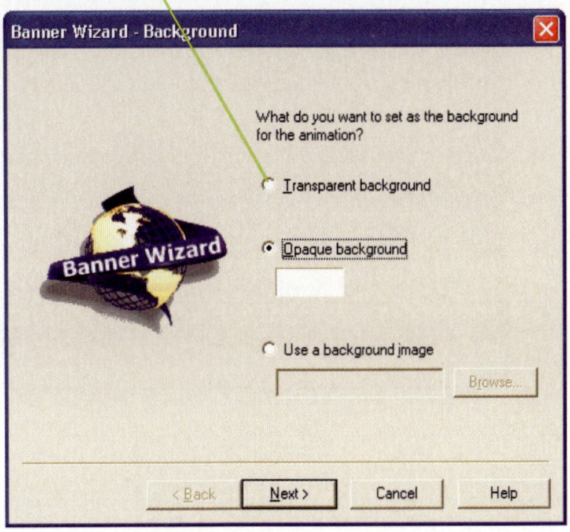

To browse files, hit Ctrl+B.

   - specifying the size of the banner
   - specifying the timing
   - specifying the text color
   - specifying a transition

You can export frames as picture tubes. Just hit Shift+U and work thru the dialog.

3. To run your animation, choose View, Animation

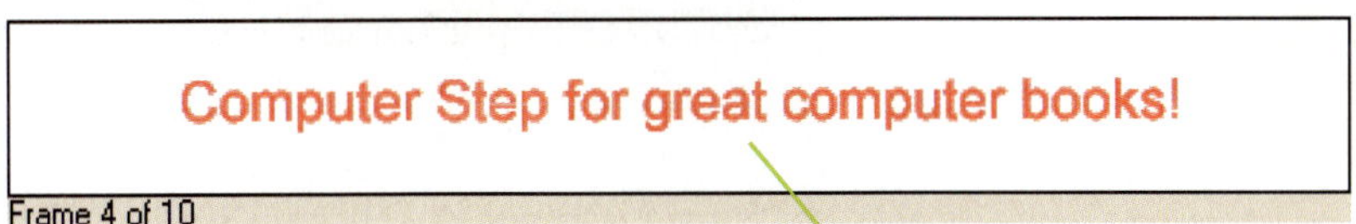

A completed banner

Working with frames

Transitions control how the animation moves from one frame to the next. Effects manipulate frames in dramatic ways – many effects are similar to those in Paint Shop Pro itself but there are additions (e.g. Shaky Cam).

Applying transitions always results in new frames but effects can add or amend frames.

Inserting transitions or effects adds the specified number of frames. However, you can also "apply" effects. Essentially, this substitutes the changes you make in the specified number of frames. To do this, choose Apply Image Effect in Step 2 then complete the dialog.

You can also insert or apply text effects. Select Insert Text Effect or Apply Text Effect. Complete the dialog which launches.

Once you've created an animation, you can customize it. This principally involves selecting individual frames and applying or modifying transitions or effects.

Applying transitions and effects

1 Right-click a frame

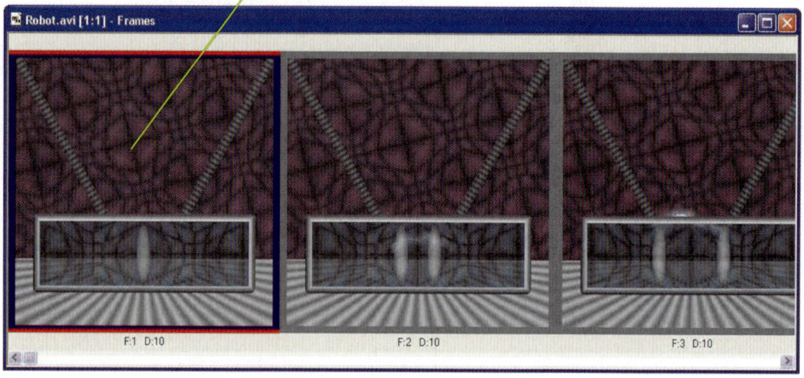

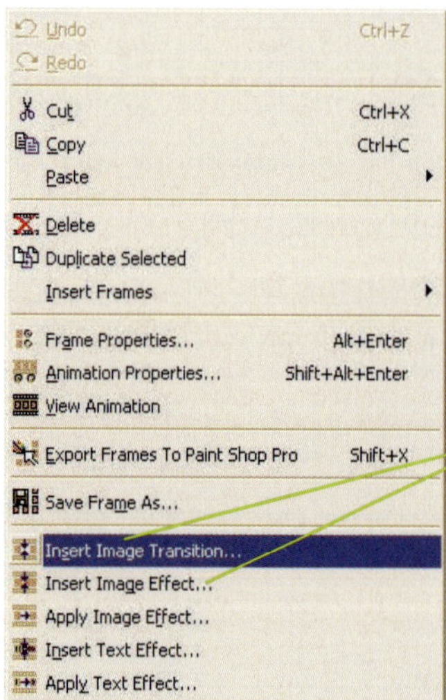

2 Select Insert Image Transition or Insert Image Effect

3 Complete steps 4–6 for transitions, or 7–9 for effects

...cont'd

It's sometimes appropriate to have the start or end of a transition as a color rather than a frame. If you want this, click Canvas Color under Start with or End with. Or click Custom Color, click in the box and select a color in the dialog.

You can export frames directly to Paint Shop Pro for editing there. Right-click a frame then hit Shift+X. Make any editing changes in Paint Shop Pro then choose Update Back to Animation Shop in the Edit menu.

Customizing the transition

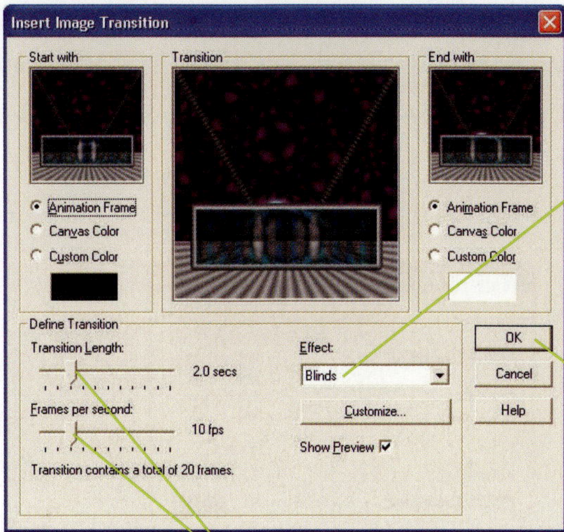

5 Select a new transition

6 Click here

4 Drag the sliders to amend the transition duration and the frames per second value

Customizing the effect

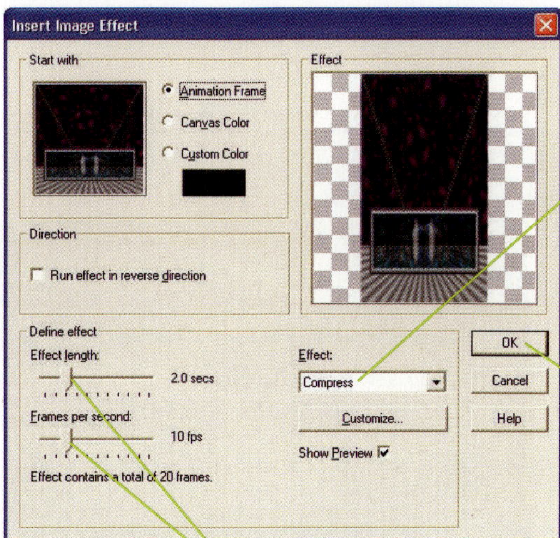

8 Select a new effect

9 Click here

7 Drag the sliders to amend the effect duration and the frames per second value

It's sometimes appropriate to have the start of an effect as a color rather than a frame. If you want this, click Canvas Color under Start with. Or click Custom Color, click in the box and select a color in the dialog that launches.

Previewing animations

Since animations are especially useful on the Web, it's handy to be able to view them in your browser before uploading.

1. Finish creating and modifying your animation, then choose Preview in Web Browser in the View menu

2. Select a format

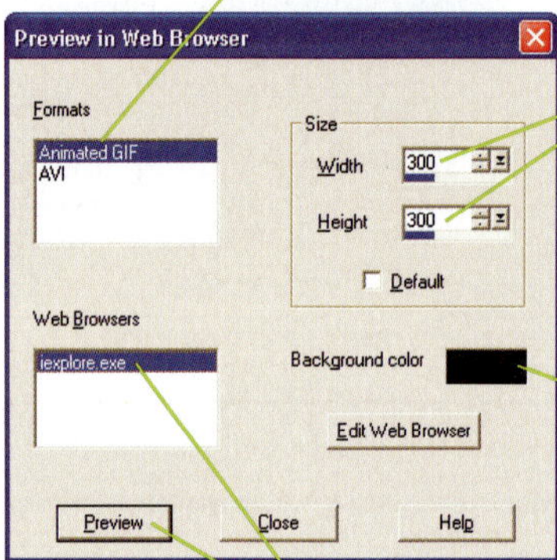

3. Optionally, amend the size

4. Optionally, select a background color

5. Select a browser then click Preview

6. Complete any further dialogs – the process may take some time

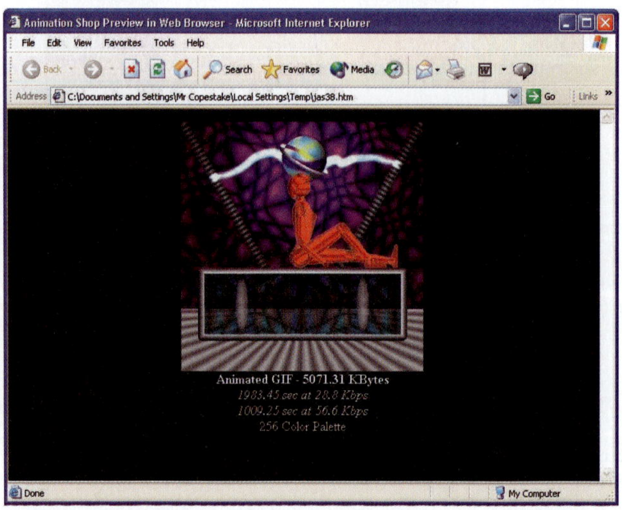

Internet Explorer previewing an animation

Animation Shop supports workspaces.

If you intend to use your animations on Web pages or in presentations, you can run a special wizard to optimize them.

Hit Shift+Z. Complete the Wizard screens (some of them are identical to processes carried out by the Animation Wizard).

You can resize animations. Press Shift+S then complete the Resize dialog. Be careful how much you resize: too much can distort images/text.

Want to print out your animation (or individual frames)? In the File menu, choose Print, Animation or Print, Frames.

Index

H

I

J

K

L

M

N

O

P

T

U

V

W

Z